1978 Supplement to the SUPREME COURT AND THE CRIMINAL PROCESS—

Cases and Comments

PETER W. LEWIS
Associate Professor, University of South Florida, Tampa

KENNETH D. PEOPLES
State of Missouri, Department of Education, Jefferson City

1978 W. B. SAUNDERS COMPANY
Philadelphia · London · Toronto

W. B. Saunders Company: West Washington Square
Philadelphia, PA 19105

1 St. Anne's Road
Eastbourne, East Sussex BN21 3UN, England

1 Goldthorne Avenue
Toronto, Ontario M8Z 5T9, Canada

1978 Supplement to The Supreme Court and the
Criminal Process—Cases and Comments   ISBN 0-7216-5770-2

© 1978 by W. B. Saunders Company. Copyright under the International Copyright Union. All rights reserved. This book is protected by copyright. No part of it may be reproduced, stored in a retrieval system, or transmitted in any form or by any means, electronic, mechanical, photocopying, recording, or otherwise, without written permission from the publisher. Made in the United States of America. Press of W. B. Saunders Company. Library of Congress catalog card number 76-50155.

Last digit is the print number: 9   8   7   6   5   4   3   2   1

PREFACE

This supplement contains all the significant United States Supreme Court decisions relevant to the criminal process—up to the end of the 1976-1977 Term of Court (ending June 29, 1977)—that were not included in the principal text because of space limitations and manuscript deadlines.

In addition to recent articles by Justices Rehnquist and Brennan and former Justice Arthur Goldberg, seventeen principal cases from the 1976-1977 Term are included, eight of which are preceded by the oral arguments. Tables summarizing recent Supreme Court decisions in the areas of gender-based discrimination, illegitimacy, the right of privacy, and double jeopardy are provided for the convenience of the reader. We trust that these and the other materials are illuminating and instructive.

The dissenting opinion of Mr. Justice White in *Moore* v. *City of East Cleveland* is included in Chapter Three because of its historical discussion of substantive and procedural due process. *Craig* v. *Boren,* the 3.2 per cent beer drinking case, is presented in Chapter Four because the Supreme Court has apparently developed a third equal protection test which may become important in cases involving the criminal process. Mr. Justice Rehnquist's dissenting opinion in *Trimble* v. *Gordon* is included in Chapter Four because he has taken a more restrictive view of the Equal Protection Clause than any other Justice in recent memory.

Although we have refrained from adding *Comments* following the principal cases, as was done in the principal text, a section on "Other Decisions of Interest" from the 1976-1977 Term is included when appropriate.

Finally, Appendix A contains the most recent nationwide survey of judges and lawyers on the Burger Court.

A note of explanation concerning the organization of material is necessary here: So that the supplementary material can be easily integrated with the contents of the principal text, it is presented within the appropriate chapters and sections used in the main text. Since new cases were not decided in all areas covered in the main text, certain chapters and sections have been omitted.

Special thanks is extended to Ellen Murray and Magdalene Deutsch for their aid in the preparation of this supplement.

PETER W. LEWIS
KENNETH D. PEOPLES

December, 1977

CONTENTS

PART ONE THE FEDERAL COURTS, THE BILL OF RIGHTS, THE CRIMINAL PROCESS, DUE PROCESS, AND EQUAL PROTECTION OF THE LAWS

1

INSIDE THE SUPREME COURT: JUDICIAL REVIEW, THE DECISION-MAKING PROCESS, AND THE BILL OF RIGHTS

1.01 The Modern Supreme Court 3
      The Notion of a Living Constitution —
        William H. Rehnquist 3
      State Constitutions and the Protection of Individual
        Rights — William J. Brennan, Jr. 9

1.02 The Federal Courts 16
      There Shall Be "One Supreme Court" —
        Arthur J. Goldberg 16

1.04 Granting Supreme Court Review 19
      Supreme Court Review of State Court
        Decisions — Charles A. Wright 19

1.05 Some Additional Limitations on Supreme Court Review 26
      Standing to Sue — Gilmore v. Utah 26

1.06 Decision-Making in the Supreme Court 30
      What the Justices Are Saying 30
      Supreme Embarrassment 34

3

DUE PROCESS AND THE FIFTH AND FOURTEENTH AMENDMENTS 35

3.03 Procedural Due Process 35
      Due Process and the Revocation of Driver's Licenses —
        Dixon v. Love 35

3.05 Burden of Proof.. 37
   Due Process and Causation
      Oral Arguments Before the U.S. Supreme Court............... 37
         Henderson v. Kibbe 40
   Due Process and Extreme Emotional Disturbance—
      Patterson v. New York.. 44
   Retroactivity of *Mullaney* v. *Wilbur*
      Oral Arguments Before the U.S. Supreme Court............... 49
         Hankerson v. North Carolina... 51

3.06 Other Decisions of Interest Involving Due Process 53
   Statutory Construction... 53
   Appeal Dismissed "for Want of a Substantial Federal
      Question"... 54
   The Right of Privacy and Zoning Regulations........................ 54

4
EQUAL PROTECTION OF THE LAWS AND THE CRIMINAL PROCESS 62

4.02 Invidious Classifications
   Gender-Based Discrimination and the Right to Drink
      Beer—Craig v. Boren 62

4.03 The "State Action" Requirement... 66
   Equal Protection and Illegitimacy—Trimble v. Gordon 66

4.05 Other Decisions of Interest Involving Equal Protection
   of the Laws and the Criminal Process 69

PART TWO CONSTITUTIONAL SAFEGUARDS OF AN ACCUSED: FOURTH, FIFTH, AND SIXTH AMENDMENT PROBLEMS

6
FIFTH AMENDMENT PROBLEMS: DOUBLE JEOPARDY, SELF-INCRIMINATION, AND THE GRAND JURY 75

6.02 The Guarantee Against Double Jeopardy.............................. 75
   A. Prior Convictions... 75
      Felony Murder and Double Jeopardy—
         Harris v. Oklahoma... 75
   E. Government Appeals in Criminal Cases—U.S.C. § 3731 76
      Judgments of Acquittal and Governmental Appeals
         Oral Arguments Before the U.S. Supreme Court......... 76
         United States v. Martin Linen Supply Co. 79
      When the Trial Court Dismisses the Charges—
         Finch v. United States... 83
   F. Other Decisions of Interest Involving Double Jeopardy 86

6.04 The Grand Jury... 88

C. Racial Discrimination and the Selection of Grand Jurors...... 88
   The "Substantial Under-representation" Test
      Oral Arguments Before the U.S. Supreme Court......... 88
      Casteneda v. Partida 90

7
SIXTH AMENDMENT PROBLEMS: THE RIGHT TO COUNSEL, JURY TRIALS, SPEEDY TRIALS, THE CONFRONTATION CLAUSE, DEFENSE WITNESSES, AND PUBLIC TRIALS 100

7.02 The Right to Counsel 100
   Informers and the Effective Assistance of Counsel
      Oral Arguments Before the U.S. Supreme Court............... 100
      Weatherford v. Bursey... 103

PART THREE   JUVENILE JUSTICE, LEGAL RIGHTS OF THE CONVICTED FELON, THE CIVIL RIGHTS ACT OF 1964, AND THE CONSTITUTIONAL RIGHTS OF LAW ENFORCEMENT AUTHORITIES

9
LEGAL RIGHTS OF CONVICTED FELONS... 111

9.05 Other Decisions of Interest: Legal Rights of Convicted
   Felons – 1976–1977 Term of Court..................................... 111
   Parole Hearings and Due Process... 111
   Parole Revocation Hearings 111

10
THE CIVIL RIGHTS ACT OF 1964 AND THE CONSTITUTIONAL RIGHTS OF LAW ENFORCEMENT AUTHORITIES............................ 113

10.04 Other Decisions of Interest: The Civil Rights Act and
   the Constitutional Rights of Law Enforcement Authorities –
   1976–1977 Term of Court... 113
   § 1983 Actions Involving Off-Duty Policemen........................ 113
   The Measure of Damages Under § 1983 Actions 114

PART FOUR   SPECIAL PROBLEMS IN THE ADMINISTRATION OF JUSTICE

13
GUILTY PLEAS AND THE PLEA BARGAINING PROCESS 117

13.01 Introduction... 117
   Plea Bargaining and the Transformation of the
      Criminal Process 117

13.02 Problems in Pleading.. 122
        Collateral Attacks on Guilty Pleas
            Oral Arguments Before the U.S. Supreme Court............... 122
            Blackledge v. Allison... 125
        The Plea Bargaining System and Confessions —
            Hutto v. Ross 128

15

THE FIRST AMENDMENT IN ITS CRIMINAL CONTEXT: FREEDOM OF THE PRESS, SPEECH, RELIGION, AND ASSEMBLY... 130

15.02 Freedom of the Press 130
        Retroactivity of *Miller* v. *California*
            Oral Arguments Before the U.S. Supreme Court............... 130
            Marks v. United States.. 134
        The "Human Cannonball" Case — Zacchini v.
            Scripps-Howard Broadcasting Co. 137

15.03 Freedom of Speech
        The License Plate Case
            Oral Arguments Before the U.S. Supreme Court............... 140
            Wooley v. Maynard... 143

15.06 Other Decisions of Interest: The First Amendment in
        Its Criminal Context — 1976–1977 Term of Court.................... 146
        Obscenity and Pornography.. 146

APPENDIX A A REPORT CARD ON THE SUPREME COURT........... 149

TABLE OF CASES

Note: Principal cases are in **boldface** and the page on which they appear in *italic*. Only United States Supreme Court cases are listed.

Abney v. United States, 86, 98

Baker v. Carr, 9, 10
Beal v. Doe, 57
Belcher v. Stengel, 113
Bell v. Burson, 35
Black v. United States, 101, 102
Blackledge v. Allison, 122, *125*
Bouie v. City of Columbia, 132, 146
Bounds v. Smith, 111
Boyd v. United States, 10, 11
Boykin v. Alabama, 123
Brady v. United States, 103
Brown v. Bd. of Education, 7
Brown v. Ohio, 87, 99

Califano v. Webster, 71
Carey v. Population Services International, 57
Castaneda v. Partida, 88, *90*
Cleveland Bd. of Education v. La Fleur, 70
Cohen v. Beneficial Industrial Loan Corp., 86
Craig v. Boren, *62*, 71
Cupp v. Naughten, 38

Dixon v. Love, *35*
Doe v. Bolton, 56
Dothard v. Rawlinson, 71, 113
Dred Scott v. Sanford, 7

Eisenstadt v. Baird, 56
Estelle v. Gamble, 111

Faretta v. California, 120
Finch v. United States, *83*, 86, 99
Fong Foo v. United States, 78
Francis v. Henderson, 88
Frontiero v. Richardson, 70

Geduldig v. Aiello, 70
General Electric Co. v. Gilbert, 71
Gilmore v. Utah, *26*
Ginzburg v. United States, 146
Glona v. American Guarantee & Liability Insur. Co., 72
Gomez v. Perez, 72
Griswold v. Connecticut, 56

Hamling v. United States, 132, 133, 146
Hankerson v. North Carolina, 49, *51*
Harris v. Oklahoma, *75*, 86, 99
Henderson v. Kibbe, 37, *40*
Henry v. Mississippi, 21–22
Hicks v. Miranda, 54
Hutto v. Ross, *128*

Ianelli v. United States, 87
Illinois v. Somerville, 78

Jeffers v. United States, 87, 99
Jenkins v. Georgia, 131
Jimenez v. Weinberger, 72
Jones v. Hildebrant, 114
Jones v. North Carolina Prisoners' Union, 111

Kahn v. Shevin, 70

Labine v. Vincent, 72
Lee v. United States, 86, 98
Leland v. Oregon, 50, 54
Levy v. Louisiana, 72
Lochner v. New York, 7

Maher v. Roe, 57

TABLE OF CASES

Marbury v. Madison, 4
Marks v. United States, 130, *134*
Mathews v. Lucas, 72
McCarthy v. United States, 123
Memoirs v. Massachusetts, 130–31, 132
Miller v. California, 130, 131, 132, 146, 147
Miranda v. Arizona, 12
Missouri v. Holland, 3
Moody v. Daggett, 111
Moore v. City of East Cleveland, Ohio, 54, 57
Morrissey v. Brewer, 112
Mullaney v. Wilbur, 49, 50, 54

New Jersey Welfare Rights Organization v. Cahill, 72

O'Brien v. United States, 101, 102

Patterson v. New York, *44*
Phillips v. Martin Marietta Corp., 70
Planned Parenthood of Central Missouri v. Danforth, 56
Poelker v. Doe, 57

Redrup v. New York, 132
Reed v. Reed, 70
Rivera v. Delaware, 54
Rizzo v. Goode, 142
Roe v. Wade, 56
Roth v. United States, 130, 131, 132

Scarborough v. United States, 53
Schlesinger v. Ballard, 70
Scott v. Kentucky Parole Bd., 111
Serafass v. United States, 76
Smith v. United States, 146
Splawn v. California, 146
Stanley v. Illinois, 70
Stanton v. Stanton, 71

Taylor v. Louisiana, 70
Time, Inc. v. Hill, 137
Townsend v. Sain, 123, 124
Trimble v. Gordon, *66,* 72
Turner v. Dept. of Employment Security, 71

United States v. Antelope, 69
United States v. Dieter, 99
United States v. Dinitz, 87
United States v. Jenkins, 76, 78
United States v. Jorn, 77
United States v. Kopp, 76, 86, 98
United States v. Martin Linen Supply Co., 76, *79,* 99
United States v. Morrison, 86, 98
United States v. O'Brien, 142, 143
United States v. Rose, 76, 86, 98
United States v. Sanford, 76, 77, 78, 86, 98
United States v. Sisson, 78

Village of Belle Terre v. Boraas, 54, 56

Ward v. Illinois, 147
Weatherford v. Bursey, 100, *103*
Weber v. Aetna Casualty & Surety Co., 72
Weinberger v. Salfi, 71
Weinerer v. Wiesenfeld, 71
Whalen v. Roe, 57
Wilson v. United States, 76, 77, 78
Winship, In re, 50, 54
Wooley v. Maynard, 140, *143*

Younger v. Harris, 141

Zacchini v. Scripps-Howard Broadcasting Co., *137*

Part One

THE FEDERAL COURTS, THE BILL OF RIGHTS,
THE CRIMINAL PROCESS, DUE PROCESS
AND EQUAL PROTECTION OF THE LAWS

1

INSIDE THE SUPREME COURT: JUDICIAL REVIEW, THE DECISION-MAKING PROCESS, AND THE BILL OF RIGHTS

1.01 THE MODERN SUPREME COURT

THE NOTION OF A LIVING CONSTITUTION*

William H. Rehnquist†

At least one of the more than half-dozen persons nominated during the past decade to be an Associate Justice of the Supreme Court of the United States has been asked by the Senate Judiciary Committee at his confirmation hearings whether he believed in a living Constitution.[1] It is not an easy question to answer; the phrase "living Constitution" has about it a teasing imprecision that makes it a coat of many colors.

One's first reaction tends to be along the lines of public relations or ideological sex appeal, I suppose. At first blush it seems certain that a *living* Constitution is better than what must be its counterpart, a *dead* Constitution. It would seem that only a necrophile could disagree. If we could get one of the major public opinion research firms in the country to sample public opinion concerning whether the United States Constitution should be *living* or *dead*, the overwhelming majority of the responses doubtless would favor a *living* Constitution....

The first meaning [of "living Constitution"] was expressed over a half-century ago by Mr. Justice Holmes in *Missouri* v. *Holland*[5] with his customary felicity when he said:

...When we are dealing with words that also are a constituent act, like the Constitution of the United States, we must realize that they have called into life a being the development of which could not have been foreseen completely by the most gifted of its begetters. It was enough for them to realize or to hope that they had created an organism; it has taken a century and has cost their successors much sweat and blood to prove that they created a nation.[6]

---

*From 54 Tex. L. Rev. 693 (1976). Reproduced by permission. This article is a revised version of an address given by Justice Rehnquist during the ninth annual Will E. Orgain Lectures at the University of Texas School of Law on March 12, 1976.

†William H. Rehnquist has served as an Associate Justice of the Supreme Court since 1972.

I shall refer to this interpretation of the phrase "living Constitution," with which scarcely anyone would disagree, as the Holmes version.

The framers of the Constitution wisely spoke in general language and left to succeeding generations the task of applying that language to the unceasingly changing environment in which they would live. Those who framed, adopted, and ratified the Civil War amendments[7] to the Constitution likewise used what have been aptly described as "majestic generalities"[8] in composing the fourteenth amendment. Merely because a particular activity may not have existed when the Constitution was adopted, or because the framers could not have conceived of a particular method of transacting affairs, cannot mean that general language in the Constitution may not be applied to such a course of conduct. Where the framers of the Constitution have used general language, they have given latitude to those who would later interpret the instrument to make that language applicable to cases that the framers might not have foreseen.

In my reading and travels I have sensed a second connotation of the phrase "living Constitution," however, one quite different from what I have described as the Holmes version, but which certainly has gained acceptance among some parts of the legal profession. Embodied in its most naked form, it recently came to my attention in some language from a brief that had been filed in a United States District Court on behalf of state prisoners asserting that the conditions of their confinement offended the United States Constitution. The brief urged:

> We are asking a great deal of the Court because other branches of government have abdicated their responsibility.... Prisoners are like other discrete and insular minorities for whom the Court must spread its protective umbrella because no other branch of government will do so.... This Court, as the voice and conscience of contemporary society, as the measure of the modern conception of human dignity, must declare that the [named prison] and all it represents offends the Constitution of the United States and will not be tolerated.

Here we have a living Constitution with a vengeance. Although the substitution of some other set of values for those which may be derived from the language and intent of the framers is not urged in so many words, that is surely the thrust of the message. Under this brief writer's version of the living Constitution, non-elected members of the federal judiciary may address themselves to a social problem simply because other branches of government have failed or refused to do so. These same judges, responsible to no constituency whatever, are nonetheless acclaimed as "the voice and conscience of contemporary society."

If we were merely talking about a slogan that was being used to elect some candidate to office or to persuade the voters to ratify a constitutional amendment, elaborate dissection of a phrase such as "living Constitution" would probably not be warranted. What we are talking about, however, is a suggested philosophical approach to be used by the federal judiciary, and perhaps state judiciaries, in exercising the very delicate responsibility of judicial review. Under the familiar principle of judicial review, the courts in construing the Constitution are, of course, authorized to invalidate laws that have been enacted by Congress or by a state legislature but that those courts find to violate some provision of the Constitution. Nevertheless, those who have pondered the matter have always recognized that the ideal of judicial review has basically antidemocratic and antimajoritarian facets that require some justification in this Nation, which prides itself on being a self-governing representative democracy.

All who have studied law, and many who have not, are familiar with John Marshall's classic defense of judicial review in his opinion for the Court in *Marbury* v. *Madison*.[9] I will summarize very briefly the thrust of that answer, with which I fully agree, because while it supports the Holmes version of the phrase "living Constitution," it also suggests some outer limits for the brief writer's version.

The ultimate source of authority in this Nation, Marshall said, is not Congress, not the states, not for that matter the Supreme Court of the United States. The people are the ultimate source of authority; they have parceled out the authority that originally resided entirely with them by adopting the original Constitution and by later amending it. They have granted some authority to the federal government and have reserved authority not granted it to the states or to the people individually. As between the branches of the federal government, the people have given certain authority to the President, certain authority to Congress, and certain authority to the federal government. From today's perspective we might add that they have placed restrictions on the authority of the state governments in the thirteenth, fourteenth, and fifteenth amendments.

In addition, Marshall said that if the popular branches of government—state legislatures, the Congress, and the Presidency—are operating within the authority granted to them by the Constitution, their judgment and not that of the Court must obviously prevail. When these branches overstep the authority given them by the Constitution, in the case of the President and Congress, or invade protected individual rights, and a constitutional challenge to their action is raised in a lawsuit brought in federal court, the Court must prefer the Constitution to the government acts.

John Marshall's justification for judicial review makes the provision for an independent federal judiciary not only understandable but also thoroughly desirable. Since the judges will be merely interpreting an instrument framed by the people, they should be detached and objective. A mere change in public opinion since the adoption of the Constitution, unaccompanied by a constitutional amendment, should not change the meaning of the Constitution. A merely temporary majoritarian groundswell should not abrogate some individual liberty truly protected by the Constitution.

Clearly Marshall's explanation contains certain elements of either ingenuousness or ingeniousness, which tend to grow larger as our constitutional history extends over a longer period of time. The Constitution is in many of its parts obviously not a specifically worded document but one couched in general phraseology. There is obviously wide room for honest difference of opinion over the meaning of general phrases in the Constitution; any particular Justice's decision when a question arises under one of these general phrases will depend to some extent on his own philosophy of constitutional law. One may nevertheless concede all of these problems that inhere in Marshall's justification of judicial review, yet feel that his justification for nonelected judges exercising the power of judicial review is the only one consistent with democratic philosophy of representative government....

... [T]he brief writer's version seems instead to be based upon the proposition that federal judges, perhaps judges as a whole, have a role of their own, quite independent of popular will, to play in solving society's problems. Once we have abandoned the idea that the authority of the courts to declare laws unconstitutional is somehow tied to the language of the Constitution that the people adopted, a judiciary exercising the power of judicial review appears in a quite different light. Judges then are no longer the keepers of the covenant; instead they are a small group of fortunately situated people with a roving commission to second-guess Congress, state legislatures, and state and federal administrative officers concerning what is best for the country. Surely there is no justification for a third legislative branch in the federal government, and there is even less justification for a federal legislative branch's reviewing on a policy basis the laws enacted by the legislatures of the fifty states. Even if one were to disagree with me on this point, the members of a third branch of the federal legislature at least ought to be elected by and responsible to constituencies, just as in the case of the other two branches of Congress. If there is going to be a council of revision, it ought to have at least some connection with popular feeling. Its members either ought to stand for reelection on occasion, or their terms should expire and they should be allowed to continue serving only if reappointed by a popularly elected Chief Executive and confirmed by a popularly elected Senate.

The brief writer's version of the living Constitution is seldom presented in its most naked form, but is instead usually dressed in more attractive garb. The argument in favor of this approach generally begins with a sophisticated wink—why pretend that there is any ascertainable content to the general phrases of the Constitution as they are written since, after all, judges constantly disagree about their meaning? We are all familiar with Chief Justice Hughes' famous aphorism that "We are under a Constitution, but the Constitution is what the judges say it is."[14] We all know the basis of Marshall's justification for judicial review, the argument runs, but it is necessary only to keep the window dressing in place. Any sophisticated student of the subject knows that judges need not limit themselves to the intent of the framers, which is very difficult to determine in any event. Because of the general language used in the Constitution, judges should not hesitate to use their authority to make the Constitution relevant and useful in solving the problems of modern society. The brief writer's version of the living Constitution envisions all of the above conclusions.

At least three serious difficulties flaw the brief writer's version of the living Constitution. First, it misconceives the nature of the Constitution, which was designed to enable the popularly elected branches of government, not the judicial branch, to keep the country abreast of the times. Second, the brief writer's version ignores the Supreme Court's disastrous experiences when in the past it embraced contemporary, fashionable notions of what a living Constitution should contain. Third, however socially desirable the goals sought to be advanced by the brief writer's version, advancing them through a freewheeling, nonelected judiciary is quite unacceptable in a democratic society.

It seems to me that it is almost impossible, after reading the record of the Founding Fathers' debates in Philadelphia, to conclude that they intended the Constitution itself to suggest answers to the manifold problems that they knew would confront succeeding generations. The Constitution that they drafted was indeed intended to endure indefinitely, but the reason for this very well-founded hope was the general language by which national authority was granted to Congress and the Presidency. These two branches were to furnish the motive power within the federal system, which was in turn to coexist with the state governments; the elements of government having a popular constituency were looked to for the solution of the numerous and varied problems that the future would bring. Limitations were indeed placed upon both federal and state governments in the form of both a division of powers and express protection for individual rights. These limitations, however, were not themselves designed to solve the problems of the future, but were instead designed to make certain that the constituent branches, when *they* attempted to solve those problems, should not transgress these fundamental limitations.

Although the Civil War Amendments[15] were designed more as broad limitations on the authority of state governments, they too were enacted in response to practices that the lately seceded states engaged in to discriminate against and mistreat the newly emancipated freed men. To the extent that the language of these amendments is general, the courts are of course warranted in giving them an application coextensive with their language....

The brief writer's version of the living Constitution, however, suggests that if the states' legislatures and governors, or Congress and the President, have not solved a particular social problem, then the federal court may act. I do not believe that this argument will withstand rational analysis. Even in the face of a conceded social evil, a reasonably competent and reasonably representative legislature may decide to do nothing. It may decide that the evil is not of sufficient magnitude to warrant any governmental intervention. It may decide that the financial cost of eliminating the evil is not worth the benefit which would result from its elimination. It may decide that the evils which might ensue from the proposed solution are worse than the evils which the solution would eliminate.

Surely the Constitution does not put either the legislative branch or the executive branch in the position of a television quiz show contestant so that when a given period of time has elapsed and a problem remains unsolved by them, the federal judiciary may press a buzzer and take its turn at fashioning a solution.

The second difficulty with the brief writer's version of the living Constitution lies in its inattention to or rejection of the Supreme Court's historical experience gleaned from similar forays into problem solving.

Although the phrase "living Constitution" may not have been used during the nineteenth century and the first half of this century, the idea represented by the brief writer's version was very much in evidence during both periods. The apogee of the living Constitution doctrine during the nineteenth century was the Supreme Court's decision in *Dred Scott* v. *Sanford*.[17] In that case the question at issue was the status of a Negro who had been carried by his master from a slave state into a territory made free by the Missouri Compromise. Although thereafter taken back to a slave state, Dred Scott claimed that upon previously reaching free soil he had been forever emancipated. The Court, speaking through Chief Justice

Taney, held that Congress was without power to legislate upon the issue of slavery even in a territory governed by it, and that therefore Dred Scott had never become free. Congress, the Court held, was virtually powerless to check or limit the spread of the institution of slavery....

The *Dred Scott* decision, of course, was repealed in fact as a result of the Civil War and in law by the Civil War amendments. The injury to the reputation of the Supreme Court that resulted from the *Dred Scott* decision, however, took more than a generation to heal. Indeed, newspaper accounts long after the *Dred Scott* decision bristled with attacks on the Court, and particularly on Chief Justice Taney, unequalled in their bitterness even to this day.

The brief writer's version of the living Constitution made its next appearance, almost as dramatically as its first, shortly after the turn of the century in *Lochner* v. *New York*.[29] The name of the case is a household word to those who have studied constitutional law, and it is one of the handful of cases in which a dissenting opinion has been overwhelmingly vindicated by the passage of time. In *Lochner*, a New York law that limited to ten the maximum number of hours per day that could be worked by bakery employees was assailed on the ground that it deprived the bakery employer of liberty without due process of law. A majority of the Court held the New York maximum hour law unconstitutional, saying, 'Statutes of the nature of that under review, limiting the hours in which grown and intelligent men may labor to earn their living, are mere meddlesome interferences with the rights of the individual....'"[30]

The fourteenth amendment, of course, said nothing about any freedom to make contracts upon terms that one thought best, but there was a very substantial body of opinion outside the Constitution at the time of *Lochner* that subscribed to the general philosophy of social Darwinism as embodied in the writing of Herbert Spencer in England and William Graham Sumner in this country. It may have occurred to some of the Justices who made up a majority in *Lochner*, hopefully subconsciously rather than consciously, that since this philosophy appeared eminently sound and since the language in the due process clause was sufficiently general not to rule out its inclusion, why not strike a blow for the cause? The answer, which has been vindicated by time, came in the dissent of Mr. Justice Holmes:

A constitution is not intended to embody a particular economic theory, whether of paternalism and the organic relation of the citizen to the state or of *laissez faire*. It is made for people of fundamentally differing views, and the accident of our finding certain opinions natural and familiar or novel and even shocking ought not to conclude our judgment upon the question whether statutes embodying them conflict with the Constitution of the United States.[31]

One reads the history of these episodes in the Supreme Court to little purpose if he does not conclude that prior experimentation with the brief writer's expansive notion of a living Constitution has done the Court little credit. There remain today those, such as wrote the brief from which I quoted, who appear to cleave nevertheless to the view that the experiments of the Taney Court before the Civil War, and of the Fuller and Taft Courts in the first part of this century, ended in failure not because they sought to bring into the Constitution a principle that the great majority of objective scholars would have to conclude was not there but because they sought to bring into the Constitution the *wrong* extraconstitutional principle. This school of thought appears to feel that while added protection for slave owners was clearly unacceptable and safeguards for businessmen threatened with ever-expanding state regulation were not desirable, expansion of the protection accorded to individual liberties against the state or to the interest of "discrete and insular" minorities,[32] such as prisoners, must stand on a quite different, more favored footing. To the extent, of course, that such a distinction may legitimately be derived from the Constitution itself, these latter principles do indeed stand on an entirely different footing. To the extent that one must, however, go beyond even a generously fair reading of the language and intent of that document in order to subsume these principles, it seems to me that they are not really distinguishable from those espoused in *Dred Scott* and *Lochner*.

The third difficulty with the brief writer's notion of the living Constitution is that it seems to ignore totally the nature of political value judgments in a democratic society. If such a society adopts a constitution and incorporates in that constitution safeguards for individual liberty, these safeguards indeed do take on a generalized moral rightness or goodness. They assume a general social acceptance neither because of any intrinsic worth nor because of any unique origins in someone's idea of natural justice but instead simply because they have been incorporated in a constitution by the people. Within the limits of our Constitution, the representatives of the people in the executive branches of the state and national governments enact laws. The laws that emerge after a typical political struggle in which various individual value judgments are debated likewise take on a form of moral goodness because they have been enacted into positive law. It is the fact of their enactment that gives them whatever moral claim they have upon us as a society, however, and not any independent virtue they may have in any particular citizen's own scale of values.

Beyond the Constitution and the laws in our society, there simply is no basis other than the individual conscience of the citizen that may serve as a platform for the launching of moral judgments. There is no conceivable way in which I can logically demonstrate to you that the judgments of my conscience are superior to the judgments of your conscience, and vice versa. Many of us necessarily feel strongly and deeply about our own moral judgments, but they remain only personal moral judgments until in some way given the sanction of law....

This is not to say that individual moral judgments ought not to afford a springboard for action in society, for indeed they are without doubt the most common and most powerful wellsprings for action when one believes that questions of right and wrong are involved. Representative government is predicated upon the idea that one who feels deeply upon a question as a matter of conscience will seek out others of like view or will attempt to persuade others who do not initially share that view. When adherents to the belief become sufficiently numerous, he will have the necessary armaments required in a democratic society to press his views upon the elected representatives of the people, and to have them embodied into positive law.

Should a person fail to persuade the legislature, or should he feel that a legislative victory would be insufficient because of its potential for future reversal, he may seek to run the more difficult gauntlet of amending the Constitution to embody the view that he espouses. Success in amending the Constitution would, of course, preclude succeeding transient majorities in the legislature from tampering with the principle formerly added to the Constitution.

I know of no other method compatible with political theory basic to democratic society by which one's own conscientious belief may be translated into positive law and thereby obtain the only general moral imprimatur permissible in a pluralistic, democratic society. It is always time consuming, frequently difficult, and not infrequently impossible to run successfully the legislative gauntlet and have enacted some facet of one's own deeply felt value judgments. It is even more difficult for either a single individual or indeed for a large group of individuals to succeed in having such a value judgment embodied in the Constitution. All of these burdens and difficulties are entirely consistent with the notion of a democratic society. It should not be easy for any one individual or group of individuals to impose by law their value judgments upon fellow citizens who may disagree with those judgments. Indeed, it should not be easier just because the individual in question is a judge. We all have a propensity to want to do it, but there are very good reasons for making it difficult to do....

The brief writer's version of the living Constitution, in the last analysis, is a formula for an end run around popular government. To the extent that it makes possible an individual's persuading one or more appointed federal judges to impose on other individuals a rule of conduct that the popularly elected branches of government would not have enacted and the voters have not and would not have embodied in the Constitution, the brief writer's version of the living Constitution is genuinely corrosive of the fundamental values of our democractic society.

References*

1. *Hearings on Nominations of William H. Rehnquist and Lewis F. Powell, Jr., Before the Senate Comm. on the Judiciary,* 92d Cong., 1st Sess. 87 (1971).

---

*Numbers do not follow in consecutive order owing to deletion of portions of the original article.

5. 252 U.S. 416 (1920).
6. Id. at 433.
7. U.S. Const. amends. XIII, XIV, XV.
8. *Fay* v. *New York*, 332 U.S. 261, 282 (1947) (Jackson, J.).
9. 5 U.S. (1 Cranch) 137 (1803).
14. C. Hughes, ADDRESSES 139 (1908).
15. U.S. Const. amends. XIII, XIV, XV.
17. 60 U.S. (19 How.) 393 (1857).
29. 198 U.S. 45 (1905).
30. Id. at 61.
31. Id at 75-76 (Holmes, J., dissenting).
32. *United States* v. *Carolene Prods. Co.*, 304 U.S. 144, 152 n.4 (1938).

STATE CONSTITUTIONS AND THE PROTECTION OF INDIVIDUAL RIGHTS*

William J. Brennan, Jr.†

... [State] courts cannot rest when they have afforded their citizens the full protections of the federal Constitution. State constitutions, too, are a font of individual liberties, their protections often extending beyond those required by the Supreme Court's interpretation of federal law. The legal revolution which has brought federal law to the fore must not be allowed to inhibit the independent protective force of state law—for without it, the full realization of our liberties cannot be guaranteed.

* * *

The decisions of the Supreme Court enforcing the protections of the fourteenth amendment generally fall into one of three categories. The first concerns enforcement of the federal guarantee of equal protection of the laws. While the best known, of course, are *Brown* v. *Board of Education*[2] and *Baker* v. *Carr*,[3] perhaps even more the concern of state bench and bar in terms of state court litigation are decisions invalidating state legislative classifications that impermissibly impinge on the exercise of fundamental rights, such as the rights to vote,[4] to travel interstate,[5] or to bear or beget a child.[6]

---

*From 90 Harv. L. Rev. 489 (1977). Copyright 1977 by the Harvard Law Review Association.

†William J. Brennan, Jr., has served as an Associate Justice of the Supreme Court since 1956.

Equally important are decisions that require exacting judicial scrutiny of classifications that operate to the peculiar disadvantage of politically powerless groups whose members have historically been subjected to purposeful discrimination—racial minorities[7] and aliens[8] are two examples.

The second category of decisions concerns the fourteenth amendment's guarantee against the deprivation of life, liberty or property where that deprivation is without due process of law. The root requirement of due process is that, except for some extraordinary situations, an individual be given an opportunity for a hearing before he is deprived of any significant "liberty" or "property" interest. Our decisions enforcing the guarantee of the due process clause have elaborated the essence of that "liberty" and "property" in light of conditions existing in contemporary society. For example, "property" has come to embrace such crucial expectations as a driver's license[9] and the statutory entitlement to minimal economic support, in the form of welfare, of those who by accident, birth or circumstance find themselves without the means of subsistence.[10] The due process safeguard against arbitrary deprivation of these entitlements, as well as the more traditional forms of property, such as a workingman's wages[11] and his continued possession and use of goods purchased under conditional sales contracts,[12] has been recognized as mandating prior notice and the opportunity to be heard. At the same time, conceptions of 'liberty" have come to recognize the undeniable proposition that prisoners and parolees retain some vestiges of human dignity, so that prison regulations and parole procedures must provide some form of notice and hearing prior to confinement in solitary[13] or the revocation of parole.[14] Moreover, the concepts of liberty and property have combined in recognizing that under modern conditions tenured public employees may not have their reasonable expectation of continued employment,[15] and school children their right to a public education,[16] revoked without notice and opportunity to be heard.

I suppose, however, that it is mostly the third category of decisions by the United States Supreme Court during the last twenty years—those enforcing the specific guarantees of the Bill of Rights against encroachment by state action—that has required the special consideration of state judges, particularly as those decisions affect the administration of the criminal justice system. After his retirement, Chief Justice Earl Warren was asked what he regarded to be the decision during his tenure that would have the greatest consequence for all Americans. His choice was *Baker* v. *Carr,* because he believed that if each of us has an equal vote, we are equally armed with the indispensable means to make our views felt. I feel at least as good a case can be made that the series of decisions binding the states to almost all of the restraints of the Bill of Rights will be even more significant in preserving and furthering the ideals we have fashioned for our society.

Before the fourteenth amendment was added to the Constitution, the Supreme Court held that the Bill of Rights did not restrict state, but only federal, action.[17] In the decades between 1868, when the fourteenth amendment was adopted, and 1897, the Court decided in case after case that the amendment did not apply various specific restraints in the Bill of Rights to state action.[18] The breakthrough came in 1897 when the prohibition against taking private property for public use without payment of just compensation was held embodied in the fourteenth amendment's proscription, "nor shall any state deprive any person of ... property without due process of law."[19] But extension of the rest of the specific restraints of the first amendment applied to state action.[20] Then in 1949 the fourth amendment's prohibition of unreasonable searches and seizures was extended,[21] but the extension was made virtually meaningless because the states were left free to decide for themselves whether any effective means of enforcing the guarantee was to be made available. It was not until 1961 that the Court applied the exclusionary rule to state proceedings.[22]

It was in the years from 1962 to 1969 that the face of the law changed. Those years witnessed the extension to the states of nine of the specifics of the Bill of Rights; decisions which have had a profound impact on American life, requiring the deep involvement of state courts in the application of federal law....

These decisions over the past two decades gave full effect to the principle of *Boyd* v. *United States,*[34] the case Mr. Justice Brandeis hailed as "a case that will be remembered so long as civil liberty lives in the United States."[35] That principle, stated by Mr. Justice Bradley, was "... constitutional provisions for the security of person and property should be liberally construed.... It is the duty of courts to be watchful for the constitutional rights of the citizen, and against any stealthy encroachments thereon."[36]

The thread of this series of Bill of Rights holdings reflects a conclusion—arrived at only after a long series of decisions grappling with the pros and cons of the question—that there exists in modern America the necessity for protecting all of us from arbitrary action by governments more powerful and more pervasive than any in our ancestors' time. Only if the amendments are construed to preserve their fundamental policies will they ensure the maintenance of our constitutional structure of government for a free society. For the genius of our Constitution resides not in any static meaning that it had in a world that is dead and gone, but in the adaptability of its great principles to cope with the problems of a developing America. A principle to be vital must be of wider application than the mischief that gave it birth. Constitutions are not ephemeral documents, designed to meet passing occasions. The future is their care, and therefore, in their application, our contemplation cannot be only of what has been but of what may be.

* * *

Of late, however, more and more state courts are construing state constitutional counterparts of provisions of the Bill of Rights as guaranteeing citizens of their states even more protection than the federal provisions, even those identically phrased. This is surely an important and highly significant development for our constitutional jurisprudence and for our concept of federalism. I suppose it was only natural that when during the 1960's our rights and liberties were in the process of becoming increasingly federalized, state courts saw no reason to consider what protections, if any, were secured by state constitutions. It is not easy to pinpoint why state courts are now beginning to emphasize the protections of their states' own bill of rights. It may not be wide of the mark, however, to suppose that these state courts discern, and disagree with, a trend in recent opinions of the United States Supreme Court to pull back from, or at least suspend for the time being, the enforcement of the *Boyd* principle with respect to application of the federal Bill of Rights and the restraints of the due process and equal protection clauses of the fourteenth amendment.

Under the equal protection clause, for example, the Court has found permissible laws that accord lesser protection to over half of the members of our society due to their susceptibility to the medical condition of pregnancy,[37] as well as laws that impose special burdens on those of our citizens who are of illegitimate birth.[38] The Court has also found uncompelling the claims of those barred from judicial forums due to their inability to pay access fees,[39] and has further handicapped the indigent by limiting their right to free trial transcripts when challenging the legality of their imprisonment.[40]

Under the due process clause, the Supreme Court has found no liberty interest in the reputation of an individual—never tried and never convicted—who is publicly branded as a criminal by the police without benefit of notice, let alone a hearing.[41] The Court has recently indicated that tenured public employees might not be entitled to any more process before deprivation of their employment than the government sees fit to give them.[42] It has approved the termination of payments to disabled individuals who are completely dependent upon those payments, prior to an oral hearing, a form of hearing statistically shown to result in a huge rate of reversals of preliminary administrative determinations.[43] And it has veered from its promise to recognize that prisoners, too, have liberty interests that cannot be ignored.[44]

The same trend is repeated in the category of the specific guarantees of the Bill of Rights. The Court has found the first amendment insufficiently flexible to guarantee access to essential public forums when in our evolving society those traditional forums are under private ownership in the form of suburban shopping centers,[45] and at the same time has found the amendment's prohibitions insufficient to invalidate a system of restrictions on motion picture theatres based upon the content of their presentations.[46] It has found that the warrant requirement plainly appearing on the face of the fourth amendment does not require the police to obtain a warrant before arrest, however easy it might have been to get an arrest warrant.[47] It has declined to read the fourth amendment to prohibit searches of an individual by police officers following a stop for a traffic violation, although there exists no probable cause to believe the individual has committed any other legal infraction.[48] The Court has held permissible police searches grounded upon consent regardless of whether the consent was a knowing and intelligent one,[49] and has found that none of us has a legitimate expectation of privacy in the contents of our bank records, thus permitting governmental seizure of those records without our knowledge or consent.[50] Even when the Court has found searches to violate fourth amendment rights, it has—on occasion—declared exceptions to the exclusionary rule and allowed the use of such evidence.[51]

Moreover, the Court has held, contrary to *Boyd* v. *United States,* that we may not interpose the privilege against self-incrimination to bar government attempts to obtain our personal papers, no matter how private the nature of their contents.[52] And the privilege, said the Court, is not violated when statements unconstitutionally obtained from an individual are used for purposes of impeaching his testimony,[53] or securing his indictment by a grand jury.[54]

The sixth amendment guarantee has fared no better. The guarantee of assistance of counsel has been held unavailable to an accused in custody when shuffled through pre-indictment identification procedures, no matter how essential counsel might be to the avoidance of prejudice to his rights at later stages of the criminal process.[55] In addition, the Court has countenanced a state's placing significant burdens—in the form of a "two-tier" trial system—on the constitutional right to trial by jury in criminal cases.[56] And in the face of our requirement of proof of guilt beyond a reasonable doubt, the Court has upheld the permissibility of less than unanimous jury verdicts of guilty.[57]

Also, a series of decisions has shaped the doctrines of jurisdiction, justiciability, and remedy, so as increasingly to bar the federal courthouse door in the absence of showings probably impossible to make.[58] At the same time, the *Younger* doctrine has been extended to allow state officials to block federal court protection of constitutional rights simply by answering a plaintiff's federal complaint with a state indictment.[59] And the centuries-old remedy of habeas corpus was so circumscribed last Term as to weaken drastically its ability to safeguard individuals from invalid imprisonment.[60]

It is true, of course, that there has been an increasing amount of litigation of all types filling the calendars of virtually every state and federal court. But a solution that shuts the courthouse door in the face of the litigant with a legitimate claim for relief, particularly a claim of deprivation of a constitutional right, seems to be not only the wrong tool but also a dangerous tool for solving the problem. The victims of the use of that tool are most often the litigants most in need of judicial protection of their rights—the poor, the underprivileged, and deprived minorities. The very lifeblood of courts is popular confidence that they mete out even-handed justice and any discrimination that denies these groups access to the courts for resolution of their meritorious claims unnecessarily risks loss of that confidence.

* * *

Some state decisions have indeed suggested a connection between these recent decisions of the United States Supreme Court and the state court's reliance on the state's bill of rights. For example, the California Supreme Court, in holding that statements taken from suspects before first giving them *Miranda* warnings are inadmissible in California courts to impeach an accused who testifies in his own defense, stated: 'We ... declare that [the decision to the contrary of the United States Supreme Court[61] is not persuasive authority in any state prosecution in California. ... We pause ... to reaffirm the independent nature of the California Constitution and our responsibility to separately define and protect the rights of California citizens despite conflicting decisions of the United States Supreme Court interpreting the federal Constitution."[62]

Enlightenment comes also from the New Jersey Supreme Court. In 1973 the United States Supreme Court held that where the subject of a search was not in custody and the prosecution attempts to justify the search by showing the subject's consent, the prosecution need not prove that the subject knew he had a right to refuse to consent to the search.[63] The Court expressly rejected the contention that the validity of consent to a non-custodial search should be tested by a waiver standard requiring the state to demonstrate that the individual consented to the search knowing he did not have to, and that he intentionally relinquished or abandoned that right. In *State* v. *Johnson*,[64] Mr. Justice Sullivan, writing for New Jersey's high court, first acknowledged that the United States Supreme Court decision was controlling on state courts in construing the fourth amendment and was therefore dispositive of the defendant's federal constitutional argument.[65] But Mr. Justice Sullivan went on to consider whether the identically phrased provision of the New Jersey Constitution, Art. I, para. 7, "should be interpreted to give the individual greater protection than is provided by" the federal provision.[66] Counsel had not made this argument either to the trial court or on appeal, but the supreme court, *sua sponte,* posed the issue and afforded counsel the opportunity for argument on the question. Mr. Justice Sullivan held for the court that, while Art. I, para. 7 was *in haec verba* with the fourth amendment and until then had not been held to impose higher or different standards than the fourth amendment, "we have the right to construe our state constitutional provision in accordance with what we conceive to be its plain meaning."[67] That meaning, he went on to hold, was "that under Art. I, para. 7 of our State Constitution the validity of a consent to search, even in a non-custodial situation, must be measured in terms of waiver, i.e., where the state seeks to justify a search on the basis of consent it has the burden of showing that the consent was voluntary, an essential element of which is knowledge of the right to refuse consent."[68]

Among other instances of state courts similarly rejecting United States Supreme Court decisions as unpersuasive, the Hawaii[69] and California[70] Supreme Courts have held that searches incident to lawful arrest are to be tested by a standard of reasonableness rather than automatically validated as incident to arrest,[71] the Michigan Supreme Court has held that a suspect is entitled to the assistance of counsel at any pretrial lineup or photographic identification procedure,[72] and the South Dakota[73] and Maine[74] Supreme Courts have held that there is a right to trial by jury even for petty offenses.[75]

Other examples abound where state courts have independently considered the merits of constitutional arguments and decline to follow opinions of the United States Supreme Court they find unconvincing, even where the state and federal constitutions are similarly or identically phrased.[76] As the Supreme Court of Hawaii has observed, "while this results in a divergence of meaning between words which are the same in both federal and state constitutions, the system of federalism envisaged by the United States Constitution tolerates such divergence where the result is greater protection of individual rights under state law than under federal law...."[77] Some state courts seem apparently even to be anticipating contrary rulings by the United States Supreme Court and are therefore resting decisions solely on state law grounds. For example, the California Supreme Court held, as a matter of state constitutional law, that bank depositors have a sufficient expectation of privacy in their bank records to invalidate the voluntary disclosure of such records by a bank to the police without the knowledge or consent of the depositor.[78] Thereafter, the United States Supreme Court ruled that federal law was to the contrary.[79]

And of course state courts that rest their decisions wholly or even partly on state law need not apply federal principles of standing and justiciability that deny litigants access to the courts. Moreover, the state decisions not only cannot be overturned by, they indeed are not even reviewable by, the Supreme Court of the United States. We are utterly without jurisdiction to review such state decisions.[80] This was precisely the circumstance of Mr. Justice Hall's now famous *Mt. Laurel* decision,[81] which was grounded on the New Jersey Constitution and on state law. The review sought in that case in the United States Supreme Court was, therefore, completely precluded.

This pattern of state court decisions puts to rest the notion that state constitutional provisions were adopted to mirror the federal Bill of Rights. The lesson of history is otherwise; indeed, the drafters of the federal Bill of Rights drew upon corresponding provisions in the various state constitutions. Prior to the adoption of the federal Constitution, each of the rights eventually recognized in the federal Bill of Rights had previously been protected in one or more state constitutions.[82] And prior to the adoption of the fourteenth amendment, these state bills of rights, independently interpreted, were the primary restraints on state action since the federal Bill of Rights had been held inapplicable.

The essential point I am making, of course, is not that the United States Supreme Court is necessarily wrong in its interpretation of the federal Constitution, or that ultimate constitutional truths invariably come prepackaged in the dissents, including my own, from decisions of the Court. It is simply that the decisions of the Court are not, and should not be, dispositive of questions regarding rights guaranteed by counterpart provisions of state law.[83] Accordingly, such decisions are not mechanically applicable to state law issues, and state court judges and the members of the bar seriously err if they so treat them. Rather, state court judges, and also practitioners, do well to scrutinize constitutional decisions by federal courts, for only if they are found to be logically persuasive and well-reasoned, paying due regard to precedent and the policies underlying specific constitutional guarantees, may they properly claim persuasive weight as guideposts when interpreting counterpart state guarantees. I suggest to the bar that, although in the past it might have been safe for counsel to raise only federal constitutional issues in state courts, plainly it would be most unwise these days not also to raise the state constitutional questions.

* * *

Every believer in our concept of federalism, and I am a devout believer, must salute this development in our state courts. Unfortunately, federalism has taken on a new meaning of late. In its name, many of the door-closing decisions described above have been rendered.[84] Under the banner of the vague, undefined notions of equity, comity and federalism the Court has condoned both isolated[85] and systematic[86] violations of civil liberties. Such decisions hardly bespeak a true concern for equity. Nor do they properly understand the nature of our federalism. Adopting the premise that state courts can be trusted to safeguard individual rights,[87] the Supreme Court has gone on to limit the protective role of the federal judiciary. But in so doing, it has forgotten that one of the strengths of our federal system is that it provides a double source of protection for the rights of our citizens. Federalism is not served when the federal half of that protection is crippled.

Yet, the very premise of the cases that foreclose federal remedies constitutes a clear call to state courts to step into the breach. With the federal locus of our double protections weakened, our liberties cannot survive if the states betray the trust the Court has put in them. And if that trust is, for the Court, strong enough to override the risk that some states may not live up to it, how much more strongly should we trust state courts whose manifest purpose is to expand constitutional protections. With federal scrutiny diminished, state courts must respond by increasing their own.

Moreover, it is not only state-granted rights that state courts can safeguard. If the Supreme Court insists on limiting the content of due process to the rights created by state law,[88] state courts can breathe new life into the federal due process clause by interpreting their common law, statutes and constitutions to guarantee a "property" and "liberty" that even the federal courts must protect. Federalism need not be a mean-spirited doctrine that serves only to limit the scope of human liberty. Rather, it must necessarily be furthered significantly when state courts thrust themselves into a position of prominence in the struggle to protect the people of our nation from governmental intrusions on their freedoms....

References*

2. 347 U.S. 483 (1954) (invalidating state laws requiring public schools to be racially segregated).
3. 369 U.S. 186 (1962) (invalidating state laws diluting individual voting rights by legislative malapportionments). See also *Reynolds* v. *Sims*, 377 U.S. 533
4. *Harper* v. *Virginia State Bd.*, 383 U.S. 663 (1966).
5. *Shapiro* v. *Thompson*, 394 U.S. 618 (1969).
6. *Eisenstadt* v. *Baird*, 405 U.S. 438 (1972); *Griswold* v. *Connecticut*, 381 U.S. 479 (1965).
7. *Brown* v. *Board of Educ.*, 347 U.S. 483 (1954).
8. *Sugarman* v. *Dougall*, 413 U.S. 634 (1973); *Graham* v. *Richardson*, 403 U.S. 365 (1971).
9. *Bell* v. *Burson*, 402 U.S. 535 (1971).
10. *Goldberg* v. *Kelly*, 397 U.S. 254 (1970).
11. *Sniadach* v. *Family Fin. Corp.*, 395 U.S. 337 (1969).

---

*Numbers do not follow in consecutive order owing to deletion of portions of the original article.

12. *Fuentes* v. *Shevin*, 407 U.S. 67 (1972).
13. *Wolff* v. *McDonnell*, 418 U.S. 539 (1974).
14. *Morrissey* v. *Brewer*, 408 U.S. 471 (1972).
15. *Perry* v. *Sindermann*, 408 U.S. 593 (1972).
16. *Goss* v. *Lopez*, 419 U.S. 556 (1975).
17. *Barron* v. *Baltimore*, 32 U.S. (7 Pet.) 243 (1833).
18. See *O'Neil* v. *Vermont*, 144 U.S. 323, 332 (1892); *McElvaine* v. *Brush*, 142 U.S. 155, 158–59 (1891); *In re Kemmler*, 136 U.S. 436, 446 (1890); *Presser* v. *Illinois*, 116 U.S. 252, 263–68 (1886); *Hurtado* v. *California*, 110 U.S. 516 (1884); *United States* v. *Cruikshank*, 92 U.S. 542, 552–56 (1875); *Walker* v. *Sauvinet*, 92 U.S. 90 (1875).
19. *Chicago B. & O.R.R.* v. *Chicago*, 166 U.S. 226, 241 (1897).
20. Compare *Gitlow* v. *New York*, 268 U.S. 652, 666 (1925), with *Prudential Ins. Co.* v. *Cheek*, 259 U.S. 530, 543 (1922).
21. *Wolf* v. *Colorado*, 338 U.S. 25, 27–28 (1949).
22. *Mapp* v. *Ohio*, 367 U.S. 643 (1961).
34. 116 U.S. 616 (1886).
35. *Olmstead* v. *United States*, 277 U.S. 438, 474 (1928) (dissenting opinion).
36. 116 U.S. at 635.
37. *Geduldig* v. *Aiello*, 417 U.S. 484 (1974); *cf., General Electric Co.* v. *Gilbert*, 45 U.S.L.W. 4031 (U.S. Dec. 7, 1976) (decided under Title VII).
38. Compare *Mathews* v. *Lucas*, 96 S. Ct. 2755 (1976), with *Weber* v. *Aetna Cas. & Sur. Co.*, 406 U.S. 164, 175 (1972) ("... imposing disabilities on the illegitimate child is contrary to the basic concept of our system that legal burdens should bear some relationship to individual responsibility or wrongdoing."). Recent decisions have also given rise to some doubt as to the Court's continuing commitment to the eradication of racial discrimination in employment and education. See *Washington* v. *Davis*, 96 S. Ct. 2040 (1976); *Pasadena City Bd. of Educ.* v. *Spangler*, 96 S. Ct. 2697 (1976); *Milliken* v. *Bradley*, 418 U.S. 717 (1974).
39. Compare *Ortwein* v. *Schwab*, 410 U.S. 656 (1972), and *United States* v. *Kras*, 409 U.S. 434 (1973), with *Boddie* v. *Connecticut*, 401 U.S. 371 (1971).
40. *United States* v. *MacCollom*, 96 S. Ct. 2086 (1976).
41. *Paul* v. *Davis*, 424 U.S. 693 (1976).
42. *Arnett* v. *Kennedy*, 416 U.S. 134 (1974); *Bishop* v. *Wood*, 96 S. Ct. 2074 (1976).
43. *Mathews* v. *Eldridge*, 424 U.S. 319 (1976).
44. Compare *Meachum* v. *Fano*, 96 S. Ct. 2532 (1976) (finding no liberty interest implicated in the transfer of a prisoner to a maximum security facility), with *Wolff* v. *McDonnell*, 418 U.S. 539 (1974).
45. *Hudgens* v. *NLRB*, 424 U.S. 507 (1976), overruling *Food Employees Union Local 590* v. *Logan Valley Plaza, Inc.*, 391 U.S. 308 (1968); *Lloyd Corp.* v. *Tanner*, 407 U.S. 551 (1972).
46. Compare *Young* v. *American Mini-Theatres, Inc.*, 96 S. Ct. 2440 (1976), with *Erznoznick* v. *City of Jacksonville*, 422 U.S. 205 (1975).
47. *United States* v. *Watson*, 423 U.S. 411 (1976). See also *United States* v. *Santana*, 96 S. Ct. 2406 (1976) (holding that in a *Watson*-like situation, police may pursue a suspect into his or her home).
48. *United States* v. *Robinson*, 414 U.S. 218 (1973);

Gustafson v. *Florida*, 414 U.S. 260 (1973). The Court has also declined to read the amendment to prohibit warrantless searches of the glove compartments of automobiles impounded for mere parking violations. *South Dakota* v. *Opperman*, 96 S. Ct. 3092 (1976).

49. *United States* v. *Watson*, 423 U.S. 411 (1976); *Schneckloth* v. *Bustamonte*, 412 U.S. 218 (1973).
50. *United States* v. *Miller*, 96 S. Ct. 1619 (1976).
51. *E.g., United States* v. *Janis*, 96 S. Ct. 3021 (1976).
52. *Andresen* v. *Maryland*, 96 S. Ct. 2737 (1976); *Fisher* v. *United States*, 96 S. Ct. 1569 (1976).
53. *Harris* v. *New York*, 401 U.S. 222 (1971).
54. *United States* v. *Calandra*, 414 U.S. 338 (1974).
55. Compare *Kirby* v. *Illinois*, 406 U.S. 682 (1972), with *United States* v. *Wade*, 388 U.S. 218 (1967).
56. *Ludwig* v. *Massachusetts*, 96 S. Ct. 2781 (1976) (approving trial de novo system).
57. *Apodaca* v. *Oregon*, 406 U.S. 404 (1972).
58. *Rizzo* v. *Goode*, 423 U.S. 362 (1976); *Simon* v. *Eastern Ky. Welfare Rights Org.*, 96 S. Ct. 1917 (1976); *Warth* v. *Seldin*, 422 U.S. 490 (1975); *O'Shea* v. *Littleton*, 414 U.S. 488 (1974).
59. *Hicks* v. *Miranda*, 422 U.S. 332 (1975).
60. *Stone* v. *Powell*, 96 S. Ct. 3037 (1976); *Francis* v. *Henderson*, 96 S. Ct. 1708 (1976).
61. *Harris* v. *New York*, 401 U.S. 222 (1971).
62. *People* v. *Disbrow*, 16 Cal. 3d 101, 113, 114–15, 545 P.2d 272, 280, 127 Cal. Rptr. 360, 368 (1976). The Hawaii and Pennsylvania Supreme Courts have taken similar positions. See *State* v. *Santiago*, 53 Hawaii 254, 492 P. 2d 657 (1971); *Commonwealth* v. *Triplett*, 341 A.2d 62 (Pa. 1975).
63. *Schneckloth* v. *Bustamonte*, 412 U.S. 218 (1973).
64. 68 N.J. 349, 346 A.2d 66 (1975).
65. See *Oregon* v. *Hass*, 420 U.S. 714, 719 (1975).
66. 68 N. J. at 353, 346 A.2d at 67–68.
67. *Id.* at 353 n.2, 346 A.2d at 68 n.2.
68. *Id.* at 353–54, 346 A.2d at 68.
69. *State* v. *Kaluna*, 55 Hawaii 361, 520 P.2d 51 (1974).
70. *People* v. *Brisendine*, 13 Cal. 3d 528, 531 P. 2d 1099, 119 Cal. Rptr. 315 (1975).
71. Compare cases cited notes 69 and 70 *supra*, with *United States* v. *Robinson*, 414 U.S. 218 (1973).
72. Compare *People* v. *Jackson*, 391 Mich. 323, 217 N.W. 2d 22 (1974), with *United States* v. *Ash*, 413 U.S. 300 (1973).
73. *Parham* v. *Municipal Court*, 199 N.W.2d 501 (S.D. 1972).
74. *State* v. *Sklar*, 317 A. 2d 160 (Me. 1974). See also *Baker* v. *City of Fairbanks*, 471 P.2d 386 (Alaska 1970).
75. Compare cases cited notes 73 and 74 *supra*, with *Baldwin* v. *New York*, 399 U.S. 66 (1970), and *Duncan* v. *Louisiana*, 391 U.S. 145 (1968).
76. For a listing of such examples, see the cases collected in the following articles: Falk, *The Supreme Court of California 1971–1972, Foreword: The State Constitution: A More than "Adequate" Nonfederal Ground*, 61 Calif. L. Rev. 273 (1973); Howard, *State Courts and Constitutional Rights in the Day of the Burger Court*, 62 Va. L. Rev. 873 (1976); Wilkes, *The New Federalism in Criminal Procedure: State Court Evasion of the Burger Court*, 62 Ky. L.J. 421, 437–43 (1974); Wilkes, *More on the New Federalism in Criminal Procedure*, 63 Ky. L.J. 873 (1975); *Project Report, Toward an Activist Role for State Bills of Rights*, 8 Harv. C.R.-C.L. L. Rev. 271 (1973).
77. *State* v. *Kaluna*, 55 Hawaii 361, 369 n.6, 520 P.2d 51, 58 n.6 (1974).
78. *Burrows* v. *Superior Court*, 13 Cal. 3d 238, 529 P.2d 590, 118 Cal. Rptr. 166 (1974).
79. *United States* v. *Miller*, 96 S. Ct. 1619 (1976).
80. The Supreme Court's jurisdiction over state cases is limited to the correction of errors related solely to questions of federal law. It cannot review state court determinations of state law even when the case also involves federal issues. *Murdock* v. *City of Memphis*, 87 U.S. (20 Wall.) 590 (1875). Moreover, if a state ground is independent and adequate to support a judgment, the Court has no jurisdiction at all over the decision despite the presence of federal issues. *Fox Film Corp.* v. *Muller*, 396 U.S. 207 (1935); *Murdock* v. *City of Memphis*, 87 U.S. (20 Wall.) 590 (1875). One reason for the refusal to review such decisions, even where the state court also decides a federal question erroneously, was explained by Mr. Justice Jackson in *Herb* v. *Pitcairn*, 324 U.S. 117, 125–26 (1945):

> Our only power over state judgments is to correct them to the extent that they incorrectly adjudge federal rights. And our power is to correct wrong judgments, not to revise opinions. We are not permitted to render an advisory opinion, and if the same judgment would be rendered by the state court after we corrected its views of federal laws, our review could amount to nothing more than an advisory opinion.

81. *Southern Burlington County NAACP* v. *Township of Mt. Laurel*, 67 N.J. 151, 336 A.2d 713 (invalidating town's exclusive zoning ordinance), *appeal dismissed and cert. denied*, 423 U.S. 808 (1975).
82. See generally Brennan, *The Bill of Rights and the States*, in THE GREAT RIGHTS (E. Cahn ed. 1963).
83. The Court has made this point clear on a number of occasions. See *Oregon* v. *Hass*, 420 U.S. 714, 719 (1975) (" . . . a State is free *as a matter of its own law* to impose greater restrictions on police activity than those this Court holds to be necessary upon federal constitutional standards"); *Cooper* v. *California*, 386, U.S. 58, 62 (1967).
84. See *Stone* v. *Powell*, 96 S. Ct. 3037 (1976); *Francis* v. *Henderson*, 96 S. Ct. 1708 (1976); *Hicks* v. *Miranda*, 422 U.S. 332 (1975).
85. See *Paul* v. *Davis*, 424 U.S. 693 (1976); cases cited note 84 *supra*.
86. See *Rizzo* v. *Goode*, 423 U.S. 362 (1976); *O'Shea* v. *Littleton*, 414 U.S. 488 (1974).
87. See *Stone* v. *Powell*, 96 S. Ct. 3037, 3051 n.35 (1976); *Doran* v. *Salem Inn, Inc.*, 422 U.S. 922, 930 (1975).
88. See p. 496 and notes 41 and 42 *supra*.

1.02. THE FEDERAL COURTS

THERE SHALL BE "ONE SUPREME COURT"*

Arthur J. Goldberg†

In discussing the proposal for a National Court of Appeals[1] (the Mini-Supreme Court) I start, as one must, with the Constitution of the United States. Article III, section 1 of the Constitution states: "The judicial Power of the United States, shall be vested in one Supreme Court...." Opponents of the proposed National Court of Appeals have argued that the creation of such a court would violate this article in that a delegation of the exercise of the Supreme Court's jurisdiction would create, in effect, two Supreme Courts.[2]

To some extent, Congress can alter the specific substantive areas that fall within the Court's appellate jurisdiction. But once Congress vests jurisdiction in the Supreme Court, can it delegate to another court responsibility for deciding cases which are properly filed in the Supreme Court? Does not the power to decide cases presuppose the power to consider them and to make a final decision with respect to them when properly filed? In other words, is delegation to another court of cases properly before the Supreme Court consistent with the Constitution's command that there be "one Supreme Court"?

Even if these constitutional doubts are not well-founded, what the Constitution does not command, it may still inspire. There is the greatest value in citizens being able to believe that, as a matter of principle, every person has a right to take a claim involving basic rights and liberties to the Supreme Court of the United States for final action, without reference to any other tribunal. It is this belief that in part inspires the great popular belief of the Supreme Court as a palladium of liberty and a citadel of justice.

---

*From 3 Hastings Const. L.Q. 339 (1976). Reproduced by permission.

†Arthur J. Goldberg served as an Associate Justice of the Supreme Court from 1962 to 1965.

The controversy relating to the mini-court commenced on December 19, 1972, with the release of a Federal Judicial Center study group report, popularly known as the Freund Report.[3] Mr. Freund, a distinguished Harvard professor and constitutional scholar, and his colleagues on the study group recommended a major change in the structure of our judicial system. After examining the workload of the Supreme Court, the group concluded that the rising caseload has imposed a "staggering burden" upon the justices.[4] The group proposed that Congress create a new National Court of Appeals, made up of a rotating panel of seven presently sitting federal appellate judges. This new court would screen the 4,000 or so petitions for review that are now filed each year with the Supreme Court; the great majority would be finally denied, but about 400 petitions would be certified to the Supreme Court itself for further screening and disposition. The new court would also hear and determine on the merits cases involving conflicts among the federal courts of appeal, a function traditionally performed by the Supreme Court.[5]

There were other recommendations in the Freund Report which did not arouse the same degree of controversy: the abolition of three-judge courts in special cases with direct appeal to the Supreme Court,[6] and the establishment of an ombudsman, rather than an untutored prison lawyer, to advise prisoners as to their prospects of success in seeking review by the Court.[7]

As a result of considerable opposition to the Freund Report's recommendations, Congress created the Commission on Revision of the Federal Court Appellate System.[8] This distinguished commission heard testimony, sponsored studies, and on June 20, 1975, submitted its report and recommendations to Congress for change in the structure and internal procedures of the federal appellate system.[9] In this commentary I shall not deal with the part of the commission report regarding the internal procedures of the existing courts of appeal. I shall confine myself to the commission's recommendations affecting the Supreme Court.

The commission recommended that Congress establish a National Court of Appeals, consisting of seven judges appointed by the President with the advice and consent of the Senate.[10] The National Court of Appeals would have jurisdiction to screen or hear cases (a) referred to it by the Supreme Court (reference jurisdiction), or (b) transferred to it from the regional courts of appeal, the Court of Claims, and the Court of Customs and Patent Appeals (transfer jurisdiction).[11]

With respect to any case before it on petition for certiorari, the Supreme Court would be authorized:

(1) to retain the case and render a decision on the merits;

(2) to deny certiorari, thus terminating the litigation;

(3) to deny certiorari and refer the case to the National Court of Appeals for that court to decide the merits of the case; or

(4) to deny certiorari and refer the case to the National Court of Appeals, giving that court discretion either to decide the case on the merits or to deny review.[12]

If a case filed in a court of appeals, the Court of Claims, or the Court of Customs and Patent Appeals is one in which an immediate decision by the National Court of Appeals is in the public interest, it may be transferred to the National Court of Appeals provided it falls within one of the following categories:

(1) the case turns on a rule of federal law and the federal courts have reached inconsistent determinations with respect to it; or

(2) the case turns on a rule of federal law applicable to a recurring factual situation, and a showing is made that the advantages of a prompt and definitive determination of that rule by the National Court of Appeals outweigh any potential disadvantages of transfer; or

(3) the case turns on a rule of federal law which has theretofore been announced by the National Court of Appeals, and there is a substantial question about the proper interpretation or application of that rule in the pending case.[13]

The National Court of Appeals would be empowered to decline the transfer, and decisions by the National Court of Appeals accepting or rejecting cases would not be reviewable under any circumstances.[14] Any case decided by the National Court of Appeals, whether upon reference or after transfer, would be subject to review by the Supreme Court upon petition for certiorari.[15]

The underlying rationale of the commission's report is that the Court is overburdened and as a consequence is unable adequately to deal with transcendent constitutional issues, to resolve conflicts between the circuits, and to determine national law authoritatively and efficiently.

The recommendations of the commission have, in the main, received the support of the Chief Justice of the United States, Mr. Justice White, Mr. Justice Blackmun, Mr. Justice Powell, and Mr. Justice Rehnquist. Mr. Justice Brennan, Mr. Justice Stewart, and Mr. Justice Marshall have, by and large, opposed the recommendations of the commission as did Mr. Justice Douglas while he was on the Court.[16] Almost everyone who has sat on the Supreme Court has agreed that three-judge courts with direct appeals to the Supreme Court should be abolished[17] and that federal diversity jurisdiction also should be terminated.

Let me first deal with the question of the "staggering burden" on Supreme Court justices. During my tenure, the Court's caseload was not as heavy as it is today; filings have increased from approximately 2,400 during the 1962 term to approximately 4,000 during the 1974 term.[18] Although the number of filed cases that the Court must screen has risen dramatically, I am of the view that certiorari petition screening, though highly important, represents one of the less time-consuming aspects of a justice's work. The vast majority of certiorari petitions raise no significant legal issue, and under existing legislation, the Court has discretion to deny petitions without a hearing or a formal opinion. Indeed, an astonishing number of filed cases present questions that a third-year law student can immediately recognize as inappropriate for the Supreme Court.

The more historically important and time-consuming aspect of a justice's work — the hearing and determination of cases on the merits — has not become correspondingly more burdensome over the years. The number of decided cases has remained relatively constant, averaging about 150 annually during recent times.[19]

I frankly do not see how the recommendations of the commission would diminish the workload of the Supreme Court. Rather it seems that were this procedure to be adopted, the workload of the Supreme Court would be increased. The Court would be required to undertake review of certiorari cases twice; first, on the original application for certiorari, and subsequently, after the National Court of Appeals decides these cases on the merits or by denial of review.[20]

The commission apparently hopes that the Supreme Court would allocate less time and work for the second review than it did for the first. But my experience teaches that some, or even all, of the Supreme Court justices would conclude that a second review similar to the first probably would be necessary in fairness to the litigants and in discharge of the Court's responsibility. It seems to me unlikely that the Supreme Court by rule would dispense with the first review in particular cases or in groups of cases.

The commission's referral proposal seems to imply that the Supreme Court should concern itself primarily with constitutional issues, and that the National Court of Appeals should deal with other important issues of national law and conflicts between the regional circuits. Yet Supreme Court justices are interested in various areas of the law, and rightly so. Questions of statutory interpretation are illustrative of the scope of appropriate exercise of jurisdiction by the Supreme Court. I doubt very much that the proposed procedure would materially alter the Court's decision-making process with respect to certiorari application of these kinds of cases.

I further adhere to the view that resolving conflicts between the circuits and therefore necessarily overruling a particular court of appeals is a sensitive process even when performed by the Supreme Court. To vest this function in a court of lesser stature than the Supreme Court, however distinguished it may be, would inevitably create tension in the appellate system. Further, the Supreme Court often delays resolution of a conflict situation until the problem is ripe for adjudication.

In summary, it is my belief that the recommendations of the commission would not alleviate the workload of the Supreme Court, but would add to it. Despite the disclaimer of the commission, its recommendations would create a "fourth tier" in our federal judicial system, leading to greater delays and greater expense than now exist. The proposed transfer jurisdiction for the National Court of Appeals likewise seems unrealistic. The commission obviously hopes that in both reference and transfer jurisdiction the Supreme Court would refuse to review decisions and actions of the National Court of Appeals except in the most summary fashion. I do not conceive that regional courts of appeal would readily yield their jurisdiction except to the Supreme Court.[21]

It is perhaps the greatest virtue of the Supreme Court that it is designed to serve, as it now functions, as a guarantee to all citizens of whatever estate, race or color that our highest court is open for consideration of their claims that they are being denied equal and relevant justice under the Constitution. I am convinced that grave injury would be done by creation of a National Court of Appeals to the great concept engraved at the very entrance of the noble edifice which houses the Court: Equal Justice Under Law.

I believe that to create a National Court of Appeals would be a serious mistake. The commission's proposal, if implemented according to its intent, would deny to Americans their historic right to take any case raising substantial constitutional questions or significant matters of national law to the highest court in the land for the final resolution by the Supreme Court and by the Supreme Court alone. I profoundly believe that the Supreme Court as it now functions is discharging its great responsibilities as the ultimate guardian of our liberties under the Constitution. Let us maintain the purpose and spirit of the institution.

References

1. *See* Federal Judicial Center, Report of the Study Group on the Case Load of the Supreme Court (1972) [hereinafter cited as Freund Report].
2. *See, e.g.,* Goldberg, *One Supreme Court,* The New Republic, Feb. 10, 1973, at 14; Warren, *A Response to Recent Proposals to Dilute the Jurisdiction of the Supreme Court,* 20 Loyola L. Rev. (New Orleans) 221, 229 (1974).
3. Freund Report, *supra* note 1.
4. *Id.* at 5.
5. *Id.* at 18–19.
6. *Id.* at 27.
7. *Id.* at 14.
8. Act of Oct. 13, 1972, Pub. L. No. 92-489, §§ 1–7, 86 Stat. 807, *as amended,* Pub. L. No. 93-420, 88 Stat. 1153 (1974).
9. U.S. Commission on Revision of the Federal Court Appellate System, Structure and Internal Procedures: Recommendations for Change (1975) [hereinafter cited as Commission Report].
10. *Id.* at 30.
11. *Id.* at 32, 34.

12. *Id.* at 32–33.
13. *Id.* at 34–35.
14. *Id.* at 35.
15. *Id.* at 38.
16. *See id.* at 172–88.
17. Recent legislation has eliminated three-judge courts except in cases challenging the constitutionality of the apportionment of legislative districts and a few other cases. Pub. L. No. 94-381, §§ 2284, 2403, 45 U.S.L.W. 1 (Aug. 12, 1976).
18. Freund Report, *supra* note 1, at A2.
19. Commission Report, *supra* note 9, at 6.
20. *Id.* at 32–38.
21. The proposed transfer jurisdiction has been eliminated in S. 3423, 94th Cong., 2d Sess. (1976), introduced by Senator Hruska, the chairman of the commission. Senator Hruska correctly states in his explanatory statement relating to this proposal that it has aroused intense and widespread dissent. My own discussions with various judges of the courts of appeals and others confirm this statement by Senator Hruska. It is my opinion that elimination of transfer jurisdiction in S. 3423 is well advised.

1.04 GRANTING SUPREME COURT REVIEW

Supreme Court Review of State Court Decisions*[1]

The Constitution does not, in terms, authorize the Supreme Court to review decisions of state courts. It does, however, extend the judicial power of the United States to defined classes of cases, some of which are as likely to arise in the courts of a state as in a federal court, and it gives to the Supreme Court appellate jurisdiction over all such cases, other than those within the original jurisdiction of the Court, with such exceptions and under such regulations as the Congress shall make.[2] It is unusual for the court of one sovereign to have appellate jurisdiction over the courts of other sovereigns, but federalism itself is—or was when the Constitution was adopted—an unusual system, and the Supremacy Clause is a sufficient basis on which to rest the appellate jurisdiction over state court decisions. Thus the First Congress, in the famous section 25 of the Judiciary Act of 1789, authorized such review.[3] . . .

* * *

Under the present statute, review is possible of the final judgment of the highest court of a state in which a decision could be had in any case where the validity of a treaty or statute of the United States is drawn in question or where the validity of a state statute is drawn in question on the ground of its being repugnant to the Constitution, treaties, or laws of the United States, or where any title, right, privilege, or immunity is specially set up or claimed under the Constitution, treaties, or statutes of, or commission held or authority exercised under, the United States.[15] The jurisdiction does not depend on the amount in controversy[16] or the citizenship of the parties.[17] It rests entirely on the existence of what is always referred to as a "federal question" in the case. The distinction that persisted from 1789 to 1914 between cases where the state court had rejected the federal claim and cases in which it had honored it still remains, as will be seen, in distinguishing those cases where an appeal may be taken from those that are reviewable only on petition for certiorari.

The state court decision to be reviewable must be that of the highest court of the state in which a decision could be had. This by no means restricts review to decisions of the highest state court. Even a trial court decision is reviewable in the United States Supreme Court if there is no higher state court to which the party can resort. In a well-known case certiorari was granted to review a decision of the Police Court of Louisville, Kentucky, where the fines imposed were so small that no review was available in any Kentucky court.[18] If discretionary review is available in some higher state court, such review must be sought, no matter how unlikely it may seem that it will be granted.[19] The attempt to secure further review will extend the time in which to resort to the Supreme Court, but if further discretionary review is refused, the judgment is that of the court below that rendered it, and it is this that must be taken to the Supreme Court.[20] However if the higher state court takes action that amounts to an affirmance of what has been done below, it is the judgment of the higher court that must be taken to the Supreme Court.[21]

---
*From Wright, Charles A., *Law of Federal Courts*, § 107 (3d ed. 1976). Reproduced by permission from West Publishing Co.

Review can only be had of "final judgments or decrees." Obviously there can be no final judgment unless there has been a judgment. Here however the Court has been liberal, and has even been willing to regard a letter from the clerk of the state court to the appellant, refusing to docket his appeal, as being a judgment of the state court.[22] In some states the highest court sits in divisions. If, after decision by a division, the party may obtain review by the whole court as a matter of right, the decision of the division is not a final judgment of the court and is not reviewable.[23] But if reconsideration by the whole court is discretionary, the decision of the division will be regarded as a final judgment, and reviewable, even though the party did not seek reconsideration by the whole court.[24] On the same principle, a party need not petition for rehearing by a court in order to have a final judgment of that court,[25] though if he does so unsuccessfully the pendency of his petition extends the time in which to seek review in the Supreme Court of the original decision.[26]

* * *

The Court decides for itself whether the decision of the state court is a final judgment. State law and state practice are of importance in determining what has been done and what may still be done within the state judicial system, but the Court will then make its own determination of whether under such circumstances the judgment has that finality requisite for Supreme Court review.[32] Although the early practice was contrary, and did not permit the Court even to consider the opinion of the state court in determining whether the state decision was final,[33] it is now quite settled that the Court may look not only to the opinion but also to any other relevant matter, in or out of the record, in determining finality.[34] The test, as in other instances where finality must be determined, is increasingly a pragmatic one. A judgment is final for purposes of review if it leaves only ministerial acts, such as entry of judgment accordingly in the lower court, to be done.[35] The traditional rule has been that judgment is not final for purposes of review, though it settles the important issue in the case, if it leaves open something not merely ministerial that might itself raise a federal question.[36]

In recent years the Court has departed strikingly from this traditional view. As it said in Cox Broadcasting Corp. v. Cohn,[37] "as the cases have unfolded, the Court has recurringly encountered situations in which the highest court of a State has finally determined the federal issue present in a particular case, but in which there are further proceedings in the lower state courts to come. There are now at least four categories of such cases in which the Court has treated the decision on the federal issue as a final judgment for the purposes of 28 U.S.C. § 1257 and has taken jurisdiction without awaiting the completion of the additional proceedings anticipated in the lower state courts."

The first of these categories, as defined by the Court in Cox, includes those cases in which there are further proceedings yet to occur in the state courts but for one reason or another the federal issue is conclusive or the outcome of further proceedings preordained.[38] The second category is the cases in which the federal issue, finally decided by the highest court in the state, will survive and require decision regardless of the outcome of future state proceedings.[39] The third category is those situations in which the federal claim has been finally decided, with further proceedings on the merits in the state courts to come, but in which later review of the federal issue cannot be had, whatever the ultimate outcome of the case.[40]

The fourth of the Cox categories was described by the Court as "those situations where the federal issue has been finally decided in the state courts with further proceedings pending in which the party seeking review here might prevail on the merits on nonfederal grounds, thus rendering unnecessary review of the federal issue by this Court, and where reversal of the state court on the federal issue would be preclusive of any further litigation on the relevant cause of action rather than merely controlling the nature and character of, or determining the admissibility of evidence in, the state proceedings still to come. In these circumstances, if a refusal immediately to review the state court decision might seriously erode federal policy, the Court has entertained and decided the federal issue, which itself has been finally determined by the state courts for purposes of the state litigation."[41]

* * *

...The Court will not review a case, even though it contains a federal question, if there is an adequate state ground that supports the decision of the state court. Further, the court will accept as binding upon it the state court's decision of questions of state law.

There has recently been an elaborate argument made that the framers of the Constitution intended that the Supreme Court would speak authoritatively on questions of state law as well as on questions of federal law.[62] The historical evidence for this proposition is unconvincing, and the uniform practice of the Court has been to the contrary. It has considered that the state courts speak with final authority on questions of state law.[63] The exceptions to this principle are very few. Decisions of the state court as to state law are only persuasive, rather than controlling, where state law is incorporated by reference in a federal statute,[64] or where protection of a federal constitutional right would be thwarted if the state had the last word on state questions, as in determining whether there is a "contract" within the meaning of the clause of the Constitution prohibiting impairment of the obligation of contracts,[65] or where the state court interpretation of state law appears to be an "obvious subterfuge to evade consideration of a federal issue."[66]

The other aspect of the rule . . . is that the Supreme Court cannot review a state decision at all if that decision rests on an adequate state ground. Thus there can be no review if the state court has decided the case exclusively on some ground of state law, and has never reached a federal question present in the case.[67] Nor can there be review where the state court has decided both the state and federal questions, if its decision of the federal question was unnecessary in the light of its disposition of the state question.[68] But if the state court has decided the case entirely on the federal question presented, the Supreme Court can review, even though there was a state question in the case that could have been the basis for decision.[69] In such a case, if the state court's resolution of the federal question is erroneous, the Supreme Court will remand the case to the state court, which can then pass on the state question.[70] And it is held, though on shaky theoretical ground, that where a state statute incorporates federal law by reference, the Supreme Court may review a state court decision as to that statute, pass on the federal question that is incorporated by reference, and remand for the state court to reconsider its interpretation of the statute in the light of the Supreme Court's interpretation of the underlying federal law.[71]

In order to bar Supreme Court review, the state ground must be "adequate."[72] If there is no fair and substantial support in the facts for the state court's ruling on the state ground, the Supreme Court can disregard it.[73] A new state rule cannot be invented for the occasion in order to defeat the federal claim.[74] If the state court's refusal to consider the merits of a case is based on a rule "more properly deemed discretionary than jurisdictional" this does not bar review in the Supreme Court.[75] Even a state procedural rule of general applicability may be thought not an adequate state ground if it is so strict that it interferes unduly with the presentation of federal questions.[76] In the familiar words of Justice Holmes, "whatever springs the State may set for those who are endeavoring to assert rights that the State confers, the assertion of Federal rights, when plainly and reasonably made, is not to be defeated under the name of local practice."[77]

Review will not be defeated by a state court decision that a case that otherwise would turn on a federal question is moot or that the party lacked standing to raise the federal claim.[78] The Court considers that these are not state grounds at all but rather questions of federal law on which only it can pronounce final judgment.

The question of the adequate state ground is much confused by the decision in Henry v. Mississippi.[79] Although the majority in that case spoke of applying "settled principles,"[80] three of the dissenters thought that the decision "portends a severe dilution, if not complete abolition, of the concept of 'adequacy' as pertaining to state procedural grounds,"[81] while a commentator suggests that "the implication that a change in doctrine is under consideration is manifest, yet the holding is sufficiently narrow that retreat is not foreclosed."[82]

It is difficult to determine what was held in Henry, much less what effect, if any, it has on previous notions of the adequate state ground. Henry's conviction was affirmed by the Mississippi Supreme Court, despite the admission of evidence that arguably had been illegally obtained, on the ground that his counsel had failed to object to the evidence when it was introduced, as normally required by state procedure.

The Court first recognized the adequate state ground rule but drew a distinction between state substantive grounds and state procedural grounds, and declared it to be settled that "a litigant's procedural defaults in state proceedings do not prevent vindication of his federal rights unless the State's insistence on compliance with its procedural rule serves a legitimate state interest."[83] This indicates that the Court could review the case if it found that the state rule served no legitimate state interest. The Court immediately agreed that the state requirement of a contemporaneous objection clearly serves a legitimate state interest, but it pointed out other ways in which Henry's counsel had made his position known at a time when corrective action was possible. In those circumstances, the Court said, the delay in making the objection could not have frustrated the state's interest in avoiding delay and waste of time. Thus to enforce the contemporaneous objection rule would be to force resort to an arid ritual rather than to serve a substantial state interest.[84]

At this point it sounded as if the Court was prepared to declare the state ground inadequate and consider the merits, but it then expressly stated that it was not holding that the state ground was inadequate nor was it looking into the merits.[85] It saw some reason to think that counsel might have withheld objection to the evidence in question as a matter of strategy. If he had deliberately bypassed the opportunity to make timely objection, Henry would be deemed to have forfeited his state court remedies.[86] The case was, accordingly, remanded to the state court to determine whether there had been such a waiver.

If there had been a waiver, that would bar Henry from a decision on the merits of his federal claim either in state or federal court. But if the state court found no waiver, it was still free to insist on its procedural requirements and could, if it wished, again affirm the conviction. In that case, however, Henry "could have a federal court apply settled principles to test the effectiveness of the procedural default to foreclose consideration of his constitutional claim."[87] Whether the federal court referred to was the Supreme Court, on direct review, or a district court on habeas corpus, was not made clear.

Subsequent developments in the Henry case shed no additional light. In the course of three more years of litigation, the state court found that there had been a deliberate waiver by Henry and his counsel, and it again affirmed his conviction.[88] The Supreme Court denied certiorari "without prejudice to the bringing of a proceeding for relief in federal habeas corpus."[89] The case clearly must be studied in any consideration of the doctrine of the adequate state ground but the few obscure cases in which it has since been involved go in opposite directions[90] and suggest that Henry was not a significant break with the past but only an unusual case heavily influenced by its facts.[91]

It is often difficult to determine whether there is an adequate state ground that bars Supreme Court review because of failure of the state decision to indicate with sufficient clarity whether that court was relying on a federal ground or a state ground. This can occur either where the state court has not written an opinion or where its opinion is ambiguous. It is not surprising that there should be such ambiguous state decisions. The state courts have power to pass on both state and federal questions, and there is no need for them to draw a sharp distinction between the two. The matter is, of course, very different when review is sought in the Supreme Court.[92] One remedy in such a situation is for counsel to seek clarification from the state court, either by amendment of its judgment[93] or by a certificate from the court or the presiding judge.[94] If the state court does give such clarification and it appears from it that the decision rested on the federal ground, review can then be had.

Where there is no such clarification from the state court, four techniques are available to the Supreme Court: (1) since the burden is on the party invoking the jurisdiction of the Supreme Court to establish that that Court has jurisdiction, it may dismiss if its jurisdiction is ambiguous;[95] (2) it may vacate the judgment below and remand so that the state court will have an opportunity to clarify what it has ruled;[96] (3) it may continue the case to give the parties an opportunity to apply to the court below for clarification;[97] or (4) if it considers that any state ground that might be advanced for the decision is insubstantial, it may take jurisdiction and decide the federal question.[98] Although there has been no coherent pattern in the Court's choice of one device rather than another,[99] the second course seems to be the one followed most often in recent cases.

The statute for review of state court decisions in the Supreme Court permits review by certiorari in any case within its terms, but allows review by appeal if the state court has held a statute or treaty of the United States invalid[100] or if the state court has held valid a statute of the state against a claim that it is repugnant to the Constitution, treaties or laws of the United States.[101] In order to be entitled to appeal under these provisions it is not necessary that the statute be challenged in its entirety. It is enough that there is a claim that the statute is invalid as applied to a particular situation.[102] This somewhat doubtful rule gives rise to extremely subtle distinctions. Thus appeal does not lie, and review is only on certiorari, if the claim is that there is an erroneous exercise of authority under a valid statute,[103] or that a statute is being applied in a constitutionally discriminatory fashion.[104] Fortunately these distinctions are not of very great practical importance. Though the chance of obtaining review is better on appeal than on certiorari, and counsel would prefer appeal for that reason, both modes of review are now essentially discretionary.[105] In addition, since 1925 there has been statutory provision that if appeal has been improvidently taken in a case in which the proper mode of review is by certiorari, the papers on which the appeal was taken shall be considered as if they were a petition for certiorari.[106] Thus it is not uncommon for the Court to dismiss the appeal but grant certiorari.[107]

For purposes of appeal, the term "statute" refers to every enactment, legislative in character, to which the state gives the force of law.[108] These range from the state constitution, on the one hand,[109] to a municipal ordinance, on the other hand,[110] and include such things as an order by the regents of the state university,[111] a traffic regulation promulgated by the city police commissioner,[112] and a court order establishing an integrated bar.[113]

References*

1. Robertson & Kirkham, Jurisdiction of the Supreme Court of the United States, Wolfson & Kurland ed. 1951, pp. 1–15; Stern & Gressman, Supreme Court Practice, 4th ed. 1969, pp. 80–146; Brennan, State Court Decisions and the Supreme Court, 1960, 31 Pa. B.A.Q. 393.
2. See Berger, Congress v. Supreme Court, 1969, pp. 225–296; Merry, Scope of the Supreme Court's Appellate Jurisdiction: Historical Basis, 1962, 47 Minn. L. Rev. 53.
3. Act of Sept. 24, 1789, § 25, 1 Stat. 73, 85.
15. 28 U.S.C.A. § 1257(3).
16. Buel v. Van Ness, 1823, 8 Wheat. 312, 5 L.Ed. 624.
17. French v. Hopkins, 1888, 8 S. Ct. 589, 124 U.S. 524, 31 L. Ed. 536.
18. Thompson v. City of Louisville, 1960, 80 S. Ct. 624, 362 U.S. 199, 4 L.Ed.2d 654. In Cohens v. Virginia, 1821, 6 Wheat. 264, 5 L.Ed. 257, the judgment reviewed was that of the Quarterly Session Court for the Borough of Norfolk, Virginia. Decision of a magistrate was reviewed in Stanford v. Texas, 1965, 85 S.Ct. 506, 379 U.S. 476, 13 L.Ed.2d 43.
19. Costarelli v. Massachusetts, 1975, 95 S.Ct. 1534 421 U.S. 193, 44 L.Ed.2d 76; Banks v. California, 1969, 89 S.Ct. 1901, 395 U.S. 708, 23 L.Ed.2d 653; Gotthilf v. Sills, 1963, 84 S.Ct. 187, 375 U.S. 79, 11 L.Ed.2d 159; Stratton v. Stratton, 1915, 36 S. Ct. 26, 239 U.S. 55, 60 L.Ed. 142.
20. Michigan-Wisconsin Pipe Line Co. v. Calvert, 1954, 74 S.Ct. 396, 347 U.S. 157, 98 L.Ed. 583; Minneapolis, St.P. & S.S.M. Ry. Co. v. Rock, 1929, 49 S.Ct. 363, 279 U.S. 410, 73 L.Ed. 766; Virginian Ry. Co. v. Mullens, 1926, 46 S.Ct. 526, 271 U.S. 220, 70 L.Ed. 915.
21. Tumey v. Ohio, 1926, 47 S.Ct. 437, 273 U.S. 510, 71 L.Ed. 749, 50 A.L.R. 1243.
22. Burns v. Ohio, 1959, 79 S.Ct. 1164, 360 U.S. 252, 3 L.Ed.2d 1209. Orders characterized as "informal" were held reviewable in Smith v. Hooey, 1969, 89 S.Ct. 575, 576, 393 U.S. 374, 375, 21 L.Ed.2d 607, and in In re Summers, 1945, 65 S.Ct. 1307, 1309, 325 U.S. 561, 564, 89 L.Ed. 1795.
23. Gorman v. Washington University, 1942, 62 S.Ct. 962, 316 U.S. 98, 86 L.Ed. 1300.
24. Local 174, Teamsters, Chauffeurs, Warehousemen and Helpers of America v. Lucas Flour Co., 1962, 82 S.Ct. 571, 369 U.S. 95, 7 L.Ed.2d 593.
25. Southern Ry. Co. v. Clift, 1922, 43 S.Ct. 126, 260 U.S. 316, 67 L.Ed. 283; cf. Market St. Ry. Co. v. Railroad Comm. of State of Cal., 1945, 65 S.Ct. 770, 324 U.S. 548, 89 L.Ed. 1171.
26. Chicago, G. W. R. Co. v. Basham, 1919, 39 S.Ct. 213, 249 U.S. 164, 64 L.Ed. 534. But a motion to clarify the mandate by certifying that a federal

---

*Numbers do not follow in consecutive order owing to deletion of portions of the original article.

question was decided does not extend the time. Department of Banking, State of Nebraska v. Pink, 1942, 63 S.Ct. 233, 317 U.S. 264, 87 L.Ed. 254.

32. Department of Banking, State of Nebraska v. Pink 1942, 63 S.Ct. 233, 317 U.S. 264, 87 L.Ed. 254; Cole v. Violette, 1943, 63 S.Ct. 1204, 319 U.S. 581, 87 L.Ed. 1599; Richfield Oil Corp. v. State Bd. of Equalization, 1946, 67 S.Ct. 156, 329 U.S. 69, 91 L.Ed. 80.
33. E.g., Haseltine v. Central Nat. Bank, 1901, 22 S.Ct. 49, 183 U.S. 130 46 L.Ed. 117. This rule was abandoned in Clark v. Williard, 1934, 54 S.Ct. 615, 292 U.S. 112, 78 L.Ed. 1160.
34. Gospel Army v. City of Los Angeles, 1947, 67 S.Ct. 1428, 1430, 331 U.S. 543, 547, 91 L.Ed. 1662; Local No. 438 Construction & General Laborers' Union, AFL-CIO v. Curry, 1963, 83 S. Ct. 531, 537, 371 U.S. 542, 551, 9 L.Ed. 2d 514.
35. Board of Com'rs of Tippecanoe County v. Lucas, 1876, 93 U.S. 108, 23 L.Ed. 822; Department of Banking, State of Nebraska v. Pink , 1942, 63 S. Ct. 233, 317 U.S. 264, 87 L.Ed. 254; Cole v. Violette, 1943, 63 S.Ct. 1204, 319 U.S. 581, 87 L.Ed. 1599.
36. Republic Natural Gas Co. v. Oklahoma, 1948, 68 S.Ct. 972, 334 U.S. 62, 92 L.Ed. 1212; State of Washington ex rel. Grays Harbor Logging Co. v. Coats-Fordney Logging Co., 1917, 37 S.Ct. 295, 243 U.S. 251, 61 L.Ed. 702; Houston v. Moore, 1818, 3 Wheat. 433, 4 L.Ed. 428.
37. 1975, 95 S.Ct. 1029, 1037, 420 U.S. 469, 502–503, 43 L.Ed.2d 328.
38. 95 S.Ct. at 1038, 420 U.S. at 479. As examples the Court cited Organization for a Better Austin v. Keefe, 1971, 91 S. Ct. 1575, 1577 n. 1, 402 U.S. 415, 418 n. 1, 29 L.Ed.2d 1; Mills v. Alabama, 1966, 86 S.Ct. 1434, 384 U.S. 214, 16 L.Ed. 2d 484; Local No. 438 v. Curry, 1963, 83 S.Ct. 531, 536–537, 371 U.S. 542, 550–551 9 L.Ed.2d 514; Pope v. Atlantic C.L.R. Co., 1953, 73 S.Ct. 749, 750, 345 U.S. 579, 382, 97 L.Ed. 1094; Richfield Oil Corp. v. State Bd. of Equalization, 1946, 67 S.Ct. 156, 158–159, 329 U.S. 69, 73–74, 91 L.Ed. 80.
39. 95 S.Ct. at 1038–1039, 420 U.S. at 480–481. As examples the Court cited Brady v. Maryland, 1963, 83 S.Ct. 1194, 1195 n. 1, 373 U.S. 83, 85 n. 1, 10 L.Ed.2d 215; Radio Station WOW, Inc. v. Johnson, 1945, 65 S.Ct. 1475, 1479–1480, 326 U.S. 120, 126–127, 89 L.Ed. 2092; Carondelet Canal & Nav. Co. v. Louisiana, 1914, 34 S.Ct. 627, 233 U.S. 362, 58 L.Ed. 1001; Forgay v. Conrad, 1848, 6 How. 201, 47 U.S. 201, 12 L.Ed. 404.
40. 95 S.Ct. at 1039–1040, 420 U.S. at 481–482. As examples the Court cited North Dakota State Bd. of Pharmacy v. Snyder's Drug Stores, Inc., 1973, 94 S.Ct. 407, 414 U.S. 156, 38 L.Ed.2d 379; California v. Stewart, 1966, 86 S.Ct. 1602, 1640 n. 71, 384 U.S. 436, 498 n. 71, 16 L.Ed.2d 694 (decided sub nom. Miranda v. Arizona).
41. 95 S.Ct. at 1041, 420 U.S. at 482–483. As examples the Court cited Miami Herald Publishing Co. v. Tornillo, 1974, 94 S.Ct. 2831, 2834 n. 6, 418 U.S. 241, 247 n. 6, 41 L.Ed.2d 730; Hudson Distributors v. Eli Lilly, 1964 84 S.Ct. 1273, 1276 n. 4, 377 U.S. 386, 389 n.4, 12 L.Ed.2d 394; Local No. 438 v. Curry, 1963, 83 S.Ct. 531, 536, 371 U.S. 542, 550 9 L.Ed.2d 514; Mercantile Nat. Bank v. Langdeau, 1963, 83 S.Ct. 520, 522, 371 U.S. 555, 558, 9 L.Ed.2d 523.
62. 2 Crosskey, Politics and the Constitution in the History of the United States, 1953, pp. 23–26.
63. E.g., Mullaney v. Wilbur, 1975, 95 S.Ct. 1881, 1885–1886, 421 U.S. 684, 689, 44 L.Ed.2d 508; Scripto, Inc. v. Carson, 1960, 80 S.Ct. 619, 362 U.S. 207, 4 L.Ed.2d 660; Sutter Butte Canal Co. v. Railroad Comm. of Cal., 1929, 49 S.Ct. 325, 279 U.S. 125, 73 L.Ed. 637; American Ry. Express Co. v. Kentucky, 1927, 47 S.Ct. 353, 273 U.S. 269, 71 L.Ed. 639; Murdock v. Memphis, 1875, 20 Wall. 590, 22 L.Ed. 429; cf. Caldarola v. Eckert, 1947, 67 S.Ct. 1569, 332 U.S. 155, 91 L.Ed. 1968.
64. Reconstruction Finance Corp. v. Beaver County, 1946, 66 S.Ct. 992, 328 U.S. 204, 90 L.Ed. 1172.
65. Indiana ex rel. Anderson v. Brand, 1938, 58 S.Ct. 443, 303 U.S. 95, 82 L.Ed. 685, 113 A.L.R. 1482.
66. Radio Station WOW, Inc. v. Johnson, 1945, 65 S.Ct. 1475, 1480, 326 U.S. 120, 129, 89 L.Ed. 2092; Ward v. Board of County Com'rs of Love County, 1920, 40 S.Ct. 419, 253 U.S. 17, 64 L.Ed. 751; Terre Haute & I.R. Co. v. Indiana ex rel. Ketcham, 1904, 24 S.Ct. 767, 194 U.S. 579, 48 L.Ed. 1124.

This was held to be the situation when the pronouncement of state law by the state court, even if novel, would not frustrate consideration of the federal issue. Mullaney v. Wilbur, 1975, 95 S.Ct. 1881, 1886 n. 11, 421 U.S. 684, 691 n. 11, 44 L.Ed.2d 508.
67. McCoy v. Shaw, 1928, 48 S.Ct. 519, 277 U.S. 302, 72 L.Ed. 891; Johnson v. New Jersey, 1966, 86 S.Ct. 1772, 1782, 384 U.S. 719, 735, 16 L.Ed.2d 882.
68. Fox Film Corp. v. Muller, 1935, 56 S.Ct. 183, 296 U.S. 207, 80 L.Ed. 158; Jankovich v. Indiana Toll Road Comm., 1965, 85 S.Ct. 493, 379 U.S. 487, 13 L.Ed.2d 439. But see Sandalow, Henry v. Mississippi and the Adequate State Ground; Proposals for a Revised Doctrine, 1965 Sup.Ct. Rev. 187, 201–203.
69. United Air Lines, Inc. v. Mahin, 1973, 93 S.Ct. 1186, 410 U.S. 623, 35 L.Ed.2d 545; Beecher v. Alabama, 1967, 88 S.Ct. 189, 190 n.3, 389 U.S. 35, 37 n.3, 19 L.Ed.2d 35; International Steel & Iron Co. v. National Surety Co., 1936, 56 S.Ct. 619, 297 U.S. 657, 89 L.Ed. 961; Red Cross Line v. Atlantic Fruit Co., 1924, 44 S.Ct. 274, 275–276, 264 U.S. 109, 120, 68 L.Ed. 582.
70. Indiana ex rel. Anderson v. Brand, 1938, 58 S.Ct 443, 303 U.S. 95, 82 L.Ed. 685, 113 A.L.R. 1482. See Evans v. Newton, 1966, 86 S.Ct. 486, 490, 382 U.S. 296, 303, 15 L.Ed.2d 373 (White, Jr., concurring). For the later history of that case, see Evans v. Abney, 1970, 90 S.Ct. 628, 396 U.S. 435, 24 L.Ed.2d 634.

Cf. Stanton v. Stanton, 1975, 95 S.Ct. 1373, 421 U.S. 7, 43 L.Ed.2d 688; United Air Lines, Inc. v. Mahin, 1973, 93 S.Ct. 1186, 1192, 410 U.S. 623, 632, 35 L.Ed.2d 545.
71. Standard Oil Co. of California v. Johnson, 1942, 62 S.Ct. 1168, 316 U.S. 481, 86 L.Ed. 1611; cf. State Tax Comm. v. Van Cott, 1939, 59 S.Ct. 605, 306 U.S. 511, 83 L.Ed. 950, criticized

1939, 39 Col. L. Rev. 1043. See Greene, Hybrid State Law in the Federal Courts, 1970, 83 Harv. L. Rev. 289. Note, Supreme Court Review of State Interpretations of Federal Law Incorporated by Reference, 1953, 66 Harv. L. Rev. 1498.

72. Brice, Anderson and the Adequate State Ground, 1972, 45 S. Cal. L. Rev. 750; Hill, The Inadequate State Ground, 1965, 65 Col. L. Rev. 943; Sandalow, Henry v. Mississippi and the Adequate State Ground; Proposals for a Revised Doctrine, 1965 Sup. Ct. Rev. 187; Note, A Clarification of the Adequate State Ground Doctrine, 1971 Wash. U.L.Q. 485. Comment, Supreme Court Treatment of State Procedural Grounds Relied on in State Courts to Preclude Decisions of Federal Questions, 1961, 61 Col. L. Rev. 255; Note, The Untenable Non-federal Ground in the Supreme Court, 1961, 74 Harv. L. Rev. 1376.

73. Ward. v. Board of County Com'rs of Love County, 1920, 40 S.Ct. 419, 253 U.S. 17, 64 L.Ed. 751; Ancient Egyptian Arabic Order of Nobles of the Mystic Shrine v. Michaux, 1929, 49 S.Ct. 485, 279 U.S. 737, 73 L.Ed. 931; Creswill v. Grand Lodge, Knights of Pythias of Georgia, 1912, 32 S.Ct. 822, 225 U.S. 246, 56 L. Ed. 1074.

74. NAACP v. Alabama ex rel. Flowers, 1964, 84 S.Ct. 1302, 1306-1311, 377 U.S. 288, 293-302, 12 L.Ed.2d 325; NAACP v. Alabama ex rel. Patterson, 1958, 78 S.Ct. 1163, 357 U.S. 449, 2 L.Ed.2d 1488; Staub v. City of Baxley, 1958, 78 S.Ct. 277, 355 U.S. 313, 2 L.Ed.2d 302; see Parrot v. City of Tallahassee, 1965, 85 S.Ct. 1322, 381 U.S. 129, 14 L.Ed.2d 263.

75. Sullivan v. Little Hunting Park, Inc., 1969, 90 S.Ct. 400, 396 U.S. 229 24 L.Ed.2d 386. This doctrine had been suggested in Justice Black's dissent in Henry v. Mississippi, 1965, 85 S.Ct. 564, 571-573, 379 U.S. 443, 455-457, 13 L.Ed.2d 408. In the Sullivan case three members of the Court agreed that there was no adequate state ground but relied on a ground very different from that announced by the majority.

76. Brown v. Western Ry. of Alabama, 1949, 70 S.Ct. 105, 338 U.S. 294, 94 L.Ed. 100, noted 1949, 35 Va. L. Rev. 1098, 1950, 50 Col. L. Rev. 385, 21 Tenn. L. Rev. 324, 28 Tex. L. Rev. 972; Douglas v. Alabama, 1965, 85 S.Ct. 1074, 1078-1079, 380 U.S. 415, 420-423, 13 L.Ed.2d 934. See Comment, Procedural Protection for Federal Rights in State Courts, 1961, 30 U. Cin. L. Rev. 184.

Professor Hill, in the article cited note 72 above, at 971-977, argues that neither the Brown case, nor any other, supports the proposition stated in the text.

77. Davis v. Wechsler, 1923, 44 S.Ct. 13, 14, 263 U.S. 22, 24, 68 L.Ed. 143.

78. Liner v. Jafco, Inc., 1964, 84 S.Ct. 391, 375 U.S. 301, 11 L.Ed.2d 347; Cramp v. Board of Public Instruction, 1961, 82 S.Ct. 275, 368 U.S. 278, 7 L.Ed.2d 285; Allied Stores of Ohio, Inc. v. Bowers, 1959, 79 S.Ct. 437, 358 U.S. 522, 3 L.Ed.2d 480.

79. 1965, 85 S. Ct. 564, 379 U.S. 443, 13 L.Ed.2d 408. The case is extensively considered in the articles by Hill and Sandalow, note 72 above.

80. 85 S.Ct. at 568, 379 U.S. at 449.

81. 85 S.Ct. at 572, 379 U.S. at 457.

82. Sandalow, note 72 above, at 197.

83. 85 S.Ct. at 567, 379 U.S. at 447. One commentator thinks this proposition "amply supported by previous case law," Sandalow, note 72 above, at 229, while another can find "no suggestion" of it in the earlier cases, Hill, note 72 above, at 988.

84. 85 S.Ct. at 568, 379 U.S. at 448-449.

85. 85 S.Ct. at 568, 379 U.S. at 449.

86. 85 S.Ct. at 568-569, 379 U.S. at 450-452.

87. 85 S.Ct. at 570, 379 U.S. at 452.

88. Henry v. Mississippi, 1968, 88 S.Ct. 2276, 392 U.S. 931, 20 L.Ed.2d 1389. A federal court subsequently held that there had been no waiver and that Henry was entitled to relief on habeas corpus. Henry v. Williams, D.C. Miss. 1969, 299 F. Supp. 36.

90. See Camp v. Arkansas, 1971, 92 S.Ct. 307, 404 U.S. 69, 30 L.Ed.2d 223, in which the Supreme Court reversed because of remarks by the prosecutor in his summation, though no objection had been made in the trial court. The state court refused to consider the point because of the lack of objection but the Supreme Court cited Henry for the proposition that "petitioner's alleged procedural default does not bar consideration of his constitutional claim in the circumstances of this case."

Compare Monger v. Florida, 1972, 92 S.Ct. 1163, 405 U.S. 958, 31 L.Ed.2d 236, where the state court's dismissal of an appeal because notice of appeal had been given after the oral entry of judgment but before the written order was expressly held to be an adequate state ground, over the dissent of three justices who relied on Henry.

These seem to be the only cases in which the Court has discussed Henry with regard to its power to review state law decisions.

91. "...[E]ven though not mentioned by the Court, is it really immaterial that the petitioner was not merely a man charged with disturbing the peace, but Aaron Henry, a Negro resident of Clarksdale, Mississippi, and president of both the Coahoma County Branch of the National Association for the Advancement of Colored People and of its State Conference of Branches? Is it, moreover, immaterial that the prosecution was commenced in 1962 in Mississippi and not at another time and another place?" Sandalow, note 72 above, at 190.

92. See Comment, Supreme Court Treatment of State Court Cases Exhibiting Ambiguous Grounds of Decision, 1962, 62 Col. L. Rev. 822.

93. E.g., Kedroff v. St. Nicholas Cathedral of Russian Orthodox Church in North America, 1952, 72 S.Ct. 143, 145, 344 U.S. 94, 97, 97 L.Ed. 120.

94. E.g., Allenberg Cotton Co., Inc. v. Pittman, 1974, 95 S.Ct. 260, 262 n.2, 419 U.S. 20, 23 n.2, 42 L.Ed.2d 195. Indiana ex rel. Anderson v. Brand, 1938, 58 S.Ct. 443, 445, 303 U.S. 95, 99, 82 L.Ed. 685, 113 A.L.R. 1482; cf. Marvin v. Trout, 1905, 26 S.Ct. 31, 199 U.S. 212, 50 L.Ed. 157; Wolfson & Kurland, Certificate by State Courts of the Existence of a Federal Question, 1949, 63 Har. L. Rev. 111. A letter from the clerk of the court is insufficient for this purpose. Dixon v. Duffy, 1952, 73 S.Ct. 193, 194, 344 U.S. 143, 145, 97 L.Ed. 153.

95. E.g., Johnson v. Risk, 1890, 11 S.Ct. 111, 137 U.S.

300, 34 L.Ed. 683; Lynch v. New York ex rel. Pierson, 1934, 55 S.Ct. 16, 293 U.S. 52, 79 L.Ed. 191; Stembridge v. Georgia, 1952, 72 S.Ct. 834, 343 U.S. 541, 96 L.Ed. 1130; Durley v. Mayo, 1956, 76 S.Ct. 806, 351 U.S. 277, 100 L.Ed. 1178; Black v. Cutter Laboratories, 1956, 76 S.Ct. 824, 351 U.S. 292, 100 L.Ed. 1188; cf. Jankovich v. Indiana Toll Road Comm., 1965, 85 S.Ct. 493, 379 U.S. 487, 13 L.Ed.2d 439.
96. E.g., Minnesota v. National Tea Co., 1949, 60 S.Ct. 676, 309 U.S. 551, 84 L.Ed. 920; Young v. Ragen, 1949, 69 S.Ct. 1073, 337 U.S. 235, 93 L.Ed. 1333; Blackburn v. Alabama, 1957, 77 S.Ct. 1098, 354 U.S. 393, 1 L.Ed.2d 1423; State Tax. Comm. of Arizona v. Murray Co. of Texas, 1960, 81 S.Ct. 53, 364 U.S. 393, 5 L.Ed.2d 39; Dept. of Mental Hygiene v. Kirchner, 1965, 85 S.Ct. 871, 380 U.S. 194, 13 L.Ed.2d 753; California v. Krivda, 1972, 92 S.Ct. 32, 409 U.S. 33, 34 L.Ed.2d 45, certiorari denied 93 S.Ct. 2734, 412 U.S. 919, 37 L.Ed.2d 145; Dept. of Motor Vehicles v. Rios, 1973, 93 S.Ct. 1019, 410 U.S. 425, 35 L.Ed.2d 398; Ohio v. Gallagher, 1976, 96 S.Ct. 1438 __U.S.__ 47 L.Ed.2d 772.
97. E.g., Herb v. Pitcairn, 1945, 65 S.Ct. 459, 324 U.S. 117, 89 L.Ed. 789, noted 1946, 94 U. Pa. L. Rev. 251; Loftus v. Illinois, 1948, 68 S.Ct. 1212, 334 U.S. 804, 92 L.Ed. 1737; Lynum v. Illinois, 1961, 82 S.Ct. 190, 368 U.S. 908, 7 L.Ed.2d 128.
98. E.G., Neilson v. Lagow, 1851, 12 How. 98, 110, 13 L.Ed. 909; Williams v. Kaiser 1945, 65 S.Ct. 363, 323 U.S. 471, 89 L.Ed. 398; Konigsberg v. State Bar of California, 1957, 77 S.Ct. 722, 723–726, 353 U.S. 252, 254–258, 1 L.Ed.2d 810; cf. Oregon v. Hass, 1975, 95 S.Ct. 1215, 420 U.S. 714, 43 L.Ed.2d 570.
99. Note, 1962, 62 Col. L. Rev. 822, 847–850.
100. 28 U.S.C.A. 1257(1).
101. 28 U.S.C.A. 1257 (2).
102. Dahnke-Walker Milling Co. v. Bondurant, 1921, 42 S.Ct. 106, 257 U.S. 282, 66 L.Ed. 239; Fiske v. Kansas, 1927, 47 S.Ct. 655, 274 U.S. 380, 71 L.Ed. 1108.
103. Philadelphia & R. Coal & Iron Co. v. Gilbert, 1917, 38 S.Ct. 58, 245 U.S. 162, 62 L.Ed. 221; Ireland v. Woods, 1918, 38 S.Ct. 319, 246 U.S. 323, 62 L.Ed. 745; Hanson v. Denckla, 1958, 78 S.Ct. 1228, 1234, 357 U.S. 235, 244, 2 L.Ed.2d 1283.
104. Zucht v. King, 1922, 43 S.Ct. 24, 260 U.S. 174, 67 L.Ed. 194; Charleston Federal Savings & Loan Ass'n v. Alderson, 1945, 65 S.Ct. 624, 324 U.S. 182, 89 L.Ed. 857.
105. See note 108 below.
106. 28 U.S.C.A. 2103.
107. E.g., Palmore v. U.S., 1973, 93 S.Ct. 1670, 411 U.S. 389, 36 L.Ed.2d 342; Garrity v. New Jersey, 1967, 87 S.Ct. 616, 618, 385 U.S. 493, 496, 17 L.Ed.2d 562; Slagle v. Ohio, 1961, 81 S.Ct. 1076, 1079, 368 U.S. 259, 264, 6 L.Ed.2d 277.
108. Williams v. Bruffy, 1877, 96 U.S. 176, 182–183, 24 L.Ed. 716. But the District of Columbia Code is not a state statute for purposes of 28 U.S.C.A. § 1257, and decisions of the District of Columbia Court of Appeals upholding provisions of that code are reviewable only by certiorari. Palmore v. U.S., 1973, 93 S.Ct. 1670, 411 U.S. 389, 36 L.Ed.2d 342.
109. E.g., Railway Express Agency v. Virginia, 1931, 51 S.Ct. 201, 282 U.S. 440, 75 L.Ed. 450.
110. E.g., Erznoznik v. City of Jacksonville, 1975, 95 S.Ct. 2268, 422 U.S. 205, 45 L.Ed.2d 125.
111. Hamilton v. Regents of the University of California, 1934, 55 S.Ct. 197, 293 U.S. 245, 79 L.Ed. 343.
112. Railway Express Agency v. New York, 1949, 69 S.Ct. 463, 336 U.S. 106, 93 L.Ed. 533.
113. Lathrop v. Donohue, 1961, 81 S.Ct. 1826, 1828–1829, 367 U.S. 820, 824–827, 6 L.Ed.2d 1191.

1.05 SOME ADDITIONAL LIMITATIONS ON SUPREME COURT REVIEW

Standing to Sue?

GILMORE v. UTAH

Supreme Court of the United States, 1976
429 U.S. 1012, 97 S. Ct. 436, 50 L. Ed. 2nd 636

The facts are stated in the opinion.

ORDER

On October 7, 1976, Gary Mark Gilmore was convicted of murder and sentenced to death by a judgment entered after a jury trial in a Utah court. On December 3, 1976, this Court granted an application for a stay of execution of the judgment and sentence, pending the filing here by the State of Utah of a response to the application together with transcripts of various specified hearings in the Utah courts and Board of Pardons, and until "further action of the Court on the application for stay."

The State of Utah has now filed its response and has substantially complied with the Court's request for transcripts of the specified hearings. After carefully examining the materials submitted by the State of Utah, the Court is convinced that Gary Mark Gilmore made a knowing and intelligent waiver of any and all federal rights he might have asserted after the Utah trial court's sentence was imposed, and, specifically, that the State's determinations of his competence knowingly and intelligently to waive any and all such rights were firmly grounded.

Accordingly, the stay of execution granted on December 3, 1976, is hereby terminated.

Mr. Chief Justice BURGER, with whom Mr. Justice POWELL joins, concurring.

On December 2, 1976, Bessie Gilmore, claiming to act as "next friend" on behalf of her son, Gary Mark Gilmore, filed with this Court an application for stay of execution of the death sentence then scheduled for December 6, 1976.[1] Since only a limited record was then before the Court, we granted a temporary stay of execution on December 3, 1976[*] in order to secure a response from the State of Utah. That response was received on December 7, 1976. On December 8, 1976, a response was filed by Gary Mark Gilmore, by and through his attorneys of record, Ronald R. Stanger and Robert L. Moody, challenging the standing of Bessie Gilmore to initiate any proceedings in his behalf.

When the application for a stay was initially filed on December 2, a serious question was presented as to whether Bessie Gilmore had standing to seek the requested relief or any relief from this Court. Assuming the Court would otherwise have jurisdiction with respect to a "next friend" application, that jurisdiction would arise only if it were demonstrated that Gary Mark Gilmore is unable to seek relief in his own behalf. See Rosenberg v. United States, 346 U.S. 273, 291, 73 S. Ct. 1152, 1161, 97 L. Ed. 1607 (1953) (separate opinion of Mr. Justice Jackson for six Members of the Court). However, in view of Gary Mark Gilmore's response on December 8, 1976, it is now clear that the "next friend" concept is wholly inapplicable in this case. Since Gary Mark Gilmore has now filed a response and appeared in his own behalf, through his retained attorneys, any basis for the standing of Bessie Gilmore to seek relief in his behalf is necessarily eliminated. The only possible exception to this conclusion would be if the record suggested, despite the representations of Gary Mark Gilmore's attorneys, that he was incompetent to waive his right of appeal under state law as he was at the present time incompetent to assert rights or to challenge Bessie Gilmore's standing to assert rights in his behalf as "next friend."[2]

After examining with care the pertinent portions of the transcripts and reports of state proceedings, and the response of Gary Mark Gilmore filed on December 8, I am in complete agreement with the conclusion expressed in the Court's order that Gary Mark Gilmore knowingly and intelligently, with full knowledge of his right to seek an appeal in the Utah Supreme Court, has waived that right.[3] I further agree that the State's determinations of his competence to

---

[1] This case may be unique in the annals of the Court. Not only does Gary Mark Gilmore request no relief himself; on the contrary he has expressly and repeatedly stated since his conviction in the Utah courts that he had received a fair trial and had been well treated by the Utah authorities. Nor does he claim to be innocent of the crime for which he was convicted. Indeed, his only complaint against Utah or its judicial process, including that raised in the state habeas corpus petition mentioned in note 3, infra, has been with respect to the delay on the part of the State in carrying out the sentence.

[*] The Chief Justice [BURGER], Mr. Justice REHNQUIST, and Mr. Justice STEVENS dissented from issuance of the stay.

[2] When Bessie Gilmore's application for a stay first came before the Court, we did not have before us for consideration transcripts of the various hearings at which Gary Mark Gilmore was said to have waived his federal constitutional rights. As today's order makes clear, each Justice has now had an opportunity to review the relevant transcripts and reports concerning mental competence and waiver.

[3] At a hearing on November 1, 1976, on a motion for a new trial, Gilmore's attorneys informed the trial court that they had been told by Gilmore not to file an appeal and not to seek a stay of execution of sentence on his behalf. They also informed the trial court that they had advised Gilmore of his rights to appeal, that they believed there were substantial grounds for appeal, that

Footnote continued on page 28

waive his rights knowingly and intelligently were firmly grounded.[4]

When the record establishing a knowing and intelligent waiver of Gary Mark Gilmore's right to seek appellate review is combined with the December 8 written response submitted to this Court,[5] it is plain that the Court is without jurisdiction to entertain the "next friend" application filed by Bessie Gilmore. This Court has jurisdiction pursuant to Art. III of the Constitution only over "cases and controversies," and we can issue stays only in aid of our jurisdiction. 28 U.S.C. §§ 1651, 2101(f). There is no dispute, presently before us, between Gary Mark Gilmore and the State of Utah, and the application of Bessie Gilmore manifestly fails to meet the statutory requirements to invoke this Court's power to review the action of the Supreme Court of Utah. No authority to the contrary has been brought to our attention, and nothing suggested in dissent bears on the threshold question of jurisdiction.

In his dissenting opinion, Mr. Justice WHITE suggests that Gary Mark Gilmore is "unable" as a matter of law to waive the right to state appellate review.[6] Whatever may be

---

[4] In the pretrial period, from August 5 to October 6, 1976, the trial court appointed psychiatrists to examine Gilmore on two occasions, to determine his competency to stand trial and his sanity at the time of the offense. Three of the five psychiatrists who examined Gilmore in that period found no evidence of mental illness or insanity. The record before us does not include the findings of the other two psychiatrists, which were presented to the trial court when it concluded that Gilmore was sane for the purpose of standing trial.

After trial, at the November 1 hearing, the state trial court ordered sua sponte that the Utah State Prison psychiatrist, or other available psychiatric personnel of the prison, examine Gilmore to determine his ability to decide not to appeal. In the order, the court noted that Gilmore had instructed his attorneys not to appeal after they had informed him that there was substantial legal merit to such an appeal. On November 3 the prison psychiatrist submitted a report, based on a one-hour psychiatric interview and a review of Gilmore's medical records, concluding that Gilmore's decision to waive appeal was the "product of an organized thought process" and that Gilmore had not become "insane or mentally ill." On the same day, two prison psychologists submitted a second report, based on psychological tests and an individual interview, concluding that "[Gilmore] presently has the mental capacity and the emotional stability to make the necessary decision concerning his sentence and to understand the consequences."

Gilmore apparently attempted to take his own life on November 16. The prison psychiatrist subsequently reported to the Board of Pardons that Gilmore's mental state on November 24 was "exactly as described" in the psychiatrist's report to the court on November 3.

the constitutionality of the Utah death penalty statute had not yet been reviewed by either the Utah Supreme Court or the United States Supreme Court, and that in their view there was a chance that the statute would eventually be held unconstitutional. The trial court itself advised Gilmore that he had a right to appeal, that the constitutional issue had not yet been resolved, and that both counsel for the State and Gilmore's own counsel would attempt to expedite an appeal to avoid unnecessary delay. Gilmore stated that he did not "care to languish in prison for another day," that the decision was his own, and that he had not made the decision as a result of the influence of drugs or alcohol or as a result of the way he was treated in prison. On November 4, the state trial court concluded that Gilmore fully understood his right to appeal and the consequences of a decision not to appeal.

On November 10, the Utah Supreme Court held a hearing on the Utah Attorney General's motion to vacate a stay of execution of sentence entered two days earlier by that Court. Gilmore was present and in response to questions from several Justices, stated that he thought he had received a fair trial and a proper sentence, that he opposed any appeal in the case, and that he wished to withdraw an appeal previously filed without his consent by appointed trial counsel.

Finally, at a hearing before the trial court on December 1, Gilmore again informed the court that he opposed all appeals that had been filed.

[5] On December 8, 1976, Gilmore, by counsel, advised this Court of the filing of a petition in a Utah state court seeking habeas corpus relief. Although that petition is not in the papers before us, it is understood that the ground relied upon is not the deprivation of any constitutional right but that there is a 60-day limitation under Utah law upon the carrying out of the sentence of death, an issue which has not been presented to the Utah Supreme Court as of this date.

[6] Mr. Justice WHITE's dissent expresses the view that absent an affirmative decision by "the

Footnote continued on opposite page

said as to the merits of this suggestion, the question simply is not before us. Gilmore, duly found to be competent by the Utah courts, has had available meaningful access to this Court and has declined expressly to assert any claim here other than his explicit repudiation of Bessie Gilmore's effort to speak for him as next friend. It follows, therefore, that the Court is without jurisdiction to consider the question posed by the dissent.

Mr. Justice STEVENS, with whom Mr. Justice REHNQUIST joins, concurring.

In my judgment the record not only supports the conclusion that Gilmore was competent to waive his right to appeal, but also makes it clear that his access to the courts is entirely unimpeded and therefore a third party has no standing to litigate an Eighth Amendment claim—or indeed any other claim—on his behalf. Without a proper litigant before it, this Court is without power to stay the execution.

Mr. Justice WHITE, joined by Mr. Justice BRENNAN and Mr. Justice MARSHALL, dissenting.

As Justice Wilkins said in dissent below,[1] there are substantial questions under Furman v. Georgia, 408 U.S. 238, 92 S. Ct. 2726, 33 L. Ed. 2d 346 (1972), about the constitutionality of the Utah death penalty statute. Because of Gary Gilmore's purported waiver of his right to challenge the statute, none of these questions was resolved in the Utah courts. I believe, however, that the consent of a convicted defendant in a criminal case does not privilege a State to impose a punishment otherwise forbidden by the Eighth Amendment.[2] Until the state courts have resolved the obvious serious doubts about the validity of the state statute, the imposition of the death penalty in this case should be stayed.

Given the inability of Gary Gilmore to waive resolution in the state courts of the serious questions concerning the constitutional legality of his death sentence, there is no jurisdictional barrier to addressing the question upon the petition of the defendant's mother. See Rosenberg v. United States, 346 U.S. 273, 291, 73 S. Ct. 1152, 1161, 97 L. Ed. 1607 (1953) (separate opinion of Justice Jackson). Without examining the constitutionality of the Utah death statute, on November 10, 1976, the Utah Supreme Court vacated its stay of Gilmore's sentence and dismissed the appeal which his then attorneys had filed on his behalf.

Pending the filing of a timely petition for certiorari, I would continue the stay previously issued by this Court; and upon said filing it would appear that the judgment of the Supreme Court of Utah should be vacated and the case remanded to the state courts for reconsideration in the light of the death penalty decisions announced by this Court last Term. Cf. Collins v. Arkansas, 429 U.S. 808, 97 S. Ct. 44, 50 L. Ed. 2d 69 (1976); Neal v. Arkansas, 429 U.S. 808, 97 S. Ct. 45, 50 L. Ed. 2d 69 (1976).

Mr. Justice MARSHALL, dissenting.

I fully agree with my Brother WHITE that a criminal defendant has no power to agree to be executed under an unconstitutional statute. I believe that the Eighth Amendment not only protects the right of individuals not to be victims of cruel and unusual punishment, but that it also expresses a fundamental interest of society in ensuring that state authority is not used to administer barbaric punishments. Irrespective of this, however, I cannot agree with the view expressed by the Chief Justice [BURGER] that Gilmore has competently, knowingly, and intelligently decided to let himself be killed. Less than

---

state courts" as to the validity of Utah's capital punishment statute, "the imposition of the death penalty in this case should be stayed." However, Gilmore has not challenged the validity of the statute under which he was convicted and there is no other party before this Court with requisite standing to do so.

---

[1] Prior to Gilmore's seeming waiver, the trial judge also appeared ready to certify an appeal in order that the state Supreme Court could pass on the issue of the validity of the death penalty statute, an issue he had not himself addressed.

---

[2] Nor in the absence of a state court decision sustaining the death penalty statute would a purported waiver of the Eighth Amendment necessarily be a defense to a wrongful death action, see Utah Code Ann. § 78-11-7, based on an execution imposed under an unconstitutional statute.

five months have passed since the commission of the crime; just over two months have elapsed since sentence was imposed. That is hardly sufficient time for mature consideration of the question, nor does Gilmore's erratic behavior—from his suicide attempt to his state habeas petition—evidence such deliberation. No adversary hearing has been held to examine the experts,[1] all employed by the State of Utah, who have pronounced Gilmore sane.[2] The decision of the Utah Supreme Court finding a valid waiver can be given little weight. In the transcripts that the court prepared for us, it omitted a portion of its proceedings as having "no pertinency" to the issue of Gilmore's "having voluntarily and intelligently waived his right to appeal." That "irrelevant" portion involved a discussion by Gilmore's trial counsel of his opinion of Gilmore's competence and the constitutionality of the Utah statute. It is appalling that any court could consider these questions irrelevant to that determination. It is equally shocking that the Utah court, in a matter of such importance, failed even to have a court reporter present to transcribe the proceeding, instead relying on recordings made by dictating machines which have produced a partly unintelligible record. These inexplicable actions by a court charged with life or death responsibility underscore the failure of the State to determine adequately the validity of Gilmore's purported waiver and the propriety of imposing capital punishment.

Mr. Justice BLACKMUN, dissenting.

I am of the view that the question of Bessie Gilmore's standing and the constitutional issue are not insubstantial, and indeed, in the context of this case, are of manifest importance. I therefore would have the pending application set for expeditious hearing and given plenary, not summary, consideration. See Mr. Justice Harlan's haunting admonition, which I joined, in New York Times Co. v. United States, 403 U.S. 713, 752, 755 (1971) (Harlan, J., dissenting).

---

[1] If Gilmore's own lawyers refused to question his competence, the court could certainly ask other counsel acting as amicus curiae to present that side of the issue.

[2] As the CHIEF JUSTICE [BURGER] notes, the opinion of the prison psychiatrist, the only doctor who has considered Gilmore's competency since the waiver decision was publicly announced, was based on a review of Gilmore's medical records and a one-hour interview.

1.06 DECISION-MAKING IN THE SUPREME COURT

WHAT THE JUSTICES ARE SAYING*

Speaking at the American Bar Association's annual meeting at a luncheon sponsored by the section on labor relations law, Supreme Court Justice Lewis F. Powell, Jr., told how it is at the top, where the view is different from that he had at his old law firm. Below are excerpts from his remarks.

When I was a practicing lawyer (a long time ago, it now seems!), I wondered how appellate courts went about their business. Now that I am an appellate judge, I still wonder—sometimes even more.

The adjustment from a large, structured law firm to the Supreme Court was not easy for me. The functioning of a modern law firm and of our Court are light years apart. I had thought of the Court, in institutional terms, as a collegial body in which the most characteristic activities would be consultation and co-operative deliberation, aided by a strong supporting staff. I was in for more than a little surprise.

The Court does have strong institutional characteristics, but it is perhaps one of the last citadels of jealously preserved individualism. To be sure, we sit together for the arguments and during the long Friday conferences when votes are taken. But for the most part, perhaps as much as 90 percent of our total time, we function as nine small, independent law firms. I emphasize the words *small* and *independent*. There is the equivalent of one partner in each chambers, three or four law clerks, two secretaries, and a messenger. The informal interchange between chambers is minimal, with most exchanges of views being by correspondence or memoranda. Indeed, a justice may go through an entire term without being once in the chambers of all of the other eight members of the Court.

Even more unsettling to me was the discovery that justices do their own work. As a senior partner at Hunton, Williams, I had managed to arrange things so that my role, while perhaps not without responsibility, was light in terms of looking into books

---

*From 62 A.B.A.J. 1454 (1976). Reproduced by permission of the American Bar Association.

myself or drafting briefs or corporate documents. On major matters, I would head up a team of lawyers including the requisite specialists; I reviewed and edited what others had drafted; conferred with clients; attended meetings; and made sure that appropriate bills were sent out. To keep my hand in, I still tried a few cases—buttressed by the best legal talent money could buy.

But life began again for me at age sixty-four. I think I missed the adequate staff of a modern law firm even more than I missed sending out bills to nervous but solvent clients. The first option I was assigned to write was a tax case.[*] It had been twenty years since I looked at the Internal Revenue Code and hoped never to see it again. One of my former tax partners could have done the opinion, a relatively simple one, in three days. It took a law clerk and me three weeks. Fortunately, the case has never been cited since I handed it down.

Opinions Must Be Unsullied

In the early weeks I thought the answer was obvious: the Court needed a permanent staff of highly qualified experts in some of the more specialized fields of law: taxation, labor law, patent law, and the like. My brothers gently rejected my proposal, reminding me that I was being paid to render personal judgments, even if they were devoid of *expertise*. If there were a central staff of specialists, it would often be their judgments that ended up in the United States Reports. The wisdom of this view, although initially accepted with some chagrin, is now self-evident to me.

The justices do receive indispensable assistance from their law clerks. I have been enormously impressed by the personal qualities and professional competency of these talented young lawyers. They function as associates do in a law firm, although in a closer and perhaps more responsible relationship with the justices. But the decision making and the ultimate choice of rationale and analysis are non-delegable.

The drafting of an opinion is a process, not an event. The process is similar to the writing of a major appellate brief by a top-flight law firm: there may be a dozen

---

*Commissioner v. First Security Bank of Utah, 405 U.S. 394 (1972).

drafts within the chambers before an opinion is deemed suitable for circulation to other justices. Even then, the process of editing and revision continues—spurred by criticisms and suggestions from other chambers.

A critical comment from a colleague is accepted routinely. What really dismays a justice is to circulate a draft opinion, and receive no word at all except perhaps a cryptic note or two saying, "I will await circulation of the dissent."

Case Selection Assures Heedfulness

The extent to which the chambers function separately is illustrated by the procedure with respect to cert. petitions and jurisdictional statements. Each justice—all nine of us acting individually—considers every petition, appeal, and motion filed with the Court. Although four votes are necessary for a "grant" or a "note," a single justice has authority to bring up for full conference discussion any case or motion. Despite the enormous burden imposed by this system of individual review, it does assure the careful participation of each justice in the vital task of selecting the relatively few cases that we can take for plenary review and decision.

The regular Friday conferences, supplemented by conferences on Wednesday afternoons during argument weeks, afford the principal opportunity for discussion, debate, and group deliberation. Justices may speak as frequently and as long as they wish. I have found the conference discussions stimulating and productive, and not infrequently a conference has altered my original tentative view. It is said that a famous justice, now deceased, often would deliver lengthy and erudite arguments at conference, pacing the floor and waving his arms. One of his brothers enjoyed deflating the orator by saying at the end of an eloquent peroration: "I was with you for the petitioner until you spoke at such length. You have now persuaded me to vote for the respondent." . . .

A favorite pastime, at least for the media and the law reviews, is to do what is called "Court watching." Scores of articles and a number of books have been written comparing the Warren and Burger Courts. Perceptions, sometimes wishful, have varied widely as to whether—or to what extent, if any—the Burger Court has engineered major changes. It is said variously that we have regressed or progressed, depending on the commentator's viewpoint.

It is perhaps venturesome for a sitting judge to express any opinion on Court trends—if they may be so characterized. Nevertheless, I make these general observations. Few would deny that the Warren Court, in a fifteen-year span, vastly expanded the role of the judiciary by construing the Constitution in dramatically bold and unprecedented ways. Much of the expansion was a reaction to the sluggishness of the legislative branch in addressing urgent needs for reform.

It was perhaps inevitable, even without major changes in personnel, that a period of consolidation and leveling off would follow. Changes in personnel did bring, as they have in the past, fresh and different assumptions and perceptions as to the role of the Court and certain constitutional issues.

The present Court, mindful of preserving the vitality of democratic processes, may be more deferential to the legislative judgments, it is more likely to give some weight to federalism, and it is more conventional in demanding compliance with jurisdictional and standing requirements.

It also is true that in recent years the Court has decided a number of criminal cases differently from what might have been expected during the decade of the sixties. But it is alarmist to suggest any significant weakening of the basic right of persons accused of crime.

A more traditional and, in my view, a sounder balance is evolving between the rights of accused persons and the right of a civilized society to have a criminal justice system that is effective as well as fair.

No other country in the world, including some with ancient and respected systems of justice, is as protective of the rights of accused persons as the United States under the Bill of Rights. We may count on the bar and the judiciary to continue to be sensitive and alert, especially to safeguard the rights that assure fair trial and protect the innocent....

Whatever else may be said, the present Court is composed of eight other justices whose legal ability, fidelity to duty, and capacity for unremitting labor I profoundly respect. While we do say in dissenting opinions some rather outrageous and unflattering things about each other, we are warm personal friends. Although I left the practice of law with genuine reluctance, I cherish the privilege of serving on the Supreme Court of the United States.

Also speaking at the annual meeting, Justice Rehnquist stated that the older perception that a judgeship was something more than the sum of its parts was dimming and that judges had no more time now than to administer cases rather than decide them. The following is excerpted from his concluding remarks:

The conclusion which I draw from all of this is not that the judicial branches of our state and federal governments are embarked on an irreversible path to second-class status. It is the more practical one that those of us interested in judicial administration must do our part in advising the public if indeed such a transformation has begun and is continuing.

The composite picture that represents a judge's working life is the result of many, many decisions, usually made by legislative bodies, decisions which if examined individually might seem to contribute little or nothing to that composite. But every new cause of action and every new wrinkle which extends final disposition of an appeal in fact do contribute to the legal mosaic that is the day, month, or year of some judge. Every legislative action which gives the judiciary more cases without also supplying the additional manpower necessary to handle them similarly contributes to that mosaic. If the long-run portents for change in that mosaic are for an ever-increasing caseload with an ever larger percentage of that caseload consisting of relatively routine work which neither requires nor engages the abilities of a first-rate judge, then the prognosis is indeed gloomy.

To say that legislative decisions made or to be made will render a judge's job less attractive is, to put it mildly, unlikely to be a dispositive argument in the court of public opinion. If some higher goals are served by these decisions, and there is no way of accomplishing those goals save by making the work of federal and state judges less stimulating and more burdensome, judges may jolly well have to make the best of their new lot. After all, time and tide have totally eliminated the occupations of blacksmith and carriage maker and have converted many a skilled artisan into a minion of some assembly line. If there is some evolutionary necessity which demands that judging must become more of a mass-produced item, it would be futile to challenge it.

I do not believe that there is any such evolutionary necessity. I do believe, though, that the amount of business which legislatures commit to judges will continue to increase, perhaps at a more modest rate than in the past. I also believe that a good part of this business, however essential it may be that it be decided by some judicial officer, is not such as to require all of the ability and experience which we have traditionally sought in a top-level trial judge.

With respect to the federal judiciary, Congress could decide that these judges have enough to do as it is and leave the creation of new types of litigation to state legislatures and state courts. Most state judicial systems have already recognized the distinction to which I have adverted between kinds of trial judges, and side by side with courts of general jurisdiction commanding the top judicial talent there exist courts of special or limited jurisdiction which are by design less prestigious than the former.

While Congress could decide not to add to the work of the federal judiciary, that is certainly not the tack it has taken in the last several years. If Congress continues on that tack, and federal judges continue to be given new tasks, I think Congress should seriously consider a significant expansion of the role of the recently created corps of United States magistrates, so that they would correspond more to the courts of limited jurisdiction found in state systems than to their present and more limited functions of acting largely as masters or referees for district judges. If this course were followed, the historical eminence of the federal district judge, which has long attracted first-rate lawyers to the position, could be preserved, while Congress could still repose in the federal judicial system as a whole such additional work as it sees fit.

If, on the other hand, the public were to insist, contrary to this very sound advice which I have just given it, that there be no differentiation within the federal system of levels of judges to handle the greatly increased and varied caseload of that system, then the position of the federal judge must undergo a devaluation. An argument may be made, which has some theoretical appeal, that we ought not to distinguish between litigants and that the social security claimant and the state habeas corpus petitioner are entitled to the same full consideration of an honest-to-God Article III federal district judge that other litigants receive.

Whatever the merits of this idea in the abstract, I think it is self-defeating in practice. Its application in the long run will not give social security claimants and state habeas corpus petitioners the full attention of a judge with a first-rate professional background of ability and experience. Instead it will give them, and all other litigants, the full attention of the sort of lawyer who can be recruited to take a job which consists in large part of reviewing written records made elsewhere, not with a view of finally resolving the case but merely as a way station on the way to the court of appeals and perhaps the Supreme Court.

A Mind For All Seasons and Reasons

If such a course be persisted in, then the American Bar Association, the Justice Department, and the Senate Judiciary Committee will have to revise downward their standards for choosing federal judges. You will never convince most people that only a candidate for judicial office combining the talents of Justinian, Lord Mansfield, and Learned Hand is capable of deciding whether the finding of a social security examiner is supported by substantial evidence considered on the record as a whole. (And there is little point in stressing that a job applicant pass examinations in trigonometry and calculus if the job seldom requires those skills and far more frequently requires the ability to add long, monotonous columns of figures.)

Not all judicial work is going to be interesting or challenging in the best of systems, any more than all of the work of a private practitioner is interesting, or all of the work of any of the world's many other occupations is invariably interesting. But a judiciary overburdened with work will respond more affirmatively to the need for putting in long hours if a large portion of the work is professionally challenging. Somewhere there comes a tipping point, just where I am not sure, at which the number of routine and uninteresting tasks in the course of a long day becomes so large a portion of the whole that the number of qualified people willing to take the job diminishes sharply.

I suggest that we are beginning to approach that point with respect to a number of our most respected courts and that it behooves us to alert the public to the damaging consequences which may result if we should actually pass that point.

SUPREME EMBARRASSMENT*

There is no law requiring the U.S. Supreme Court to keep its decision-making process confidential—only tradition, common sense and good faith. But that secrecy has now been breached—in a news report that described uncompleted Court action on appeals in the Watergate cover-up trial. And the reverberations not only could help John Mitchell and H. R. Haldeman to remain free for a little while longer, but could exacerbate divisions within the nation's highest court.

The report was by Nina Totenberg of National Public Radio. She said the Justices had decided not to hear the appeals of Mitchell, Haldeman and John Ehrlichman (who is already in prison). Her scoop offered more than the precise 5–3 vote taken at a private weekly conference attended only by the Justices. She asserted that Chief Justice Warren E. Burger, a Richard Nixon appointee, had held back a final decision on the appeal so that he could lobby some of his brethren to change their votes. Justices Byron R. White and John Paul Stevens were identified as his specific targets.

Dominating Style. What is sometimes called "vote trading" is not uncommon on the Court; another way to describe such exchanges might be that the Justices practice compromise and persuasion. But apparently some Justices object to the dominating style of Burger. Although he has only a single vote, he stands, as Chief Justice, *primus inter pares.* He also has been known to assign the dullest, hardest or least significant opinions to those who do not cooperate with him.

Inevitably, the stunning breach of secrecy in the Watergate case was attributed to a deliberate "leak"—possibly from an opponent of Burger or a friend of Totenberg or both. The first name to come to almost every Court specialist's mind was Justice Potter Stewart, who is widely assumed to fit both descriptions. Totenberg, 33, calls the reports sexist. She said that she pieced together the story from seven different sources. And in fact, dozens of law clerks and secretaries have access to information about the private conferences.

Totenberg insists that far too much attention is being focused on the leak itself and not enough on what is being said about the Court's method of deliberation. The report was designed, she says, to disclose how Burger attempts to "manipulate the decision-making process" and often for "political" reasons. "It's common knowledge at the Court," charges Totenberg. "Everyone is complaining about it, Justices and clerks. But no one will confront the chief."

Tainted. Many Court observers believe that such confrontation is common. Some Justices are said to have engaged in a shouting match at the first private conference after the news leak. "There is a lot of bad feeling," says one source close to the Court. "There is less collegiality than one would suspect, or than one might hope." Another insider agrees: "It is nine people with little in common who don't respect each other all that much either politically or intellectually." No Justice will comment publicly on these reports.

Lawyers for Mitchell, Haldeman and Ehrlichman moved last week to capitalize on the furor. One of their chief arguments on appeal has been the alleged effect of prejudicial publicity during the trial; now they want time to argue that the Supreme Court itself is tainted by publicity. To tell the Justices that they cannot make an unbiased decision would seem to be grasping at straws. But if Totenberg's story was accurate—and almost everyone assumes that it was—the former Nixon aides are about to lose anyway.

Still, because Burger held up the decision, the Court remains in an embarrassing position. If the appeal is granted, it could appear that some Justices had caved in to the chief. The appeal probably will be rejected.[*] Authorities also believe that the news report will have no impact on Court customs. But legal scholars fear that the antagonistic mood among some of the Justices will grow and further erode the collegiality of the Court.

---

*From Newsweek, May 9, 1977, p. 66. Copyright 1977 by Newsweek, Inc. All rights reserved. Reprinted by permission.

*The Supreme Court denied certiorari. 45 U.S.L.W. 3762 (May 24, 1977).

3
DUE PROCESS AND THE FIFTH AND FOURTEENTH AMENDMENTS

3.03 PROCEDURAL DUE PROCESS

Due Process and the Revocation of Driver's Licenses

DIXON V. LOVE
Supreme Court of the United States, 1977
431 U.S. 105, 97 S. Ct. 1723, 52 L. Ed. 2d 172

The driver's license of appellee Dennis Love, a truck driver, was suspended under Illinois law in November, 1969, because he had been convicted of three traffic violations within a 12-month period. He was then convicted on a charge of driving while his license was suspended, and another suspension was imposed in March, 1970. In August, 1974, Love was arrested twice for speeding. He was convicted on both charges and received a third speeding citation in February, 1975. In March, 1975, he was notified by letter that he would lose his driving privileges if convicted of a third offense. On March 31, Love was convicted of the third speeding charge, and on June 3, 1975, he received a notice that his driver's license was being revoked.

Under Illinois law, the secretary of state is authorized to suspend or revoke a driver's license without a preliminary hearing upon a showing that the driver's conduct falls into any of 18 enumerated categories, one of which is that the driver has been repeatedly convicted of violations of traffic laws to a degree indicating "lack of ability to exercise ordinary and reasonable care in the safe operation of a motor vehicle . . ." [Ill. Rev. Stat. § 6-206(a)(3)]. Pursuant to this provision, the secretary issued a regulation requiring revocation in the event a driver's license is otherwise suspended three times within a 10-year-period. A full administrative hearing is available, upon request by the licensee, only after the suspension or revocation has taken effect.

Without requesting an administrative hearing, Love brought an action in federal district court challenging the constitutionality of § 6-206(a)(3) on due process grounds. A three-judge federal court, relying on *Bell* v. *Burson*, 402 U.S. 535 (1971), held that a license cannot be suspended or revoked under § 6-206(a)(3) before a hearing is held to determine whether the licensee meets the statutory criteria. The secretary of state was enjoined from enforcing the statute, and the United States Supreme Court noted probable jurisdiction.

Mr. Justice BLACKMUN delivered the opinion of the Court.

* * *

It is clear that the Due Process Clause applies to the deprivation of a driver's license by the State:

"Suspension of issued licenses thus involves state action that adjudicates important interests of the licensees. In such cases the licenses are not to be taken away without that procedural due process required by the Fourteenth Amendment." Bell v. Burson, 402 U.S., at 539.

It is equally clear that a licensee in Illinois eventually can obtain all the safeguards procedural due process could be thought to require before a discretionary suspension or revocation becomes final. Appellee does not challenge the adequacy of the administrative hearing ... available under [Illinois law]. The only question is one of timing. This case thus presents an issue similar to that considered only last Term in Mathews v. Eldridge, 424 U.S. 319, 333 (1976), namely, "the extent to which due process requires an evidentiary hearing prior to the deprivation of some type of property interest even if such a hearing is provided thereafter." We may analyze the present case, too, in terms of the factors considered in Eldridge:

"[I]dentification of the specific dictates of due process generally requires consideration of three distinct factors: first, the private interest that will be affected by the official action; second, the risk of an erroneous deprivation of such interest through the procedures used, and probable value, if any, of additional or substitute procedural safeguards; and finally, the Government's interest, including the function involved and the fiscal and administrative burdens that the additional or substitute procedural requirement would entail." Id., at 335.

The private interest affected by the decision here is the granted license to operate a motor vehicle. Unlike the social security recipients in Eldridge, who at least could obtain retroactive payments if their claims were subsequently sustained, a licensee is not made entirely whole if his suspension or revocation is later vacated. On the other hand, a driver's license may not be so vital and essential as are social insurance payments on which the recipient may depend for his very subsistence. See Goldberg v. Kelly, 397 U.S. 254, 264 (1970). The Illinois statute includes special provisions for hardship and for holders of commercial licenses, who are those most likely to be affected by the deprival of driving privileges. . . . We therefore conclude that the nature of the private interest here is not so great as to require us "to depart from the ordinary principle, established by our decisions, that something less than an evidentiary hearing is sufficient prior to adverse administrative action." Mathews v. Eldridge, 424 U.S. at 343. See Arnett v. Kennedy, 416 U.S. 134 (1974).

Moreover, the risk of an erroneous deprivation in the absence of a prior hearing is not great. Under the Secretary's regulations, suspension and revocation decisions are largely automatic. Of course, there is the possibility of clerical error, but written objection will bring a matter of that kind to the Secretary's attention. In this case appellee had the opportunity for a full judicial hearing in connection with each of the traffic convictions on which the Secretary's decision was based. Appellee has not challenged the validity of those convictions or the adequacy of his procedural rights at the time they were determined. Since appellee does not dispute the factual basis for the Secretary's decision, he is really asserting the right to appear in person only to argue that the Secretary should show leniency and depart from his own regulations. Such an appearance might make the licensee feel that he has received more personal attention, but it would not serve to protect any substantive rights. We conclude that requiring additional procedures would be unlikely to have significant value in reducing the number of erroneous deprivations.

Finally, the substantial public interest in administrative efficiency would be impeded by the availability of a pretermination hearing in every case. Giving licensees the choice thus automatically to obtain a delay in the effectiveness of a suspension or revocation would encourage drivers routinely to request full administrative hearings. See Mathews v. Eldridge, 424 U.S. at 347. Far more substantial than the administrative burden, however, is the important public interest in safety on the roads and highways, and in the prompt removal of a safety hazard. . . . [T]he

Illinois statute at issue in the instant case is designed to keep off the roads those drivers who are unable or unwilling to respect traffic rules and the safety of others.

We conclude that the public interests present under the circumstances of this case are sufficiently visible and weighty for the State to make its summary initial decision effective without a predecision administrative hearing.

The present case is a good illustration of the fact that procedural due process in the administrative setting does not always require application of the judicial model. When a governmental official is given the power to make discretionary decisions under a broad statutory standard, case-by-case decision-making may not be the best way to assure fairness. Here the Secretary commendably sought to define the statutory standard narrowly by the use of his rulemaking authority. The decision to use objective rules in this case provides drivers with more precise notice of what conduct will be sanctioned and promotes equality of treatment among similarly situated drivers....

Reversed.

[Mr. Justice BRENNAN, Mr. Justice STEVENS, and Mr. Justice MARSHALL concurred in the result]. [Mr. Justice REHNQUIST took no part in the consideration or decision of this case.]

3.05 BURDEN OF PROOF

Due Process and Causation

ORAL ARGUMENTS BEFORE THE
U.S. SUPREME COURT*

Henderson v. Kibbe, No. 75-1906; argued 3/1/77

The Court heard argument on a challenge to a federal court's power to grant habeas relief to a state inmate who had not raised the claim in trial court. The question was whether the defendant's failure to raise at trial his challenge to the sufficiency of a jury charge defeats his habeas claim.

Lillian Zeisel Cohen, Assistant Attorney General of New York, urged the Court to reverse a Second Circuit decision granting habeas relief. Nothing the state courts did here violated respondent Kibbe's federal constitutional rights, she said. Whether the jury instruction was adequate was a question of state law which the state courts properly decided against him.

The murder statute under which Kibbe was convicted speaks, in part, in terms of causation. However, the trial court did not define causation in its instruction, and Kibbe raised no objection to the instruction as delivered.

Cohen explained that Kibbe and one Roy Krall were indicted on second degree murder charges for the death of George Stafford. Stafford, who had been drinking heavily in a Rochester bar, asked several persons for a ride home. Kibbe and Krall, who had apparently already decided to steal the money that Stafford had been flashing openly, agreed to give him a lift. After a round of drinks at another bar, the trio entered Kibbe's car, ostensibly to drive Stafford home.

However, after they had been driving for a bit, Kibbe slapped Stafford several times and took his money, Cohen said. The pair then forced Stafford to lower his trousers and take off his boots to prove that he had no more money. With Stafford still partially undressed and without his eyeglasses, the two men forced him out of the car onto an

---
*From 20 Crim. L. Rptr. 4186–4189 (1977). Reprinted by permission of the Bureau of National Affairs, Inc.

unlighted road in near zero cold and drove away.

Mr. Justice Stewart: "What advice did they give Stafford?"

"They told him to get shelter." Krall and Kibbe apparently knew that there was a gas station about a quarter of a mile away on the other side of the road.

Mr. Justice Stewart: "What kind of road was this?"

"I gather that it was a country road with no artificial lighting."

Mr. Justice Stewart: "Was there traffic?"

Some, but not much, counsel answered.

Sitting in the Road

About a half hour later, Stafford, who was then sitting in the middle of the road, was struck and fatally injured by a pickup truck about a fourth of a mile away from the gas station.

Mr. Justice Stewart: "Krall is not a party here?"

That's right. He didn't pursue the case to this Court.

The Chief Justice: "This case was tried in a New York state court. The state appellate courts affirmed. The district court denied habeas. But the Second Circuit reversed, right?"

Yes, Cohen replied. The district judge found no substantial constitutional violation, and concluded that review of a state jury instruction to which no objection had been raised is not ordinarily within the scope of habeas jurisdiction.

The Chief Justice: "The decision of the federal district court was set aside?"

"Yes, sir; by a divided Second Circuit."

At trial, defense counsel argued that Blake, the driver of the pickup, had caused Kibbe's death. Both Kibbe and Krall strongly disputed any criminal liability for Stafford's death.

Mr. Justice Stewart: "Was there any evidence as to the immediate cause of Stafford's death?"

"Yes, sir."

Mr. Justice Stewart: "Was the impact of the truck the sole cause of death?"

Counsel acknowledged that it was, but she also maintained that the defendant's conduct was the proximate cause of death. Turning to the instruction, Cohen said neither defendant objected to the charge that was given to the jury, which did not explain the term "cause" as used in the murder statute. That issue was raised first by a dissenting judge in the intermediate state appellate court.

Cupp Disavowed?

The Chief Justice: "The prosecutor emphasized to a great extent the defendants' conduct in leaving the man on the side of the road, didn't he?"

Counsel agreed with this point, and stressed that the indictment and the murder statute were read to the jury. Causation was also argued indirectly to the jury, she said.

In *Cupp* v. *Naughten*, 414 U.S. 141 (1973), this Court explained that a single instruction may not be viewed in artificial isolation, but within the context of the entire trial, Cohen pointed out. In reaching its decision here, the Second Circuit effectively disavowed the *Cupp* holding; it discounted the reading of the statute and indictment to the jury. The jury charge was perfectly adequate as far as it went.

The ultimate question for the jury — whether Kibbe could have foreseen Stafford's death — was before it, even though not directly expressed in the charge.

Mr. Justice White: "That isn't what the instruction says. It mentions causation, not foreseeability."

The Chief Justice: "Did the judge charge the jury to evaluate things in light of ordinary human experience?"

Counsel was unsure on this point.

Mr. Justice Stewart: "Is it a common ground, between the petitioner and respondent, what a proper instruction would have been?"

Counsel thought the link between the two sides was that the defendants could only be convicted if Stafford's death was foreseeable as a result of the defendants' conduct.

"Is that different from the ordinary concept of proximate cause in New York law?" one Justice asked.

"Yes, sir, except as to the culpability requirement."

"This isn't negligence? We are talking about proximate cause. Do you concede that the prosecution gave an erroneous definition of cause in his argument?"

"No, sir."

Mr. Justice Stewart: "Then there isn't a

common ground between the petitioners and respondent on the causation point."

The prosecution, Cohen emphasized, discussed the "but/for" test in the context of foreseeability.

Proper Instruction

Mr. Justice Stewart: "Is it clear, at all, what the instruction should have been if properly given?"

Counsel could not point to a model definition of causation though she did discuss the LaFave-Scott definition. [See LaFave and Scott, Criminal Law, 257–263 (1972).]

Mr. Justice White: "Would you defend an instruction if the judge had defined causation in but/for terms?"

If that was the sole instruction on causation, it would be improper. But Cohen again maintained that the minor infirmities in the instruction here raise no federal constitutional questions.

Mr. Justice White: "What do you understand as the constitutional infirmity here?"

According to the Second Circuit this instruction was inadequate and denied Kibbe his due process right to have every element of the crime against him proved beyond a reasonable doubt. The state's failure to define "causation" raises at most a question of state law. This instruction simply did not taint the respondent's trial.

The Chief Justice: "Is it possible that the defense avoided the causation issue for its own benefit on appeal?"

Counsel thought this was possible.

Mr. Justice Blackmun: "What has happened to Krall? Was he convicted?"

"Yes, sir."

Key Term

Referring to the question raised by Mr. Justice Blackmun, Sheila Ginsberg of New York, counsel for the respondent, explained that Krall's pro se habeas petition is now pending in the federal courts.

Foreseeability, Ginsberg argued, is the key to determining causation, but the jury that convicted Kibbe was not told this. At trial, causation was bitterly contested.

Turning to the factual situation, Ginsberg told the Court that few cars traveled the road on which Stafford was struck. The record shows this.

The Chief Justice: "Do you mean that it wasn't foreseeable that some automobiles would be traveling on the road? If the defendant's car was there, why wasn't it foreseeable that others would be driving there?"

Kibbe knew that this road was not heavily traveled, Ginsberg stated; on the facts here, it was perfectly reasonable to expect that Stafford could get across to the nearby gas station.

Mr. Justice Marshall asked whether or not Stafford was drunk.

Ginsberg conceded that Stafford had been drinking, but did not think he was drunk.

Mr. Justice Marshall: "Do sober people walk in the road with no boots?"

Counsel disputed the state's claim that Stafford left the car without his boots. The evidence shows that the boots came off when Blake's pickup dragged Stafford's body after the collision.

Mr. Justice Marshall: "Do you dispute that he was drunk?"

"I would dispute that he was so drunk as to be unaware"; he was moderately drunk. He was intoxicated.

Mr. Justice Marshall: "The difference is?"

Stafford was aware of his need to protect his safety, counsel responded.

The problem with the instruction, Ginsberg submitted, was that the jury did not know how to determine causation. They did not know about superseding causes. A knowledge of foreseeability was fundamental.

Mr. Justice Stevens: "What is stricter, foreseeability or recklessness?"

Recklessness is a lesser standard; it requires a general awareness of the risk of injury or death to another, Ginsberg replied.

Mr. Justice Stevens: "Is there any other evidence of the risk of death that Stafford faced other than being hit by a car?"

The Chief Justice: "Freezing?"

"Yes, sir." However, Kibbe believed that the gas station was accessible to Stafford, who also knew that it was nearby, Ginsberg stressed.

Constitutional Question

Mr. Justice Stewart: "Certainly there can be no serious claim that the jury didn't find every element of the crime beyond a reasonable doubt. The problem is whether it was a constitutional violation not to instruct as to the meaning of 'cause.' That's what this case is all about."

Counsel submitted that the failure to give the proper instruction denied Kibbe his due process rights.

In response to another question from Mr. Justice Stewart, Ginsberg stated that the New York courts didn't rule on the sufficiency of the jury charge.

The Chief Justice: "What is there to suggest that counsel's failure to object to the instruction was not a trial tactic?"

The Second Circuit concluded that the failure to raise the objection was inadvertent. Even from the state's own assessment, the defendant couldn't help but benefit from an instruction on causation, Ginsberg replied.

The Chief Justice: "Isn't it remarkable to suggest that this failure was inadvertent?"

"No, sir." In the heat of the moment and counsel's other concerns, such inadvertence was not unlikely. There is no question that a definition of cause would have helped Kibbe.

Mr. Justice Stevens: "Do you question the adequacy of the charge on 'intent'?"

"No, sir."

Mr. Justice Stevens: "Then we must accept the adequacy of the jury finding on intent."

The Justice also asked counsel what the correct instruction should have been.

Fashioning such an instruction, counsel stated: "The jury may not find the defendant guilty of having caused Stafford's death if the jury believes Blake's operation of the truck was a superseding cause, if the jury finds Blake's operation was negligent, and if the jury determines that Blake was the sole cause of Stafford's death."

Mr. Justice Marshall: "Do you find any case for that charge?"

"Yes, sir," counsel answered, citing a New York case. A proper charge must include language as to foreseeability and superseding cause, she added.

Responding to the Chief Justice, Ginsberg stated the trial judge had an obligation to give a proper charge even though no objection was raised to the instruction.

Mr. Justice White: "Where in the Constitution do you find the requirement that cause must be defined in terms of foreseeability?"

Our point, counsel asserted, is that the trial judge's failure to define causation communicated the misconception that causation existed.

Mr. Justice White: "Let's assume that the judge instructed on but/for causation. Would you be here? I assume you would be claiming the but/for phrasing was unconstitutional?"

"The use of the but/for test encourages the jury to assume that causation could be presumed." The Constitution requires that each element of a crime be proved.

Mr. Justice Stevens: "Would the following charge be okay: The chain of causation would be broken if the death was caused by an intervening agent that wasn't foreseeable?"

Counsel did not think that such a charge would have put Kibbe at a disadvantage.

HENDERSON v. KIBBE

Supreme Court of the United States, 1977
431 U.S. 145, 97 S. Ct. 1730, 52 L. Ed. 2d 203

The facts are stated in the opinion.

Mr. Justice STEVENS delivered the opinion of the Court.

* * *

On the evening of December 30, 1970, respondent and his codefendant encountered a thoroughly intoxicated man named Stafford in a bar in Rochester, N.Y. After observing Stafford display at least two $100 bills, they decided to rob him and agreed to drive him to a nearby town. While in the car, respondent slapped Stafford several times, took his money and, in a search for concealed funds, forced Stafford to lower his trousers and remove his boots. They then abandoned him on an unlighted, rural road, still in a state of partial undress, and without his coat or his glasses. The temperature was near zero, visibility was obscured by blowing snow, and snow banks flanked the roadway. The time was between 9:30 and 9:40 P.M.

At about 10 P.M., while helplessly seated in a traffic lane about a quarter-mile from the nearest lighted building, Stafford was struck by a speeding pickup truck. The driver testified that while he was traveling 50 miles per hour in a 40 mile zone, the first of two approaching cars flashed its lights — presumably as a warning which he did not understand. Immediately after the cars passed, the driver saw Stafford sitting in the road with his hands in the air. The driver neither swerved nor braked his vehicle before it hit Stafford. Stafford was pronounced dead upon arrival at the local hospital.

Respondent and his accomplice were convicted of grand larceny, robbery and second-degree murder.[3] Only the conviction for murder, as defined in New York Penal Law § 125.25, Subd. 2, is now challenged. That statute provides that "[a] person is guilty of murder" when "[u]nder circumstances evincing a depraved indifference to human life, he recklessly engages in conduct which creates a grave risk of death to another person, *and thereby causes the death of another person.*" (Emphasis added.)

Defense counsel argued that it was the negligence of the truck driver, rather than the defendants' action, that had caused Stafford's death, and that the defendants could not have anticipated the fatal accident.[4] On the other hand, the prosecution argued that the death was foreseeable and would not have occurred but for the conduct of the defendants who therefore were the cause of death.[5] Neither party requested the trial judge to instruct the jury on the meaning of the statutory requirement that the defendants' conduct "thereby cause[d] the death of another person," and no such instruction was given. The trial judge did, however, read the indictment and the statute to the jury and

---

[3]Respondent was sentenced to concurrent terms of 15 years to life on the murder conviction; 5–15 years on the robbery conviction; and an indeterminate term up to 4 years on the grand larceny conviction.

[4]"Let's look at this indictment. Count 1 says and I will read the important part. That the defendant, 'Feloniously and under circumstances evincing a depraved indifference to human life recklessly engaged in conduct which created a grave risk of death to another person, to wit, George Stafford, and thereby caused the death of George Stafford.' So, you can see by the accent that I put on reaching that, the elements of this particular crime, and which must be proven beyond a reasonable doubt.

* * *

"[Y]ou are going to have to honestly come to the conclusion that here three people, all three drinking, and that these two, or at least my client, were in a position to perceive this grave risk, be aware of it and disregard it. Perceive that Mr. Stafford would sit in the middle of the northbound lane, that a motorist would come by who was distracted by flashing lights in the opposite lane, who then froze at the wheel, who then didn't swerve, didn't brake, and who was violating the law by speeding, and to make matters worse, he had at that particular time, because of what the situation was, he had low beams on, that is a lot of anticipation. That is a lot of looking forward. Are you supposed to anticipate that somebody is going to break the law when you move or do something? I think that is a reasonable doubt." App. 68.

[5]"As I mentioned, not only does the first count contain reference to and require proof of a depraved indifference to a human life, it proves that the defendants recklessly engaged in conduct which created a risk of death in that they caused the death of George Stafford. Now, I very well know, members of the jury, you know, that quite obviously the acts of both of these defendants were not the only, the direct or the most preceding cause of his death. If I walked with one of you downtown, you know, and we went across one of the bridges and you couldn't swim and I pushed you over and you drowned because you can't swim, I suppose you can say, well, you drowned because you couldn't swim. But of course, the fact is that I pushed you over. The same thing here. Sure, the death, the most immediate, the most preceding, the most direct cause of Mr. Stafford's death was the motor vehicle.... But how did he get there? Or to put it differently, would this man be dead had it not been for the acts of these two defendants? And I submit to you, members of the jury, that the acts of these defendants did indeed cause the death of Mr. Stafford. He didn't walk out there on East River Road. He was driven out there. His glasses were taken and his identification was taken and his pants were around his ankles." App. 75–76.

explained the meaning of some of the statutory language. He advised the jury that a "person acts recklessly with respect to a result or to a circumstances [sic] described by a statute defining an offense *when he is aware of and consciously disregards a substantial and unjustifiable risk that such result will occur* or that such circumstances exist." App. 89 (emphasis added).

The Appellate Division of the New York Supreme Court affirmed respondent's conviction. 41 A.D.2d 228 (1973). Although respondent did not challenge the sufficiency of the instructions to the jury in that court, one judge dissented on the ground that the trial court's charge did not explain the issue of causation or include an adequate discussion of the necessary mental state. That judge expressed the opinion that "the jury, upon proper instruction, could have concluded that the victim's death by an automobile was a remote and intervening cause."

The New York Court of Appeals also affirmed. 35 N.Y.2d, 407, 321 N.E.2d 773 (1974). It identified the causation issue as the only serious question raised by the appeal, and then rejected the contention that the conduct of the driver of the pickup truck constituted an intervening cause which relieved the defendants of criminal responsibility for Stafford's death. The court held that it was "not necessary that the ultimate harm be intended by the actor. It will suffice if it can be said beyond a reasonable doubt, as indeed it can be said here, that the ultimate harm is something which should have been foreseen as being reasonably related to the acts of the accused." The court refused to consider the adequacy of the charge to the jury because that question had not been raised in the trial court.

Respondent then filed a petition for a writ of habeas corpus in the United States District Court for the Northern District of New York relying on 28 U.S.C. § 2254. The District Court held that the respondent's attack on the sufficiency of the charge failed to raise a question of constitutional dimension and that, without more, "the charge is not reviewable in a federal habeas corpus proceeding." App. 21.

The Court of Appeals for the Second Circuit reversed, 534 F.2d 493 (1976). In view of the defense strategy which consistently challenged the sufficiency of the proof of causation, the majority held that the failure to make any objection to the jury instructions was not a deliberate bypass precluding federal habeas corpus relief, but rather was an "obviously inadvertent" omission. Id., at 497. On the merits, the court held that since the Constitution requires proof beyond a reasonable doubt of every fact necessary to constitute the crime, In re Winship, 397 U.S. 358, 364 [1970], the failure to instruct the jury on an essential element as complex as the causation issue in this case created an impermissible risk that the jury had not made a finding that the Constitution requires.

Because the Court of Appeals' decision appeared to conflict with this Court's holding in Cupp v. Naughton, 414 U.S. 141 [1976], we granted certiorari....

Respondent argues that the decision of the Court of Appeals should be affirmed on either of two independent grounds: (1) that the omission of an instruction on causation created the danger that the jury failed to make an essential factual determination as required by Winship; or (2) assuming that they did reach the causation question, they did so without adequate guidance and might have rendered a different verdict under proper instructions. A fair evaluation of the omission in the context of the entire record requires rejection of both arguments.

I

The Court has held "that the Due Process Clause protects the accused against conviction except upon proof beyond a reasonable doubt of every fact necessary to constitute the crime with which he is charged." In re Winship, 397 U.S. 358, 364 [1970]. One of the facts which the New York statute required the prosecution to prove is that the defendant's conduct caused the death of Stafford. As the New York Court of Appeals held, the evidence was plainly sufficient to prove that fact beyond a reasonable doubt. It is equally clear that the record requires us to conclude that the jury made such a finding.

There can be no question about the fact that the jurors were informed that the case included a causation issue that they had to decide. The element of causation was stressed in the arguments of both counsel. The statutory language, which the trial judge read to the jury, expressly refers to the requirement that defendants' conduct "cause[d] the death of another person." The indictment tracks the statutory language; it was read to the jury and they were given a copy for use during their deliberations. The judge instructed the jury that all elements of the crime must be proven beyond a reasonable doubt. Whether or not the arguments of counsel correctly characterized the law applicable to the causation issue, they surely made it clear to the jury that such an issue had to be decided. It follows that the objection predicated on this Court's holding in Winship is without merit.

II

An appraisal of the significance of an error in the instructions to the jury requires a comparison of the instructions which were actually given with those that should have been given. Orderly procedure requires that the respective adversaries' views as to how the jury should be instructed be presented to the trial judge in time to enable him to deliver an accurate charge and to minimize the risk of committing reversible error. It is the rare case in which an improper instruction will justify reversal of a criminal conviction when no objection has been made in the trial court. The burden of demonstrating that an erroneous instruction was so prejudicial that it will support a collateral attack on the constitutional validity of a state court's judgment is even greater than the showing required to establish plain error on direct appeal. The question in such a collateral proceeding is "whether the ailing instruction by itself so infected the entire trial that the resulting conviction violates due process," Cupp v. Naughton, 414 U.S. 141, 147 [1976], not merely whether "... the instruction is undesirable, erroneous, or even 'universally condemned,'" id., at 146.

In this case, the respondent's burden is especially heavy because no erroneous instruction was given; his claim of prejudice is based on the failure to give any explanation—beyond the reading of the statutory language itself—of the causation element. An omission, or an incomplete instruction, is less likely to be prejudicial than a misstatement of the law. Since this omission escaped notice on the record until Judge Cardamone filed his dissenting opinion at the intermediate appellate level, the probability that it substantially affected the jury deliberations seems remote.

Because the respondent did not submit a draft instruction on the causation issue to the trial judge, and because the New York courts apparently had no previous occasion to construe this aspect of the murder statute, we cannot know with certainty precisely what instruction should have been given as a matter of New York law. We do know that the New York Court of Appeals found no reversible error in this case; and its discussion of the sufficiency of the evidence gives us guidance about the kind of causation instruction that would have been acceptable.

The New York Court of Appeals concluded that the evidence of causation was sufficient because it can be said beyond a reasonable doubt that the "ultimate harm" was "something which should have been foreseen as being reasonably related to the acts of the accused." It is not entirely clear whether the court's reference to "ultimate harm" merely required that Stafford's death was foreseeable, or, more narrowly, that his death by speeding vehicle was foreseeable. In either event, the court was satisfied that the "ultimate harm" was one which should have been foreseen. Thus, an adequate instruction would have told the jury that if the ultimate harm should have been foreseen as being reasonably related to defendants' conduct, that conduct should be regarded as having caused the death of Stafford.

The significance of the omission of such an instruction may be evaluated by comparison with the instructions that were given. One of the elements of respondent's offense is that he acted "recklessly," supra, at 2, 3–4. By returning a guilty verdict, the jury necessarily found, in accordance with its instruction on recklessness, that respondent was "aware of and consciously disregard[ed] a substantial and unjustifiable risk" that death would occur. A person who is "aware of and consciously disregards" a substantial risk must also foresee the ultimate harm that the risk entails. Thus, the jury's determination that the respondent acted recklessly necessarily included a determination that the ultimate harm was foreseeable to him.

In a strict sense, an additional instruction on foreseeability would not have been cumulative because it would have related to an element of the offense not specifically covered in the instructions given. But since it is logical to assume that the jurors would have responded to an instruction on causation consistently with their determination of the issues that were comprehensively explained, it is equally logical to conclude that such an instruction would not have affected their verdict. Accordingly, we reject the suggestion that the omission of more complete instructions on the causation issue "so infected the entire trial that the resulting conviction violated due process." Even if we were to make the unlikely assumption that the jury might have reached a different verdict pursuant to an additional instruction, that possibility is too speculative to justify the conclusion that constitutional error was committed.

The judgment is reversed.

Mr. Chief Justice BURGER, concurring in the judgment.

... In my view, the federal court was precluded from granting respondent's petition for collateral relief under 28 U.S.C. § 2254 because he failed to object to the jury instructions at the time they were given. By that failure he waived any claim of constitutional error. This was precisely why the New York Court of Appeals refused to consider respondent's belated claim. Cf. Henry v. Mississippi, 379 U.S. 443 (1965).

This Court has held that under certain circumstances a defendant's failure to comply with state procedural requirements will not be deemed a waiver of federal constitutional rights, unless it is shown that such bypass was the result of a deliberate tactical decision. See Fay v. Noia, 372 U.S. 391 (1963); Humphrey v. Cady, 405 U.S. 504 (1972). These cases, however, involved *post*-trial omissions of a technical nature which would be unlikely to jeopardize substantial state interests. *Mid*-trial omissions such as occurred in this case, on the other hand, are substantially different. "It is one thing to fail to utilize the [state] appeal process to cure a defect which already inheres in a judgment of conviction, but it is quite another to forego making an objection or exception which might prevent the error from ever occurring." Mullaney v. Wilbur, 421 U.S. 684, 704 note (1975) (REHNQUIST, J., concurring); see Estelle v. Williams, 425 U.S. 501, 513–514 (1976) (POWELL, J., concurring). Thus, by failing to object to the jury charge, respondent injected into the trial process the very type of error which the objection requirement was designed to avoid. Federal courts may not overlook such failure on collateral attack.

The "deliberate bypass" doctrine of Fay v. Noia, supra, should not be extended to mid-trial procedural omissions which impair substantial State interests. I would simply hold that the United States District Court was barred from examining the substance of respondent's constitutional claim, and rest our reversal of the Court of Appeals on that ground.

[Mr. Justice REHNQUIST took no part in the consideration or decision of this case.]

Due Process and Extreme Emotional Disturbance

PATTERSON v. NEW YORK

Supreme Court of the United States, 1977
432 U.S. 197, 97 S. Ct. 2319, 52 L. Ed. 2d 281

The facts are stated in the opinion.

Mr. Justice WHITE delivered the opinion of the Court.

The question here is the constitutionality under the Fourteenth Amendment's Due

Process Clause of burdening the defendant in a New York State murder trial with proving the affirmative defense of extreme emotional disturbance as defined by New York law.

I

After a brief and unstable marriage, the appellant, Gordon Patterson, became estranged from his wife, Roberta. Roberta resumed an association with John Northrup, a neighbor to whom she had been engaged prior to her marriage to appellant. On December 27, 1970, Patterson borrowed a rifle from an acquaintance and went to the residence of his father-in-law. There, he observed his wife through a window in a state of semiundress in the presence of John Northrup. He entered the house and killed Northrup by shooting him twice in the head.

Patterson was charged with second-degree murder. In New York there are two elements of this crime: (1) "intent to cause the death of another person"; and (2) "caus[ing] the death of such person or of a third person." N.Y. Penal Law 125.25 (McKinney). Malice aforethought is not an element of the crime. In addition, the State permits a person accused of murder to raise an affirmative defense that he "acted under the influence of extreme emotional disturbance for which there was a reasonable explanation or excuse."

New York also recognizes the crime of manslaughter. A person is guilty of manslaughter if he intentionally kills another person "under circumstances which do not constitute murder because he acts under the influence of extreme emotional disturbance." Appellant confessed before trial to killing Northrup, but at trial he raised the defense of extreme emotional disturbance.

The jury was instructed as to the elements of the crime of murder. Focusing on the element of intent, the trial court charged:

"Before you, considering all of the evidence, can convict this defendant or anyone of murder, you must believe and decide that the People have established beyond a reasonable doubt that he intended, in firing the gun, to kill either the victim himself or some other human being.... Always remember that you must not expect or require the defendant to prove to your satisfaction that his acts were done without the intent to kill. Whatever proof he may have attempted, however far he may have gone in an effort to convince you of his innocence or guiltlessness, he is not obliged, he is not obligated to prove anything. It is always the People's burden to prove his guilt, and to prove that he intended to kill in this instance beyond a reasonable doubt." App., at A-70 to 71.

The jury was further instructed, consistently with New York law, that the defendant had the burden of proving his affirmative defense by a preponderance of the evidence. The jury was told that if it found beyond a reasonable doubt that appellant had intentionally killed Northrup but that appellant had demonstrated by a preponderance of the evidence that he had acted under the influence of extreme emotional disturbance, it must find appellant guilty of manslaughter instead of murder.

The jury found appellant guilty of murder. Judgment was entered on the verdict, and the Appellate Division affirmed. While appeal to the New York Court of Appeals was pending, this Court decided Mullaney v. Wilbur, 421 U.S. 684 (1975), in which the Court declared Maine's murder statute unconstitutional. Under the Maine statute, a person accused of murder could rebut the statutory presumption that he committed the offense with "malice aforethought" by proving that he acted in the heat of passion on sudden provocation. The Court held that this scheme improperly shifted the burden of persuasion from the prosecutor to the defendant and was therefore a violation of due process. In the Court of Appeals appellant urged that New York's murder statute is functionally equivalent to the one struck down in Mullaney and that therefore his conviction should be reversed.

The Court of Appeals rejected appellant's argument, holding that the New York murder statute is consistent with due process. People v. Patterson, 39 N.Y.2d 288 (1976). The Court distinguished Mullaney on the ground that the New York statute involved no shifting of the burden to the defendant to disprove any fact essential to the offense charged since the New York affirmative defense of extreme emotional disturbance bears no direct relationship to any element of murder. This appeal ensued, and we noted probable jurisdiction. 429 U.S. 813 (1976). We affirm.

II

It goes without saying that preventing and dealing with crime is much more the business of the States than it is of the Federal Government, Irvine v. California, 347 U.S. 128, 134 (1954) (plurality opinion), and that we should not lightly construe the Constitution so as to intrude upon the administration of justice by the individual States. Among other things, it is "normally within the power of the State to regulate procedures under which its laws are carried out, including the burden of producing evidence and the burden of persuasion," and its decision in this regard is not subject to proscription under the Due Process Clause unless "it offends some principle of justice so deeply rooted in the traditions and conscience of our people as to be ranked as fundamental." Speiser v. Randall, 357 U.S. 513, 523 (1958); Leland v. Oregon, 343 U.S. 790, 798 (1952); Snyder v. Massachusetts, 201 U.S. 97, 105 (1934).

In determining whether New York's allocation to the defendant of proving the mitigating circumstances of severe emotional disturbance is consistent with due process, it is therefore relevant to note that this defense is a considerably expanded version of the common law defense of heat of passion on sudden provocation, and that at common law the burden of proving the latter, as well as other affirmative defenses — indeed, "all ... circumstances of justification, excuse or alleviation" — rested on the defendant. 4 Blackstone, Commentaries 201; M. Foster, Crown Law 255 (1762); Mullaney v. Wilbur, 421 U.S. 684, 693-694 (1975). This was the rule when the Fifth Amendment was adopted, and it was the American rule when the Fourteenth Amendment was ratified. Commonwealth v. York, 50 Mass. 93 (1845).

In 1895 the common law view was abandoned with respect to the insanity defense in federal prosecutions. Davis v. United States, 160 U.S. 469 (1895). This ruling had wide impact on the practice in the federal courts with respect to the burden of proving various affirmative defenses, and the prosecution in a majority of jurisdictions in this country sooner or later came to shoulder the burden of proving the sanity of the accused and of disproving the facts constituting other affirmative defenses, including provocation. Davis was not a constitutional ruling, however, as Leland v. Oregon, supra, made clear.

At issue in Leland v. Oregon was the constitutionality under the Due Process Clause of the Oregon rule that the defense of insanity must be proved by the defendant beyond a reasonable doubt. Noting that Davis "obviously established no constitutional doctrine," 343 U.S., at 797, the Court refused to strike down the Oregon scheme, saying that the burden of proving all elements of the crime beyond reasonable doubt, including the elements of premeditation and deliberation, was placed on the State under Oregon procedures and remained there throughout the trial. To convict, the jury was required to find each element of the crime beyond reasonable doubt, based on all the evidence, including the evidence going to the issue of insanity. Only then was the jury "to consider separately the issue of legal sanity per se...." Id., at 795. This practice did not offend the Due Process Clause even though among the 20 States then placing the burden of proving his insanity on the defendant, Oregon was alone in requiring him to convince the jury beyond a reasonable doubt.

In 1970, the Court declared that the Due Process Clause "protects the accused ... by requiring proof beyond a reasonable doubt of every fact necessary to constitute the crime with which he is charged." In re Winship, 397 U.S. 358, 364 (1970). Five years later, in Mullaney v. Wilbur, 421 U.S. 684 (1975), the Court further announced that under the Maine law of homicide, the burden could not constitutionally be placed on the defendant of proving by a preponderance of the evidence that the killing had occurred in the heat of passion on sudden provocation. The CHIEF JUSTICE [BURGER] and Mr. Justice REHNQUIST, concurring, expressed their understanding that the Mullaney decision did not call into question the ruling in Leland v. Oregon, supra, with respect to the proof of insanity.

Subsequently, the Court confirmed that it remained constitutional to burden the defendant with proving his insanity defense when it is dismissed, as not raising a substantial federal question, a case in which the appellant specifically challenged the continuing validity of Leland v. Oregon. This occurred in Rivera v. Delaware, [97 S. Ct. 498] (1976), an appeal from a Delaware conviction which, in reliance on Leland, had been affirmed by the Delaware Supreme Court over the claim that the Delaware statute was unconstitutional because it burdened the defendant with proving his affirmative defense of insanity by a preponderance of the evidence. The claim in this Court was that Leland had been overruled by Winship and Mullaney. We dismissed the appeal as not presenting a substantial federal question. Cf. Hicks v. Miranda, 422 U.S. 332, 344 (1975).

III

We cannot conclude that Patterson's conviction under the New York law deprived him of due process of law. The crime of murder is defined by the statute, which represents a recent revision of the State criminal code, as causing the death of another person with intent to do so. The death, the intent to kill, and causation are the facts that the State is required to prove beyond reasonable doubt if a person is to be convicted of murder. No further facts are either presumed or inferred in order to constitute the crime. The statute does provide an affirmative defense—that the defendant acted under the influence of extreme emotional disturbance for which there was a reasonable explanation—which, if proved by a preponderance of the evidence, would reduce the crime to manslaughter, an offense defined in a separate section of the statute. It is plain enough that if the intentional killing is shown, the State intends to deal with the defendant as a murderer unless he demonstrates the mitigating circumstances.

Here, the jury was instructed in accordance with the statute, and the guilty verdict confirms that the State successfully carried its burden of proving the facts of the crime beyond reasonable doubt. Nothing in the evidence, including any evidence that might have been offered with respect to Patterson's mental state at the time of the crime, raised a reasonable doubt about his guilt as a murderer; and clearly the evidence failed to convince the jury that Patterson's affirmative defense had been made out. It seems to us that the State satisfied the mandate of Winship that it prove beyond reasonable doubt "every fact necessary to constitute the crime with which [Patterson was] charged." In re Winship, 397 U.S. 358, 364 [1970].

In convicting Patterson under its murder statute, New York did no more than Leland and Rivera permitted it to do without violating the Due Process Clause. Under those cases, once the facts constituting a crime are established beyond reasonable doubt, based on all the evidence including the evidence of the defendant's mental state, the State may refuse to sustain the affirmative defense of insanity unless demonstrated by a preponderance of the evidence.

The New York law on extreme emotional disturbance follows this pattern. This affirmative defense, which the Court of Appeals described as permitting "the defendant to show that his actions were caused by a mental infirmity not rising to the level of insanity, and that he is less culpable for having committed them," App. 111, does not serve to negative any facts of the crime which the State is to prove in order to convict for murder. It constitutes a separate issue on which the defendant is required to carry the burden of persuasion; and unless we are to overturn Leland and Rivera, New York has not violated the Due Process Clause, and Patterson's conviction must be sustained.

We are unwilling to reconsider Leland and Rivera. But even if we were to hold that a State must prove sanity to convict once that fact is put in issue, it would not necessarily follow that a State must prove beyond a reasonable doubt every fact, the existence or nonexistence of which it is willing to recognize as an exculpatory or mitigating circumstance affecting the degree of culpability or the severity of the punishment. Here, in revising its criminal code, New York provided the affirmative defense of extreme emotional disturbance, a substantially expanded version of the older heat of passion concept; but it was willing to do so only if the facts making out the defense were established by the defendant with sufficient certainty. The State was itself unwilling to undertake to establish the absence of those facts beyond reasonable doubt, perhaps fearing that proof would be too difficult and that too many persons deserving treatment as murderers would escape that punishment if the evidence need merely raise a reasonable doubt about the defendant's emotional state. It has been said that the new criminal code of New York contains some 25 affirmative defenses which exculpate or mitigate but which must be established by the defendant to be operative. The Due Process Clause, as we see it, does not put New York to the choice of abandoning those defenses or undertaking to disprove their existence in order to convict for a crime which otherwise is within its constitutional powers to sanction by substantial punishment.

The requirement of proof beyond reasonable doubt in a criminal case is "bottomed on a fundamental value determination of our society that it is far worse to convict an innocent man than to let a guilty man go free." Winship, supra, at 372 (Harlan, J., concurring). The social cost of placing the burden on the prosecution to prove guilt beyond a reasonable doubt is thus an increased risk that the guilty will go free. While it is clear that our society has willingly chosen to bear a substantial burden in order to protect the innocent, it is equally clear that the risk it must bear is not without limits; and Justice Harlan's aphorism provides little guidance for determining what those limits are. Due process does not require that every conceivable step be taken, at whatever cost, to eliminate the possibility of convicting an innocent person. Punishment of those found guilty by a jury, for example, is not forbidden merely because there is a remote possibility in some instances that an innocent person might go to jail.

It is said that the common law rule permits a State to punish one as a murderer when it is as likely as not that he acted in the heat of passion or under severe emotional distress and when, if he did, he is guilty only of manslaughter. But this has always been the case in those jurisdictions adhering to the traditional rule. It is also very likely true that fewer convictions for murder would occur if New York were required to negative the affirmative defense at issue here. But in each instance of a murder conviction under the present law, New York will have proved beyond reasonable doubt that the defendant has intentionally killed another person, an act which it is not disputed the State may constitutionally criminalize and punish. If the State nevertheless chooses to recognize a factor that mitigates the degree of criminality or punishment, we think the State may assure itself that the fact has been established with reasonable certainty. To recognize at all a mitigating circumstance does not require the State to prove its nonexistence in each case in which the fact is put in issue, if in its judgment this would be too cumbersome, too expensive, and too inaccurate.

We thus decline to adopt as a constitutional imperative, operative country-wide, that a State must disprove beyond reasonable doubt every fact constituting any and all affirmative defenses related to the culpability of an accused. Traditionally, due process has required that only the most basic procedural safeguards be observed; more subtle balancing of society's interests against those of the accused have been left to the legislative branch. We therefore will not disturb the balance struck in previous cases holding that the Due Process Clause requires the prosecution to prove beyond reasonable doubt all of the elements included in the definition of the offense of which the defendant is charged. Proof of the nonexistence of all affirmative defenses has never been constitutionally required; and we perceive no reason to fashion such a rule in this case and apply it to the statutory defense at issue here.

This view may seem to permit state legislatures to reallocate burdens of proof by labeling as affirmative defenses at least some elements of the crimes now defined in their statutes. But there are obviously constitutional limits beyond which the States may not go in this regard. "[I]t is not within the province of a legislature to declare an individual guilty or presumptively guilty of a crime." McFarland v. American Sugar Refining Co., 241 U.S. 79, 86 (1916). The legislature cannot "validly command that the finding of an indictment, or mere proof of the identity of the accused, should create a presumption of the existence of all the facts essential to guilt." Tot v. United States, 319 U.S. 463, 469 (1943). See also Speiser v. Randall, 357 U.S. 513, 523–525 (1958).

Long before Winship, the universal rule in this country was that the prosecution must prove guilt beyond reasonable doubt. At the same time, the long-accepted rule was that it was constitutionally permissible to provide that various affirmative defenses were to be proved by the defendant. This did not lead to such abuses or to such widespread redefinition of crime and reduction of the prosecution's burden that a new constitutional rule was required. This was not the problem to which Winship was addressed. Nor does the fact that a majority of the States have now assumed the burden of disproving affirmative defenses—for whatever reasons—mean that those States who strike a different balance are in violation of the Constitution.

IV

Mullaney's holding, it is argued, is that the State may not permit the blameworthiness of an act or the severity of punishment authorized for its commission to depend on the presence or absence of an identified fact without assuming the burden of proving the presence or absence of that fact, as the case may be, beyond reasonable doubt. In our view, the Mullaney holding should not be so broadly read. The concurrence of two Justices in Mullaney was necessarily contrary to such a reading; and a majority of the Court refused to so understand and apply Mullaney when Rivera was dismissed for want of a substantial federal question.

Mullaney surely held that a State must prove every ingredient of an offense beyond a reasonable doubt, and that it may not shift the burden of proof to the defendant by presuming that ingredient upon proof of the other elements of the offense. This is true even though the State's practice, as in Maine, had been traditionally to the contrary. Such shifting of the burden of persuasion with respect to a fact which the State deems so important that it must be either proved or presumed is impermissible under the Due Process Clause.

It was unnecessary to go further in Mullaney. The Maine Supreme Court made it clear that malice aforethought, which was mentioned in the statutory definition of the crime, was not equivalent to premeditation and that the presumption of malice traditionally arising in intentional homicide cases carried no factual meaning insofar as premeditation was concerned. Even so, a killing became murder in Maine when it resulted from a deliberate, cruel act committed by one person against another, "suddenly, and without any, or without considerable, provocation." Premeditation was not within the definition of murder; but malice, in the sense of the absence of provocation, was part of the definition of that crime. Yet malice, i.e., lack of provocation, was presumed and could be rebutted by the defendant only by proving by a preponderance of the evidence that he acted with heat of passion upon sudden provocation. In Mullaney we held that however traditional this mode of proceeding might have been, it is contrary to the Due Process Clause as construed in Winship.

As we have explained, nothing was presumed or implied against Patterson; and his conviction is not invalid under any of our prior cases. The judgment of the New York Court of Appeals is

Affirmed.

[Mr. Justice POWELL, with whom Mr. Justice BRENNAN and Mr. Justice MARSHALL joined, dissented.]

[Mr. Justice REHNQUIST took no part in the consideration or decision of this case.]

Retroactivity of *Mullaney v. Wilbur*

ORAL ARGUMENTS BEFORE THE U.S. SUPREME COURT*

Hankerson v. North Carolina, No. 75-6568; argued 2/22/77

A murder case from North Carolina presented the Court with its first plenary look at issues arising out of its 1975 decision in

---

*20 Crim. L. Rptr. 4174–4175. Reprinted by permission of the Bureau of National Affairs, Inc.

Mullaney v. *Wilbur*, 421 U.S. 684. In *State v. Hankerson*, 288 N.C. 632, 220 S.E.2d 575, a majority of the North Carolina Supreme Court found *Mullaney* problems with time-honored jury instructions on claims of heat of passion and self-defense. In murder cases in the state, malice and unlawfulness are presumed. Under the old instructions, a defendant was required to rebut the presumption of malice by proving "to the satisfaction of the jury" that he killed in the heat of a sudden passion. The defendant bore an identical burden of proving self-defense in order to rebut the presumption of unlawfulness. These instructions, the state majority said, "violate the concept of due process announced for the first time in *Mullaney.*"

However, the majority declined to give *Mullaney* retroactive effect. Instead, it held that any trial conducted on or after the date of the *Mullaney* decision must comply with new rules, which it proceeded to formulate.

Lawrence G. Diedrick, of Rocky Mount, North Carolina, presented the argument for the defendant Hankerson. The main question the Court must resolve, he said, is whether the *Mullaney* rule implicates the truth-finding process. The state majority said that the purpose of *Mullaney* was to insure a reliable determination of guilt or degree of guilt. But it nonetheless went on to consider the other two factors of retroactivity analysis — the state's prior reliance on the old rule, and the effect of retroactive application upon the criminal justice system. Consideration of these factors led the majority to hold *Mullaney* prospective only.

We submit, counsel said, that the state majority should never have considered the second and third retroactivity factors. *Mullaney* is designed to overcome a flaw that impaired the jury's truth-finding function. Accordingly, it must be given completely retroactive effect. *Mullaney* relied on *In re Winship,* 397 U.S. 358 (1970), and that case has been applied retroactively. Moreover, Mr. Justice Powell's opinion in *Mullaney* noted that the state there had "affirmatively shifted the burden of proof to the defendant. The result, in a case such as this one where the defendant is required to prove the critical fact in dispute, is to increase further the likelihood of an erroneous murder conviction." 421 U.S. at 701.

Mr. Justice Stewart noted that the North Carolina majority treated both absence of malice and the self-defense issue as being covered by *Mullaney.* But *Mullaney* didn't involve a factor, like self-defense, that would constitute a complete defense to a murder charge.

Self-defense can be analogized to the heat-of-passion factor, counsel answered. True, the latter goes only to mitigation, while the former is a complete defense. But both involve elements of the crime — malice and unlawfulness. By statute and case law, unlawfulness is an essential element of murder. A defense of insanity or alibi is different, counsel added: such defenses do not involve elements of the offense, so the defendant may be required to shoulder the burden. [*Leland* v. *Oregon,* 343 U.S. 790 (1952).]

The North Carolina majority said that this case did not present the sudden passion issue, Mr. Justice White pointed out.

Diedrick disagreed with the state court's analysis on that point. There was evidence that the victim had put a knife to the defendant's neck — I think that raises the sudden passion issue, he said.

In any event, the retroactivity issue would remain, with regard to self-defense.

Disastrous Impact Predicted

Assistant Attorney General Charles M. Hensey presented the state's argument. We agree, he said, that retroactivity is appropriate if the purpose of the new rule is to insure the integrity of the truth-finding process. *Mullaney* had this purpose. But we argue that *Mullaney* has not wrought so dramatic an improvement in the truth-finding process as to require retroactivity. The new rule deals only with the fringes of the process. Juries are knowledgeable and sensitive, and *Mullaney* hasn't significantly improved their performance. Thus the Court may consider the other retroactivity factors — reliance and impact.

The impact of retroactive application would be almost disastrous. According to the state supreme court, there are some 700 prisoners, convicted of second-degree murder or manslaughter, who might bring post-conviction relief actions. Handling these claims would be extremely difficult, costly, and time consuming. [In his brief, counsel noted that under *Evans* v. *State,* 349 A.2d 300 (Md. App. 1975), "first-degree murder convictions would not be affected by *Mullaney* since the elements of premeditation and deliberation would have been proved beyond a reasonable doubt and thus render any *Mullaney* error harmless beyond a reasonable doubt." — ed.]

Mr. Justice White noted that the state did not file a cross-petition for certiorari with respect to the state court's holding that

Mullaney applied to the jury instructions regarding self-defense. So that question is not open here, right? he asked. Mr. Justice Blackmun later raised the same point.

Counsel agreed. He later indicated that the state perceived little harm in conforming jury instructions in further trials to the state court's requirements.

But Mr. Justice Stevens said the North Carolina majority relied on state statutory law in determining that *Mullaney* applied. He also asked counsel whether the heat of passion issue was presented in this case.

Like defense counsel, Hensey said it was. There was some evidence in the case raising the issue. Moreover, the fact that North Carolina treats heat of passion much the same as self-defense gets the issue here.

Mr. Justice Stewart asked whether counsel could offer an argument for distinguishing between heat of passion and self-defense in the *Mullaney* context.

Hensey replied that the state could not see one. In response to further questioning, he said he could see no difference between heat of passion and self-defense, on the one hand, and insanity on the other. Both self-defense and insanity go to unlawfulness. Yet *Leland* says that the defendant may be required to prove insanity.

Impact Disputed

In rebuttal, Diedrick disputed the state's analysis of the impact retroactive application would have. The statistics are meaningless without a breakdown as to how each defendant pleaded and what degree of homicide the jury found, he said.

Mr. Justice Stewart thought that even a guilty pleader could mount a collateral attack.

But counsel said that if self-defense is available, a guilty plea would amount to a waiver of the defense.

At any rate, he concluded, retroactive application is worth the price. He reemphasized that the *Mullaney* rule implicates the fact-finding process. Failure to accord *Mullaney* retroactive application raises the possibility that innocent defendants will remain incarcerated.

HANKERSON v. NORTH CAROLINA

Supreme Court of the United States, 1977
432 U.S. 233, 97 S. Ct. 2339, 52 L. Ed. 2d 306

In 1974, prior to the decision in *Mullaney* v. *Wilbur*, 421 U.S. 684 (1975), Johnnie Hankerson, the petitioner, was convicted in a North Carolina state court of second degree murder over his claim that he acted in self-defense. The trial judge had instructed the jury that if the prosecution proved beyond a reasonable doubt that the petitioner intentionally killed the victim with a deadly weapon, the law presumed that the killing was unlawful and that it was done with malice, and in order to excuse his act, the petitioner had to prove to the jury's "satisfaction" that he acted in self-defense. The North Carolina Supreme Court affirmed the conviction over petitioner's objection to such instructions and refused to apply *Mullaney* retroactively. The United States Supreme Court granted certiorari.

Mr. Justice WHITE delivered the opinion of the Court.

* * *

This Court granted Hankerson's petition for a writ of certiorari, which raised the single question whether Mullaney [v. Wilbur, 421 U.S. 684 (1975)] should be held retroactive. The State of North Carolina has filed an answering brief in which it argues (1) that the North Carolina Supreme Court was correct in holding Mullaney not retroactive; and (2) that in any event the judgment below should be affirmed because the instructions given in this case did leave the burden of disproving self-defense beyond a reasonable doubt on the prosecution, or at least did not require the accused to prove self-defense by a preponderance of the evidence in contravention of Mullaney. These are the only two issues before this Court, and we treat them in order.

II

The Supreme Court of North Carolina erred in declining to hold retroactive the rule in Mullaney v. Wilbur, supra. In Ivan V. v. City of New York, 407 U.S. 203, 204-205 (1972), this Court addressed the question whether our decision in In re Winship, 397 U.S. 358 (1970) — holding the reasonable doubt standard applicable to state juvenile proceedings — was to be applied retroactively. The Court there said:

"'Where the major purpose of a new constitutional doctrine is to overcome an aspect of the criminal trial that substantially impairs its truth-finding function and so raises serious questions about the accuracy of guilty verdicts in past trials, the new rule has been given complete retroactive effect. Neither good-faith reliance by state or federal authorities on prior constitutional law or accepted practice, nor severe impact on the administration of justice has sufficed to require prospective application in these circumstances.' Williams v. United States, 401 U.S. 646, 653 (1971). See Adams v. Illinois, 405 U.S. 278, 280 (1972); Roberts v. Russell, 392 U.S. 293, 295 (1968).

"Winship expressly held that the reasonable-doubt standard 'is a prime instrument for reducing the risk of convictions resting on factual error.' The standard provides concrete substance for the presumption of innocence — that bedrock 'axiomatic and elementary' principle whose 'enforcement lies at the foundation of the administration of our criminal law'.... 'Due process commands that no man shall lose his liberty unless the Government has borne the burden of . . . convincing the factfinder of his guilt.' To this end, the reasonable-doubt standard is indispensable, for it 'impresses on the trier of fact the necessity of reaching a subjective state of certitude of the facts in issue.' 397 U.S., at 363-364.

"Plainly, then, the major purpose of the constitutional standard of proof beyond a reasonable doubt announced in Winship was to overcome an aspect of a criminal trial that substantially impairs the truth-finding function, and Winship is thus to be given complete retroactive effect."

Ivan V. controls this case. In Mullaney v. Wilbur, as in In re Winship, the Court held that due process requires the States in some circumstances to apply the reasonable-doubt standard of proof rather than some lesser standard under which an accused would more easily lose his liberty. In Mullaney, as in Winship, the rule was designed to diminish the probability that an innocent person would be convicted and thus to overcome an aspect of a criminal trial that "substantially impairs the truth-finding function."

* * *

. . . [R]espondent claims that in deciding whether a new constitutional rule is to be applied retroactively, the Court has traditionally inquired not only, as in Ivan V., into the purpose of the rule but also into the extent of the State's justified reliance on the old rule and the impact that retroactive application of the new rule would have on the administration of justice. See, e.g., Stovall v. Denno, 388 U.S. 293 (1967); Johnson v. New Jersey, 384 U.S. 719 (1966); Tehan v. Shott, 382 U.S. 406 (1966); Linkletter v. Walker, 381 U.S. 618 (1965). It claims that even where the purpose of the new rule is to improve the "integrity of the factfinding process," the rule has been held nonretroactive when the impact of the new rule on the administration of justice would otherwise be devastating and when the States have justifiably relied on the old rule. See, e.g., Stovall v. Denno, supra (holding nonretroactive the requirement of United States v. Wade, 388 U.S. 218 [1967], that counsel be present at a pretrial line-up); Adams v. Illinois, 405 U.S. 278 (1972) (holding nonretroactive the rule of Coleman v. Alabama, 399 U.S. 1 [1970], that counsel be present at a preliminary hearing).

The force of Ivan V. may not be avoided so easily. It is true that we have said that the question of whether the purpose of a new constitutional rule is to enhance the integrity of the factfinding process is a question of "degree," Johnson v. New Jersey, supra, 384 U.S., at 729; and when the degree to which the rule enhances the integrity of the factfinding process is sufficiently small, we have looked to questions of reliance by the State on the old rule and the impact of the new rule on the administration of justice in deciding whether the new rule is to be applied retroactively. Stovall v. Denno, supra; Adams v. Illinois, supra; DeStefano v. Woods, 392 U.S. 631 (1968). But we have never deviated from the rule stated in Ivan V. that "'[w]here the *major* purpose of new constitutional doctrine is to overcome an aspect of the criminal trial that *substantially* impairs its truth-finding function and so raises *serious* questions about the accuracy of guilty verdicts in past trials, the new rule [is] given complete retroactive effect.'" Id., at 204 (emphasis added). The reasonable-doubt standard of proof is as "substantial" a requirement under Mullaney as it was in Winship. Respondent's attempt to distinguish Ivan V. is without merit.

III

Respondent next argues in support of the judgment below that the instruction in this case—that the defendant must "satisfy" the jury that he acted in self-defense—is the equivalent of an instruction that it should acquit if it entertains a reasonable doubt on the subject, or is so nearly the equivalent of such an instruction that it is not in violation of the rule announced in Mullaney, where the burden impermissibly placed on the defendant was to persuade the jury by a preponderance of the evidence. Respondent's argument is squarely contrary to the construction given by the North Carolina Supreme Court to the jury charge in this case. That court concluded that a burden to "satisfy" the jury of self-defense places a burden on a defendant "no greater and at the same time one not significantly less than persuasion by a preponderance of the evidence." The Court has no basis for disagreeing with this interpretation of the charge, which is essentially a question of state law. Since the issue of whether due process requires the prosecution to disprove self-defense beyond a reasonable doubt under North Carolina law was not raised by either party in this case, we declined to consider it now.

Reversed.

[Mr. Justice MARSHALL and Mr. Justice POWELL each wrote concurring opinions..

[Mr. Justice BLACKMUN, with whom CHIEF JUSTICE BURGER joined, wrote a concurring opinion.]

[Mr. Justice REHNQUIST took no part in the consideration or decision of this case.]

3.06 OTHER DECISIONS OF INTEREST INVOLVING DUE PROCESS

Statutory Construction

In *Scarborough* v. *United States,* 431 U.S. 563 (1977), the Supreme Court granted certiorari to decide whether proof that a possessed firearm had previously traveled in interstate commerce is sufficient to satisfy a federal statute that requires a nexus between the possession of a firearm by a convicted felon and interstate commerce. In 1972, Richard Scarborough, petitioner, pleaded guilty in a Virginia state court to the felony of possession of narcotics with intent to distribute. A year later, law enforcement officials, acting pursuant to a search warrant, seized four firearms from petitioner's bedroom. He was charged with violating 18 U.S.C. App. § 1202(a)(1), which makes it a crime for a convicted felon to "receive, possess, or transport in commerce or affecting commerce ... any firearm." The prosecution established that all the seized firearms had traveled in interstate commerce prior to the date that Scarborough became a convicted felon. The trial judge instructed the jury that the prosecution had met its burden under the statute if it showed that the firearm possessed by the convicted felon had at some time previously traveled in interstate commerce. The petitioner was convicted, and the Court of Appeals (4th Cir.) affirmed.

The Supreme Court affirmed, over the dissent of Justice Stewart, in a 7-1 decision. Writing for the Court, Mr. Justice Marshall held that:

1. Proof that the possessed firearm had previously traveled at some time in interstate commerce is sufficient to satisfy the statutorily required nexus between possession and commerce.

2. The nexus need not be "contemporaneous"—the firearm may have traveled in interstate commerce before the accused became a convicted felon.

3. The legislative history shows a congressional intent to require no more than a minimal nexus between possession and interstate commerce. The Congress, by including the phrase, "affecting commerce," meant to assert its full Commerce Clause power and to broadly outlaw possession.

Mr. Justice Stewart, dissenting, stated that § 1202(a)(1) does not become operative "unless and until a person first comes into possession of a firearm after he is convicted of a felony." Mr. Justice Rehnquist did not participate.

Appeal Dismissed "for Want of a Substantial Federal Question"

In *Rivera* v. *Delaware,* 429 U.S. 877 (1976), a majority of the Supreme Court sustained a Delaware statute that requires a criminal defendant raising an insanity defense to prove mental illness or defect by a preponderance of the evidence. There was no written opinion; rather, the Court dismissed the appeal from the Delaware Supreme Court, which had sustained the statute, "for want of a substantial federal question." Such summary disposition affords the case precedential weight. See *Hicks* v. *Miranda,* 422 U.S. 332, 344 (1975). Mr. Justice Stevens would have noted probable jurisdiction and set the case for oral argument. Mr. Justice Brennan, joined by Mr. Justice Marshall, wrote a dissenting opinion, stating that the case presented a substantial federal question; to wit, "whether *Leland* [v. *Oregon,* 343 U.S. 790 (1952), which sustained a state statute requiring an accused to prove his insanity beyond a reasonable doubt] can be reconciled with *In re Winship* [397 U.S. 358 (1970)] and *Mullaney* [v. *Wilbur,* 421 U.S. 684 (1975)]."

The Right of Privacy and Zoning Regulations

In *Moore* v. *City of East Cleveland, Ohio,* 431 U.S. 494 (1977), the Supreme Court granted review to decide the constitutionality of a city ordinance that limited occupancy of a dwelling unit to members of a single family. The appellant, a grandmother, was convicted of a criminal offense for having two grandchildren who were cousins rather than brothers permanently living with her. When she failed to remove them from the home, she was convicted under the ordinance and sentenced to five days in jail and a $25 fine. The Ohio Court of Appeals affirmed, and the Ohio Supreme Court denied review. On appeal, the United States Supreme Court noted probable jurisdiction. In a plurality opinion written by Mr. Justice Powell, joined by Justices Brennan, Marshall, and Blackmun, the ordinance was struck down as violative of appellant's liberty rights under the Due Process Clause of the Fourteenth Amendment. The Court held that:

1. The ordinance, which expressly declared that certain categories of relatives may live together while others may not, bore no "rational relationship to permissible state objectives."

2. The ordinance at best had only a tenuous relationship to the objectives cited by the city: avoiding overcrowding, traffic congestion, and undue financial burdening of the school system.

3. Freedom of personal choice in matters of family life and marriage is protected by the liberty aspect of the Fourteenth Amendment, and enjoyment of this freedom is not limited to nuclear families (i.e., a married couple and their dependent children). (See Table 3–5, infra.)

Mr. Justice Stevens wrote a concurring opinion in which he stated that the Due Process Clause includes the right to use one's property as one sees fit. Because the ordinance bore no "substantial relationship" to the maintenance of public health, safety, morals, or general welfare, the ordinance constituted the taking of property without due process. Mr. Justice Stewart, joined by Mr. Justice Rehnquist, dissented, stating that the city has the power to ordain single-family residential occupancy and the power to say what constitutes a "family." Chief Justice Burger dissented on the ground that the appellant's failure to exhaust adequate administrative remedies foreclosed federal review.

Mr. Justice White's dissent is presented below:

Mr. Justice WHITE, dissenting.

The Fourteenth Amendment forbids any

State to "deprive any person of life, liberty, or property, without due process of law," or to "deny to any person within its jurisdiction the equal protection of the laws." Both provisions are invoked in this case in an attempt to invalidate a city zoning ordinance.

I

The emphasis of the Due Process Clause is on "process." As Mr. Justice Harlan once observed, it has been "ably and consistently argued in response to what were felt to be abuses by this Court of its reviewing power . . ." that the Due Process Clause should be limited "to a guarantee of procedural due process." Poe v. Ullman, 367 U.S. 497, 540 (1961) (Harlan, J., dissenting). These arguments had seemed "persuasive" to Justices Brandeis and Holmes, Whitney v. California, 274 U.S. 357, 373 (1927), but they recognized that the Due Process Clause, by virtue of case-to-case "judicial inclusion and exclusion," Davidson v. New Orleans, 96 U.S. 97, 104 (1877), had been construed to proscribe matters of substance, as well as inadequate procedures, and to protect from invasion by the States "all fundamental rights comprised within the term liberty." Whitney v. California, supra, at 373.

Mr. Justice Black also recognized that the Fourteenth Amendment had substantive as well as procedural content. But believing that its reach should not extend beyond the specific provisions of the Bill of Rights, see Adamson v. California, 332 U.S. 46 (1947) (Black, J., dissenting), he never embraced the idea that the Due Process Clause empowered the courts to strike down merely unreasonable or arbitrary legislation, nor did he accept Mr. Justice Harlan's consistent view. See Griswold v. Connecticut, 381 U.S. 479, 507 (1965) (Black, J., dissenting), and id., at 499 (Harlan, J., concurring). Writing at length in dissent in Poe v. Ullman, 367 U.S. 497, 543 (1961), Mr. Justice Harlan stated the essence of his position as follows:

"This 'liberty' is not a series of isolated points pricked out in terms of the taking of property; the freedom of speech, press, and religion; the right to keep and bear arms; the freedom from unreasonable searches and seizures; and so on. It is a rational continuum which, broadly speaking, includes a freedom from all substantial arbitrary impositions and purposeless restraints, see Allgeyer v. Louisiana, 165 U.S. 578; Holden v. Hardy, 169 U.S. 366; Booth v. Illinois, 184 U.S. 425; Nebbia v. New York, 291 U.S. 502; Skinner v. Oklahoma, 316 U.S. 535, 544 (concurring opinion); Schware v. Board of Bar Examiners, 353 U.S. 232, and which also recognizes, what a reasonable and sensitive judgment must, that certain interests require particularly careful scrutiny of the state needs asserted to justify their abridgement. Cf. Skinner v. Oklahoma, supra; Bolling v. Sharpe, supra."

This construction was far too open ended for Mr. Justice Black. For him, Meyer v. Nebraska, 262 U.S. 390 (1923), and Pierce v. Society of Sisters, 268 U.S. 510 (1925), as substantive due process cases, were as suspect as Lochner v. New York, 198 U.S. 45 (1905), Coppage v. Kansas, 236 U.S. 1 (1915), and Adkins v. Children's Hospital, 261 U.S. 525 (1923). In his view, Ferguson v. Skrupa, 372 U.S. 726 (1963) should have finally disposed of them all. But neither Meyer nor Pierce has been overruled, and recently there have been decisions of the same genre—Roe v. Wade, 410 U.S. 113 (1973); Loving v. Virginia, 388 U.S. 1 (1967); Griswold v. Connecticut, supra; and Eisenstadt v. Baird, 405 U.S. 438 (1972). Not all of these decisions purport to rest on substantive due process grounds, compare Roe v. Wade, supra, at 152–153, with Eisenstadt v. Baird, supra, at 453–454, but all represented substantial reinterpretations of the Constitution.

Although the Court regularly proceeds on the assumption that the Due Process Clause has more than a procedural dimension, we must always bear in mind that the substantive content of the Clause is suggested neither by its language nor by preconstitutional history; that content is nothing more than the accumulated product of judicial interpretation of the Fifth and Fourteenth Amendments. This is not to suggest, at this point, that any of these cases should be overruled, or that the process by which they were decided was illegitimate or even unacceptable, but only to underline Mr. Justice Black's constant reminder to his colleagues that the Court has

TABLE 3.5 Supreme Court Decisions Involving the Right of Privacy: 1965–1977

Case	Holding	Vote	Dissenting Opinions
Griswold v. Connecticut, 381 U.S. 479 (1965)	State statute making the use of contraceptives a criminal offense held invalid as an unconstitutional invasion of the right of privacy of married persons.	7–2	Black, Stewart
Eisenstadt v. Baird, 405 U.S. 438 (1972)	State statute making it a crime to sell, lend, or give away any contraceptive drug, except by prescription by a physician to married persons, held violative of the rights of single persons to equal protection of the laws.	6–1	Burger
Roe v. Wade, 410 U.S. 113 (1973)	The right to privacy encompasses a woman's decision whether or not to terminate her pregnancy.	7–2	White, Rehnquist
Doe v. Bolton, 410 U.S. 179 (1973)	State statute restricting a woman's right to terminate her pregnancy during the first trimester held unconstitutional.	7–2	White, Rehnquist
Village of Belle Terre v. Boraas, 416 U.S. 1 (1974)	Village zoning ordinance prohibiting occupancy of one-family dwellings by more than two unrelated persons but allowing occupancy by any number of persons related by blood, adoption, or marriage held not unconstitutional.	7–2	Brennan, Marshall
Planned Parenthood of Central Missouri v. Danforth, 428 U.S. 52 (1976)	State statute requiring a woman's written consent prior to an abortion not unconstitutional; statute requiring spouse's written consent, or in the case of unmarried females under age 18 their parents' written consent, prior to abortion procedure held unconstitutional.	6–3	White, Burger, Rehnquist

Whalen v. Roe, 429 U.S. 589 (1977)	State law requiring that state be provided with a copy of every prescription for certain dangerous drugs held not unconstitutional invasion of privacy of physicians and their patients.	9–0	—
Carey v. Population Services International, 431 U.S. 678 (1977)	State law permitting only licensed pharmacists to make retail sales of nonprescription contraceptives to persons over 16 years of age held unconstitutional denial of right of privacy of those under 16 years of age.	7–2	Burger, Rehnquist
Moore v. City of East Cleveland, 431 U.S. 494 (1977)	City ordinance that limits occupancy of dwelling unit to members of a single family and defines "family" to exclude certain categories of related persons held violative of liberty aspect of Due Process Clause.	5–4	Burger, White, Stewart, Rehnquist
Beal v. Doe, 432 U.S. 438 (1977)	Title XIX of Social Security Act does not require participating states to fund nontherapeutic abortions as a condition of participation in the program.	6–3	Blackmun, Brennan, Marshall
Maher v. Roe, 432 U.S. 464 (1977)	State regulation that limits state Medicaid benefits for first trimester abortions to those that are "medically necessary" held not violative of woman's right to decide whether or not to terminate her pregnancy.	6–3	Blackmun, Brennan, Marshall
Poelker v. Doe, 432 U.S. 519 (1977)	City hospital's policy not to provide financed hospital services for nontherapeutic abortions while providing such services for therapeutic abortions held constitutional.	6–3	Blackmun, Brennan, Marshall

no license to invalidate legislation which it thinks merely arbitrary or unreasonable. And no one was more sensitive than Mr. Justice Harlan to any suggestion that his approach to the Due Process Clause would lead to judges "roaming at large in the constitutional field." Griswold v. Connecticut, supra, at 502. No one proceeded with more caution than he did when the validity of state or federal legislation was challenged in the name of the Due Process Clause.

This is surely the preferred approach. That the Court has ample precedent for the creation of new constitutional rights should not lead it to repeat the process at will. The judiciary, including this Court, is the most vulnerable and comes nearest to illegitimacy when it deals with judge-made constitutional law having little or no cognizable roots in the language or even the design of the Constitution. Realizing that the present construction of the Due Process Clause represents a major judical gloss on its terms, as well as on the anticipation of the Framers, and that much of the underpinning for the broad, substantive application of the Clause disappeared in the conflict between the executive and the judiciary in the 1930's and 1940's, the Court should be extremely reluctant to breathe still further substantive content into the Due Process Clause so as to strike down legislation adopted by a State or city to promote its welfare. Whenever the judiciary does so, it unavoidably pre-empts for itself another part of the governance of the country without express constitutional authority.

II

Accepting the cases as they are and the Due Process Clause as construed by them, however, I think it evident that the threshold question in any due process attack on legislation, whether the challenge is procedural or substantive, is whether there is a deprivation of life, liberty or property. With respect to "liberty," the statement of Mr. Justice Harlan in Poe v. Ullman, quoted supra, at 2, most accurately reflects the thrust of prior decisions—that the Due Process Clause is triggered by a variety of interests, some much more important than others. These interests have included a wide range of freedoms in the purely commercial area such as the freedom to contract and the right to set one's own prices and wages. Meyer v. Nebraska, 262 U.S. 390, 399 (1923), took a characteristically broad view of "liberty."

"While this Court has not attempted to define with exactness the liberty thus guaranteed, the term has received much consideration, and some of the included things have been definitely stated. Without doubt, it denotes not merely freedom from bodily restraint, but also the right of the individual to contract, to engage in any of the common occupations of life, to acquire useful knowledge, to marry, establish a home and bring up children, to worship God according to the dictates of his own conscience, and, generally, to enjoy those privileges long recognized at common law as essential to the orderly pursuit of happiness by free men [citing cases]."

As I have said, Meyer has not been overruled nor its definition of liberty rejected. The results reached in some of the cases cited by Meyer have been discarded or undermined by later cases, but those cases did not cut back the definition of liberty espoused by earlier decisions. They disagreed only, but sharply, as to the protection that was "due" the particular liberty interests involved. See, for example, West Coast Hotel Co. v. Parrish, 300 U.S. 379 (1937), overruling Ribnik v. McBride, 277 U.S. 350 (1928).

Just a few years ago, we recognized that while "the range of interests protected by procedural due process is not infinite," and while we must look to the nature of the interest rather than its weight in determining whether a protected interest is at issue, the term "liberty" has been given broad meaning in our cases. Board of Regents v. Roth, 408 U.S. 564, 570–571 (1972). "In a constitution for a free people there can be no doubt that the meaning of 'liberty' must be broad indeed. See, e.g., Bolling v. Sharpe, 347 U.S. 497, 499–500; Stanley v. Illinois, 405 U.S. 645." Id., at 572.

It would not be consistent with prior cases to restrict the liberties protected by the Due Process Clause to those fundamental interests "implicit in the concept of ordered liberty." Ante, at 7. Palko v. Connecticut, 302 U.S. 319 (1937), from which this much-quoted phrase is taken, id., at 325, is not to the contrary. Palko was a criminal case, and the issue was thus not whether a protected liberty interest was at stake but what protective process was "due" that interest. The Court used the quoted standard to determine which of the protections of the Bill of Rights was due a criminal defendant in a state court within the meaning of the Fourteenth Amendment. Nor do I think the broader view of "liberty" is inconsistent with or foreclosed by the dicta in Roe v. Wade, 410 U.S. 113, 152 (1973), and Paul v. Davis, 424 U.S. 693, 713 (1976). These cases at most assert that only fundamental liberties will be given substantive protection; and they may be understood as merely identifying certain fundamental interests that the Court has deemed deserving of a heightened degree of protection under the Due Process Clause.

It seems to me that Mr. Justice Douglas was closest to the mark in Poe v. Ullman, supra, at 517, when he said that the trouble with the holdings of the "old Court" was not in its definition of liberty but in its definition of the protections guaranteed to that liberty—"not in entertaining inquiries concerning the constitutionality of social legislation but in applying the standards that it did."

The term "liberty" is not, therefore, to be given a crabbed construction. I have no more difficulty than Mr. Justice POWELL apparently does in concluding that petitioner in this case properly asserts a liberty interest within the meaning of the Due Process Clause. The question is not one of liberty, vel non. Rather, there being no procedural issue at stake, the issue is whether the precise interest involved—the interest in having more than one set of grandchildren live in her home—is entitled to such substantive protection under the Due Process Clause that this ordinance must be held invalid.

III

Looking at the doctrine of "substantive" due process as having to do with the possible invalidity of an official rule of conduct rather than of the procedures for enforcing that rule, I see the doctrine as taking several forms under the cases, each differing in the severity of review and the degree of protection offered to the individual. First, a court may merely assure itself that there is in fact a duly enacted law which proscribes the conduct sought to be prevented or sanctioned. In criminal cases, this approach is exemplified by the refusal of courts to enforce vague statutes that no reasonable person could understand as forbidding the challenged conduct. There is no such problem here.

Second is the general principle that "liberty may not be interfered with, under the guise of protecting the public interest, by legislative action which is arbitrary or without reasonable relation to some purpose within the competency of the state to effect." Meyer v. Nebraska, supra, at 399–400. This means-end test appears to require that any statute restrictive of liberty have an ascertainable purpose and represent a rational means to achieve that purpose, whatever the nature of the liberty interest involved. This approach was part of the substantive due process doctrine prevalent earlier in the century, and it made serious inroads on the presumption of constitutionality supposedly accorded to state and federal legislation. But with Nebbia v. New York, 291 U.S. 502 (1934), and other cases of the 1930's and 1940's such as West Coast Hotel Co. v. Parrish, supra, the courts came to demand far less from and to accord far more deference to legislative judgments. This was particularly true with respect to legislation seeking to control or regulate the economic life of the state or Nation. Even so, "while the legislative judgment on economic and business matters is 'well-nigh conclusive' . . . , it is not beyond judicial inquiry." Poe v. Ullman, supra, at 518 (Douglas, J., dissenting). No case that I know of, including Ferguson v. Skrupa, supra, has announced that there is some legislation with respect to which there no longer exists a means-ends test as a matter of substantive due process law. This is not surprising, for otherwise a protected liberty could be infringed by a law having no purpose or utility whatsoever. Of course, the current approach is to deal more gingerly with a state statute and to insist that the challenger bear the burden of demonstrating its unconstitutionality; and there is a broad category of cases in which substantive review is indeed mild and very similar to the original thought of Munn v. Illinois, 94 U.S. 113, 132 (1877), that "if a state of facts could exist that would justify such legislation," it passes its initial test.

There are various "liberties," however, which require that infringing legislation be given closer judicial scrutiny, not only with respect to existence of a purpose and the means employed, but also with respect to the importance of the purpose itself relative to the invaded interest. Some interests would appear almost impregnable to invasion, such as the freedoms of speech, press, and religion, and the freedom from cruel and unusual punishments. Other interests, for example, the right of association, the right to vote, and various claims sometimes referred to under the general rubric of the right to privacy, also weigh very heavily against state claims of authority to regulate. It is this category of interests which, as I understand it, Mr. Justice STEWART refers to as "implicit in the concept of ordered liberty." Ante, at ___. Because he would confine the reach of substantive due process protection to interests such as these and because he would not classify in this category the asserted right to share a house with the relatives involved here, he rejects the due process claim.

Given his premise, he is surely correct. Under our cases, the Due Process Clause extends substantial protection to various phases of family life, but none requires that the claim made here be sustained. I cannot believe that the interest in residing with more than one set of grandchildren is one that calls for any kind of heightened protection under the Due Process Clause. To say that one has a personal right to live with all, rather than some, of one's grandchildren and that this right is implicit in ordered liberty is, as my Brother STEWART says, "to extend the limited substantive contours of the Due Process Clause beyond recognition." Ibid. The present claim is hardly one of which it could be said that "neither liberty nor justice would exist if [it] were sacrificed." Palko v. Connecticut, supra, at 326.

Mr. Justice POWELL would apparently construe the Due Process Clause to protect from all but quite important state regulatory interests any right or privilege that in his estimate is deeply rooted in the country's traditions. For me, this suggests a far too expansive charter for this Court and a far less meaningful and less confining guiding principle than Mr. Justice STEWART would use for serious substantive due process review. What the deeply rooted traditions of the country are is arguable; which of them deserve the protection of the Due Process Clause is even more debatable. The suggested view would broaden enormously the horizons of the Clause; and, if the interest involved here is any measure of what the States would be forbidden to regulate, the courts would be substantively weighing and very likely invalidating a wide range of measures that Congress and state legislatures think appropriate to respond to a changing economic and social order.

Mrs. Moore's interest in having the offspring of more than one dependent son live with her qualifies as a liberty protected by the Due Process Clause; but, because of the nature of that particular interest, the demands of the Clause are satisfied once the Court is assured that the challenged proscription is the product of a duly enacted or promulgated statute, ordinance, or regulation and that it is not wholly lacking in purpose or utility. That under this ordinance any number of unmarried children may reside with their mother and that this number might be as destructive of neighborhood values as one or more additional grandchildren is just another argument that children and grandchildren may not constitutionally be distinguished by a local zoning ordinance.

That argument remains unpersuasive to me. Here the head of the household may house himself or herself and spouse, their parents, and any number of their unmarried children. A fourth generation may be represented by only one set of grandchildren and then only if born to a dependent child. The ordinance challenged by petitioner prevents her from living with both sets of grandchildren only in East Cleveland, an area with a radius of three miles and a population of 40,000. Brief for Appellee 16 n. 1. The ordinance thus denies petitioner the opportunity to live with all her grandchildren in this particular suburb; she is free to do so in other parts of the Cleveland metropolitan area. If there is power to maintain the character of a single-family neighborhood, as there surely is, some limit must be placed on the reach of the "family." Had it been our task to legislate, we might have approached the problem in a different manner than did the drafters of this ordinance; but I have no trouble in concluding that the normal goals of zoning regulation are present here and that the ordinance serves these goals by limiting, in identifiable circumstances, the number of people who can occupy a single household. The ordinance does not violate the Due Process Clause.

* * *

4
EQUAL PROTECTION OF THE LAWS AND THE CRIMINAL PROCESS

4.02 INVIDIOUS CLASSIFICATIONS

Gender-Based Discrimination and the Right to Drink Beer

CRAIG v. BOREN

Supreme Court of the United States, 1976
429 U.S. 190, 97 S. Ct. 451, 50 L. Ed. 2d 397

Appellant Curtis Craig, a male then between 18 and 21 years of age, and appellant Whitener, a licensed vendor of 3.2 per cent beer, brought an action for declaratory and injunctive relief in federal district court, claiming that an Oklahoma statutory scheme that prohibited the sale of "nonintoxicating" 3.2 per cent beer to males under the age of 21 and to females under the age of 18 constituted gender-based discrimination that denied males 18 to 20 years of age the equal protection of the laws. A three-judge district court upheld the statutory scheme, 399 F. Supp. 1304 (1975), and the United States Supreme Court noted probable jurisdiction.

Mr. Justice BRENNAN delivered the opinion of the Court.

[Because Craig reached age 21 after probable jurisdiction was noted, the Supreme Court held that the case was moot as to him. The Court concluded that Whitener had jus tertii standing to make the equal protection challenge.]

A

* * *

Analysis may appropriately begin with the reminder that Reed v. Reed [404 U.S. 71 (1971)]. . . emphasized that statutory classifications that distinguish between males and females are "subject to scrutiny under the Equal Protection Clause." 404 U.S., at 75. To withstand constitutional challenge, previous cases establish that classifications by gender must serve important governmental objectives and must be substantially related to achievement of those objectives. . . . Decisions following Reed similarly have rejected administrative ease and convenience as sufficiently important objectives to justify gender-based classifications. See, e.g., Stanley v. Illinois, 405 U.S. 645, 656

(1972); Frontiero v. Richardson, 411 U.S. 677, 690 (1973); Schlesinger v. Ballard, 419 U.S. 498, 506–507 (1975). . . .

We turn then to the question whether, under Reed, the difference between males and females with respect to the purchase of 3.2% beer warrants the differential in age drawn by the Oklahoma statute. We conclude that it does not.

B

The District Court recognized that Reed v. Reed was controlling. In applying the teachings of that case, the Court found the requisite important governmental objective in the traffic-safety goal proffered by the Oklahoma Attorney General. It then concluded that the statistics introduced by the appellees established that the gender-based distinction was substantially related to achievement of that goal.

C

We accept for purposes of discussion the District Court's identification of the objective underlying §§ 241 and 245 as the enhancement of traffic safety. Clearly, the protection of public health and safety represents an important function of state and local governments. However, appellees' statistics in our view cannot support the conclusion that the gender-based distinction closely serves to achieve that objective and therefore the distinction cannot under Reed withstand equal protection challenge.

The appellees introduced a variety of statistical surveys. First, an analysis of arrest statistics for 1973 demonstrated that 18–20-year-old male arrests for "driving under the influence" and "drunkenness" substantially exceeded female arrests for that same age period. Similarly, youths aged 17–21 were found to be overrepresented among those killed or injured in traffic accidents, with males again numerically exceeding females in this regard. Third, a random roadside survey in Oklahoma City revealed that young males were more inclined to drive and drink beer than were their female counterparts. Fourth, Federal Bureau of Investigation nationwide statistics exhibited a notable increase in arrests for "driving under the influence." Finally, statistical evidence gathered in other jurisdictions, particularly Minnesota and Michigan, was offered to corroborate Oklahoma's experience by indicating the pervasiveness of youthful participation in motor vehicle accidents following the imbibing of alcohol. Conceding that "the case is not free from doubt," 399 F. Supp., at 1314, the District Court nonetheless concluded that this statistical showing substantiated "a rational basis for the legislative judgment underlying the challenged classification." Id., at 1307.

Even were this statistical evidence accepted as accurate, it nevertheless offers only a weak answer to the equal protection question presented here. The most focused and relevant of the statistical surveys, arrests of 18–20-year-olds for alcohol-related driving offenses, exemplifies the ultimate unpersuasiveness of this evidentiary record. Viewed in terms of the correlation between sex and the actual activity that Oklahoma seeks to regulate—driving while under the influence of alcohol—the statistics broadly establish that .18% of females and 2% of males in that age group were arrested for that offense. While such a disparity is not trivial in a statistical sense, it hardly can form the basis for employment of a gender line as a classifying device. Certainly if maleness is to serve as a proxy for drinking and driving, a correlation of 2% must be considered an unduly tenuous "fit." Indeed, prior cases have consistently rejected the use of sex as a decisionmaking factor even though the statutes in question certainly rested on far more predictive empirical relationships than this.

Moreover, the statistics exhibit a variety of other shortcomings that seriously impugn their value to equal protection analysis. Setting aside the obvious methodological problems, the surveys do not adequately justify the salient features of Oklahoma's gender-based traffic-safety law. None purports to measure the use and dangerousness of 3.2% beer as opposed to alcohol generally, a detail that is of particular importance since, in light of its low alcohol level, Oklahoma apparently considers the 3.2% beverage to be "non-intoxicating." 37 Okla. Stat. § 163.1 (1971); see State ex rel. Springer v. Bliss, 199 Okla. 198, 185 P.2d 220 (1947). Moreover, many of the studies, while graphically documenting the unfortunate increase in driving while under the influence of alcohol, make no effort to relate their findings to age-sex differentials as involved here. Indeed, the only survey that explicitly centered its attention upon young drivers and their use of beer—albeit apparently not of the diluted 3.2% variety—reached results that hardly can be viewed as impressive in justifying either a gender or age classification.

There is no reason to belabor this line of analysis. It is unrealistic to expect either members of the judiciary or state officials to be well versed in the rigors of experimental or statistical technique. But this merely illustrates that proving broad sociological propositions by statistics is a dubious business, and one that inevitably is in tension with the normative philosophy that underlies the Equal Protection Clause. Suffice to say that the showing offered by the appellees does not satisfy us that sex represents a legitimate, accurate proxy for the regulation of drinking and driving. In fact, when it is further recognized that Oklahoma's statute prohibits only the selling of 3.2% beer to young males and not their drinking the beverage once acquired (even after purchase by their 18-20-year-old female companions), the relationship between gender and traffic safety becomes far too tenuous to satisfy Reed's requirement that the gender-based difference be substantially related to achievement of the statutory objective.

We hold, therefore, that under Reed, Oklahoma's 3.2% beer statute invidiously discriminates against males 18-20 years of age.

D

* * *

[The Court rejected the appellee's argument that the Twenty-first Amendment (repealing Prohibition) operates to defeat the equal protection challenge. The Court held that that Amendment cannot defeat an otherwise established claim under the Equal Protection Clause.]

Reversed.

Mr. Justice STEWART, concurring.

* * *

Every State has broad power under the Twenty-first Amendment to control the dispensation of alcoholic beverages within its borders. E.g., California v. LaRue, 409 U.S. 109 [1900]; Seagram & Sons v. Hostetter, 384 U.S. 35 [1900]; Hostetter v. Idlewild Bon Voyage Liquor Corp., 377 U.S. 324, 330 [1900]; Mahoney v. Joseph Triner Corp., 304 U.S. 401 [1900]; State Board of Equalization v. Young's Market Co., 299 U.S. 59 [1900]. But "[t]his is not to say that the Twenty-first Amendment empowers a State to act with total irrationality or invidious discrimination in controlling the dispensation of liquor...." California v. LaRue, supra, at 120, (concurring opinion).

The disparity created by these Oklahoma statutes amounts to total irrationality. For the statistics upon which the State now relies, whatever their other shortcomings, wholly fail to prove or even suggest that 3.2 beer is somehow more deleterious when it comes into the hands of a male aged 18-20 than of a female of like age. The disparate statutory treatment of the sexes here, without even a colorably valid justification or explanation, thus amounts to invidious discrimination....

Mr. Justice POWELL, concurring.

* * *

[I] agree that Reed v. Reed, 404 U.S. 71 (1971), is the most relevant precedent. But I find it unnecessary, in deciding this case, to read that decision as broadly as some of the Court's language may imply. Reed and subsequent cases involving gender-based classifications make clear that the Court subjects such classifications to a more critical examination than is normally applied when "fundamental" constitutional rights and "suspect classes" are not present.

I view this as a relatively easy case. No one questions the legitimacy or importance of the asserted governmental objective: the promotion of highway safety. The decision of the case turns on whether the state legislature, by the classification it has chosen, has adopted a means that bears a "fair and substantial relation" to this objective....

It seems to me that the statistics offered by the State and relied upon by the District Court do tend generally to support the view that young men drive more, possibly are inclined to drink more, and—for various reasons—are involved in more accidents than young women. Even so, I am not persuaded that these facts and the inferences fairly drawn from them justify this classification based on a three-year age differential between the sexes, and especially one that is so easily circumvented as to be virtually meaningless. Putting it differently, this gender-based classification does not bear a fair and substantial relation to the object of the legislation.

Mr. Justice STEVENS, concurring.

There is only one Equal Protection Clause. It requires every State to govern impartially. It does not direct the courts to apply one standard of review in some cases and a different standard in other cases. Whatever criticism may be levelled at a judicial opinion implying that there are at least three such standards applies with the same force to a double standard.

I am inclined to believe that what has become known as the two-tiered analysis of equal protection claims does not describe a completely logical method of deciding cases, but rather is a method the Court has employed to explain decisions that actually apply a single standard in a reasonably consistent fashion. I also suspect that a careful explanation of the reasons motivating particular decisions may contribute more to an identification of that standard than an attempt to articulate it in all-encompassing terms. It may therefore be appropriate for me to state the principal reasons which persuaded me to join the Court's opinion.

In this case, the classification is not as obnoxious as some the Court has condemned, nor as inoffensive as some the Court has accepted. It is objectionable because it is based on an accident of birth, because it is a mere remnant of the now almost universally rejected tradition of discriminating against males in this age bracket, and because, to the extent it reflects any physical difference between males and females, it is actually perverse. The question then is whether the traffic safety justification put forward by the State is sufficient to make an otherwise offensive classification acceptable.

The classification is not totally irrational. For the evidence does indicate that there are more males than females in this age bracket who drive and also more who drink. Nevertheless, there are several reasons why I regard the justification as unacceptable. It is difficult to believe that the statute was actually intended to cope with the problem of traffic safety, since it has only a minimal effect on access to a not-very-intoxicating beverage and does not prohibit its consumption. Moreover, the empirical data submitted by the State accentuates the unfairness of treating all 18–21-year-old males as inferior to their female counterparts. The legislation imposes a restraint on 100% of the males in the class allegedly because about 2% of them have probably violated one or more laws relating to the consumption of alcoholic beverages. It is unlikely that this law will have a significant deterrent effect either on that 2% or on the law-abiding 98%. But even assuming some such slight benefit, it does not seem to me that an insult to all of the young men of the State can be justified by visiting the sins of the 2% on the 98%.

[Mr. Justice BLACKMUN concurred in the result.]

Mr. CHIEF JUSTICE BURGER, dissenting.

* * *

[I] cannot agree that appellant Whitener has standing arising from her status as a saloonkeeper to assert the constitutional rights of her customers. In this Court "a litigant may only assert his own constitutional rights or immunities." United States v. Raines, 362 U.S. 17, 21 (1960). There are a few, but strictly limited, exceptions to that rule; despite the most creative efforts, this case fits within none of them.

* * *

On the merits, we have only recently recognized that our duty is not "to create substantive constitutional rights in the name of guaranteeing equal protection of the laws." San Antonio School District v. Rodriguez, 411 U.S. 1, 33 (1976). Thus, even interests of such importance in our society as public education and housing do not qualify as "fundamental rights" for equal protection purposes because they have no textually independent constitutional status.... Though today's decision does not go so far as to make gender-based classifications "suspect," it makes gender a disfavored classification. Without an independent constitutional basis supporting the right asserted or disfavoring the classification adopted, I can justify no substantive constitutional protection other than the normal McGowan

v. Maryland, 366 U.S., at 425–426, protection afforded by the Equal Protection Clause.

The means employed by the Oklahoma Legislature to achieve the objectives sought may not be agreeable to some judges, but since eight Members of the Court think the means not irrational, I see no basis for striking down the statute as violative of the Constitution simply because we find it unwise, unneeded, or possibly even a bit foolish....

Mr. Justice REHNQUIST, dissenting.

The Court's disposition of this case is objectionable on two grounds. First is its conclusion that *men* challenging a gender-based statute which treats them less favorably than women may invoke a more stringent standard of judicial review than pertains to most other types of classifications. Second is the Court's enunciation of this standard, without citation to any source, as being that "classifications by gender must serve *important* governmental objectives and must be *substantially* related to achievement of those objectives...." The only redeeming feature of the Court's opinion, to my mind, is that it apparently signals a retreat by those who joined the plurality opinion in Frontiero v. Richardson, 411 U.S. 677 (1973), from their view that sex is a "suspect" classification for purposes of equal protection analysis. I think the Oklahoma statute challenged here need pass only the "rational basis" equal protection analysis expounded in cases such as McGowan v. Maryland, 366 U.S. 420 (1961), and Williamson v. Lee Optical Co., 348 U.S. 483 (1955), and I believe that it is constitutional under that analysis.

* * *

4.03 THE "STATE ACTION" REQUIREMENT

Equal Protection and Illegitimacy

TRIMBLE v. GORDON
Supreme Court of the United States, 1977
430 U.S. 762, 97 S. Ct. 1459, 52 L. Ed. 2d 31

In a 5–4 decision, the United States Supreme Court held that an Illinois probate law that allows illegitimate children to inherit by intestate succession only from their mothers, while legitimate children are allowed to inherit by intestate succession from both parents, violates the Equal Protection Clause of the Fourteenth Amendment.

Mr. Justice REHNQUIST, dissenting.

The Fourteenth Amendment's prohibition against "any state deny[ing] to any person ... the equal protection of the laws" is undoubtedly one of the majestic generalities of the Constitution. If, during the period of more than a century since its adoption, this Court had developed a consistent body of doctrine which could reasonably be said to expound the intent of those who drafted and adopted that Clause of the Amendment, there would be no cause for judicial complaint, however unwise or incapable of effective administration one might find those intentions. If, on the other hand, recognizing that those who drafted and adopted this language had rather imprecise notions about what it meant, the Court had evolved a body of doctrine which was both consistent and served some arguably useful purpose, there would likewise be little cause for great dissatisfaction with the existing state of the law.

Unfortunately, more than a century of decisions under this Clause of the Fourteenth Amendment have produced neither of these results. They have instead produced a syndrome wherein this Court seems to regard the Equal Protection Clause as a cat-of-nine-tails to be kept in the judicial closet as a threat to legislatures which may, in the view of the judiciary, get out of hand and pass "arbitrary," "illogical," or "unreasonable" laws. Except in the area of the law in which the Framers obviously meant it to apply—classifications based on race or on national origin, the first cousin of race, the Court's decisions can fairly be described as an endless tinkering with legislative judgments, a series of conclusions unsupported by any central guiding principle.

It is too well known to warrant more than brief mention that the Framers of the Constitution adopted a system of checks and balances conveniently lumped under the descriptive head of "federalism," whereby all power was originally presumed to reside in the people of the States who adopted the Constitution. The Constitution delegated some authority to the federal executive, some to the federal legislative, some to the federal judiciary, and reserved the remaining authority normally associated with sovereignty to the States and to the people in the States. In reaching the results that it did, the Constitutional Convention in 1787 rejected the idea that members of the federal judiciary should sit on a council of revision, and veto laws which it considered unwise; it also rejected a proposal which would have empowered Congress to nullify laws enacted by any of the several States.

Following the Civil War, Congress propounded and the States ratified the so-called "Civil War Amendments"—the Thirteenth, Fourteenth, and Fifteenth Amendments, which, together with post–Civil War legislation, sharply altered the balance of power between the federal and state governments. See Mitchum v. Foster, 407 U.S. 225, 238–242 (1972). But they were designed to accomplish this purpose not in some vague, ill-defined way which was ultimately to be discovered by this Court more than a century after their enactment. Their language contained the mechanisms by which their purpose was to be accomplished. Congress might affirmatively legislate under § 5 of the Fourteenth Amendment to carry out the purposes of that Amendment, and the courts could strike down state laws found directly to violate the dictates of any of the Amendments.

This was strong medicine, and intended to be such. But it cannot be read apart from the original understanding at Philadelphia: The Civil War Amendments did not make this Court into a council of revision, and they did not confer upon this Court any authority to nullify state laws which were merely felt to be inimical to the Court's notion of the public interest.

That much is common ground at least at the conscious level. But in providing the Court with the duty of enforcing such generalities as the Equal Protection Clause, the Framers of the Civil War Amendments placed it in the position of Adam in the Garden of Eden. As members of a tripartite institution of government which is responsible to no constituency, and which is held back only by its own sense of self-restraint, see United States v. Butler, 297 U.S. 1, 79 (1936) (Stone, J., dissenting), we are constantly subjected to the human temptation to hold that any law containing a number of imperfections denies equal protection simply because those who drafted it could have made it a fairer or a better law. The Court's opinion in the instant case is no better and no worse than the long series of cases in this line, a line which unfortunately proclaims that the Court has indeed succumbed to the temptation implicit in the Amendment.

The Equal Protection Clause is itself a classic paradox, and makes sense only in the context of a recently fought Civil War. It creates a requirement of equal treatment to be applied to the process of legislation—legislation whose very purpose is to draw lines in such a way that different people are treated differently. The problem presented is one of sorting the legislative distinctions which are acceptable from those which involve invidiously unequal treatment.

All constitutional provisions for protection of individuals involve difficult questions of line drawing. But most others have implicit within them an understandable value judgment that certain types of conduct have a favored place and are to be protected to a greater or lesser degree. Obvious examples are free speech, freedom from unreasonable search and seizure, and the right to a fair trial. The remaining judicial task in applying those guarantees is to determine whether, on given facts, the constitutional value judgment embodied in such a provision has been offended in a particular case.

In the case of equality and equal protection, the constitutional principle—the thing to be protected to a greater or lesser degree—is not even identifiable from within the four corners of the Constitution. For equal protection does not mean that all persons must be treated alike. Rather, its general principle is that persons similarly situated should be treated similarly. But that statement of the rule does little to determine whether or not a question of equality is even involved in a given case. For the crux of the problem is *whether persons are similarly situated* for purposes of the state action in issue. Nothing in the words of the Fourteenth Amendment specifically addresses this question in any way.

The essential problem of the Equal Protection Clause is therefore the one of determining where the courts are to look for guidance in defining "equality" as that word is used in the Fourteenth Amendment. Since the Amendment grew out of the Civil War and the freeing of the slaves, the core prohibition was early held to be aimed at the protection of blacks. See Strauder v. West Virginia, 100 U.S. 303 (1880); Bickel, "The Original Understanding and the Segregation Decision," 69 Harv. L. Rev. 1 (1955). If race was an invalid sorting tool where blacks were concerned, it followed logically that it should not be valid where other races were concerned either. See Yick Wo v. Hopkins, 118 U.S. 356 (1886). A logical, though not inexorable, next step, was the extension of the protection to prohibit classifications resting on national origin. See Oyama v. California, 332 U.S. 633 (1948).

The presumptive invalidity of all of these classifications has made decisions involving them, for the most part, relatively easy. But when the Court has been required to adjudicate equal protection claims not based on race or national origin, it has faced a much more difficult task. In cases involving alienage, for example, it has concluded that such classifications are "suspect" because, though not necessarily involving race or national origin, they are enough like the latter to warrant similar treatment. See Graham v. Richardson, 403 U.S. 365 (1971); Sugarman v. Dougall, 413 U.S. 634 (1973); In re Griffith, 413 U.S. 717 (1973). While there may be individual disagreement as to how such classes are to be singled out and as to whether specific classes are sufficiently close to the core area of race and national origin to warrant such treatment, one cannot say that the inquiry is not germaine to the meaning of the Clause.

Illegitimacy, which is involved in this case, has never been held by the Court to be a "suspect classification." Nonetheless, in several opinions of the Court, statements are found which suggest that although illegitimates are not members of a "suspect class," laws which treat them differently than those born in wedlock will receive a more far-reaching scrutiny under the Equal Protection Clause than will other laws regulating economic and social conditions. Levy v. Louisiana, 391 U.S. 68 (1968); Glona v. American Guarantee and Liability Insurance Co., 391 U.S. 73 (1968); Labine v. Vincent, 401 U.S. 532 (1971); Weber v. Aetna Casualty & Surety Co., 406 U.S. 164 (1972); Gomez v. Perez, 409 U.S. 535 (1973); New Jersey Welfare Rights Organization v. Cahill, 411 U.S. 619 (1973); Jimminez v. Weinberger, 417 U.S. 628 (1974). But see Mathews v. Lucas, 427 U.S. 495 (1976). The Court's opinion today contains language to that effect. In one sense this language is a source of consolation, since it suggests that parts of the Court's analysis used in this case will not be carried over to traditional "rational basis" or "minimum scrutiny" cases. At the same time, though, it is a source of confusion, since the unanswered question remains as to the precise sort of scrutiny to which classifications based on illegitimacy will be subject.

The appropriate "scrutiny," in the eyes of the Court, appears to involve some analysis of the relation of the "purpose" of the legislature to the "means" by which it chooses to carry out that purpose. The Court's opinion abounds in language of this sort. . . .

* * *

. . . It should be apparent that litigants who wish to succeed in invalidating a law under the Equal Protection Clause must have a certain schizophrenia if they are to be successful in their advocacy: They must first convince this Court that the legislature had a particular purpose in mind in enacting the law, and then convince it that the law was not at all suited to the accomplishment of that purpose.

But a graver defect than this in the Court's analysis is that it also requires a conscious second-guessing of legislative judgment in an area where this Court has no special expertise whatever. Even assuming that a court has properly accomplished the difficult task of identifying the "purpose" which a statute seeks to serve, it then sits in judgment to consider the so-called "fit" between that "purpose" and the statutory means adopted to achieve it. In most cases, and all but invariably if the court insists on singling out a unitary "purpose," the "fit" will involve a greater or lesser degree of imperfection. Then the Court asks itself how much "imperfection" between means and ends is permissible? In making this judgment it must throw into the judicial hopper the whole range of factors which were first thrown into the legislative hopper. What alternatives were reasonably available? What reasons are there for the legislature to accomplish this "purpose" in the way it did? What obstacles stood in the way of other solutions?

The fundamental flaw, to me, in this approach is that there is absolutely nothing to be implied from the fact that we hold judicial commissions that would enable us to answer any one of these questions better than the legislators to whose initial decision they were committed. Without any antecedent constitutional mandate, we have created on the premises of the Equal Protection Clause a school for legislators, whereby opinions of this Court are written to instruct them in a better understanding of how to accomplish their ordinary legislative tasks....

* * *

4.05 OTHER DECISIONS OF INTEREST INVOLVING EQUAL PROTECTION OF THE LAWS AND THE CRIMINAL PROCESS

In *United States* v. *Antelope*, 430 U.S. 641 (1977), the respondents, enrolled Coeur d'Alene Indians, broke into the home of an 81-year-old non-Indian female on a federal enclave in Idaho and robbed and murdered her. They were convicted in a federal district court of burglary, robbery, and first degree murder under the felony murder provisions of the federal enclave murder statute, 18 U.S.C. § 1111, as made applicable to Indians by the Major Crimes Act, 18 U.S.C. § 1153.

Respondents contended that their felony-murder convictions were unlawful products of invidious discrimination in that a non-Indian charged with the murder of another non-Indian within Indian country would have been subject to prosecution only under Idaho law, which does not have a felony murder statute. Under Idaho law, a conviction of first degree murder requires proof of premeditation and deliberation, which is not required under the felony murder component of 18 U.S.C. § 1111. The Court of Appeals (9th Cir.) reversed on the ground that the respondent Indians had been denied their constitutional rights under the Fifth Amendment's equal protection principles.

In a unanimous opinion by Chief Justice Burger, the United States Supreme Court reversed and held that:

1. Federal legislation singling out Indian tribes as subjects of classification is expressly provided for in the Constitution: Under Art. 1, § 8, Congress has the power "to regulate Commerce with foreign Nations, and among the several States, and with the Indian Tribes."

2. Federal legislation of Indian tribes is rooted in the unique status of Indians as "a separate people" with their own political institutions and is not to be viewed as legislation aimed at a "racial group consisting of Indians."

3. The respondents were subject to the same body of law as any other persons, Indian or non-Indian, charged with first degree murder committed on a federal enclave.

4. Congress has the constitutional authority to prescribe a criminal code applicable in Indian country.

5. Persons charged with crimes on federal military bases or other federal enclaves cannot demand that their federal prosecutions be governed by more lenient state law.

TABLE 4.1 Supreme Court Decisions Involving Gender-Based Discrimination: 1971–1977

Case	Holding	Vote	Dissenting Opinions
Phillips v. Martin Marietta Corp., 400 U.S. 542 (1971)	Section 703(a) of the Civil Rights Act of 1964 held not to permit different hiring policies for male and female parents of preschool age children in the absence of showing of relevance of job performance.	9–0	—
Reed v. Reed, 404 U.S. 71 (1971)	State law giving mandatory preference for appointment as estate administrator to male applicants over female applicants otherwise equally qualified held violative of the Equal Protection Clause.	9–0	—
Stanley v. Illinois, 405 U.S. 645 (1972)	State law whereby unwed fathers of illegitimate children are presumed to be unfit to raise such children on mother's death and are denied hearings as to fitness as a parent held violative of Due Process and Equal Protection Clauses.	5–2	Burger, Blackmun
Frontiero v. Richardson, 411 U.S. 677 (1973)	Difference in treatment of servicewomen and servicemen claiming spouse as dependent and seeking increased allowances for quarters and medical and dental benefits held violative of the equal protection of the laws.	8–1	Rehnquist
Cleveland Bd. of Education v. LaFleur, 414 U.S. 632 (1974)	School board rules requiring pregnant teachers to take mandatory leave five months before expected delivery date and barring their return before child is three months old held violative of Due Process Clause.	7–2	Rehnquist, Burger
Kahn v. Shevin, 416 U.S. 351 (1974)	State statute granting widows, but not widowers, an annual $500 property tax exemption upheld on equal protection grounds.	6–3	Brennan, Marshall, White
Geduldig v. Aiello, 417 U.S. 484 (1974)	State disability insurance program that excludes from coverage normal pregnancy and childbirth held not violative of the Equal Protection Clause.	6–3	Brennan, Douglas, Marshall
Schlesinger v. Ballard, 419 U.S. 498 (1975)	Equal protection of laws not violated by granting female Navy officers a longer tenure than male officers prior to discharge for want of promotion.	5–4	Brennan, Douglas, Marshall, White
Taylor v. Louisiana, 419 U.S. 522 (1975)	State jury selection system that excludes women unless they file a written declaration indicating a desire to serve held unconstitutional.	8–1	Rehnquist

Case	Description	Vote	Dissenting
Weinerer v. Wiesenfeld, 420 U.S. 636 (1975)	Provision of Social Security Act that grants survivors' benefits to widowed mothers with minor children but not to widowed fathers in same situation held violative of the equal protection of the laws.	8–0	—
Stanton v. Stanton, 421 U.S. 7 (1975)	State law specifying greater age of majority for males than for females for purposes of child support held violative of the equal protection of the laws.	8–1	Rehnquist
Weinberger v. Salfi, 422 U.S. 749 (1975)	Provision of Social Security Act that conditions benefits upon a showing that the respective relationships of the widow and child to the deceased wage earner existed for at least nine months prior to his death held not violative of the equal protection of the laws.	6–3	Douglas, Brennan, Marshall
Turner v. Dept of Employment Security, 423 U.S. 44 (1975)	State statute making pregnant women ineligible for unemployment compensation from 12 weeks before the expected date of childbirth until 6 weeks after childbirth held denial of due process.	8–1	Rehnquist
Craig v. Boren, 429 U.S. 190 (1976)	State law prohibiting the sale of 3.2% beer to males under the age of 21 and to females under the age of 18 held violative of the equal protection of the laws.	7–2	Burger, Rehnquist
General Electric Co. v. Gilbert, 429 U.S. 125 (1976)	Employer's disability insurance plan that excludes from coverage disabilities arising from pregnancy held not violative of Title VII of the Civil Rights Act of 1964.	6–3	Brennan, Marshall, Stevens
Califano v. Goldfarb, 430 U.S. 199 (1977)	Social Security Act provision whereby survivors' benefits are payable to widower only if he had been receiving at least half his support from his wife held violative of the equal protection of the laws.	5–4	Rehnquist, Burger, Stewart, Blackmun
Califano v. Webster, 430 U.S. 313 (1977)	Provision of Social Security Act whereby female wage earner could exclude from the computation of her "average monthly wage" three more lower-earning years than a similarly situated male wage earner held not unconstitutional.	9–0	—
Dothard v. Rawlinson, 433 U.S. 321 (1977)	Proof that state's statutory minimum height and weight requirements for prison guards disqualify a disproportionately large percentage of women establishes prima facie case of sex discrimination.	6–3	White, in part { Brennan, Marshall

TABLE 4.2 Supreme Court Decisions on Classifications Involving Illegitimacy: 1968–1977

Case	Holding	Vote	Dissenting Opinions
Levy v. Louisiana, 391 U.S. 68 (1968)	State statute prohibiting wrongful death actions on behalf of illegitimate children, but permitting such actions on behalf of legitimate children, held violative of equal protection of the laws.	6-3	Harlan, Black, Stewart
Glona v. American Guarantee & Liability Insurance Co., 391 U.S. 73 (1968)	State statute prohibiting wrongful death actions by mothers of illegitimate children, but permitting such actions on behalf of mothers of legitimate children, held violative of the equal protection of the laws.	6-3	Harlan, Black, Stewart
Labine v. Vincent, 401 U.S. 532 (1971)	State law barring acknowledged illegitimate children from sharing equally with legitimate heirs in father's estate held not violative of the Equal Protection Clause.	5-4	Brennan, Douglas, White, Marshall
Weber v. Aetna Casualty & Surety Co., 406 U.S. 164 (1972)	State workmen's compensation law that denies dependent unacknowledged illegitimate children the right to recover benefits on the death of their natural father held violative of the Equal Protection Clause.	8-1	Rehnquist
Gomez v. Perez, 409 U.S. 535 (1973)	State law that denies illegitimate children the right to child support from their natural fathers held violative of the Equal Protection Clause.	7-2	Stewart, Rehnquist
New Jersey Welfare Rights Organization v. Cahill, 411 U.S. 619 (1973)	State welfare assistance program that limits benefits to only those families that have either legitimate or adopted children held violative of the Equal Protection Clause.	8-1	Rehnquist
Jimminez v. Weinberger, 417 U.S. 628 (1974)	Social Security Act provision that denies benefits to illegitimate children born after the onset of the parent's disability held violative of the Equal Protection Clause.	8-1	Rehnquist
Mathews v. Lucas, 427 U.S. 495 (1976)	Provision of Social Security Act that conditions illegitimate child's survivorship benefits on proof of dependency on deceased held not unconstitutional.	6-3	Stevens, Brennan, Marshall
Trimble v. Gordon, 430 U.S. 732 (1977)	State law that allows illegitimate children to inherit by intestate succession only from their mother, but allows legitimate children to inherit from both their mother and father, held violative of the equal protection of the laws.	5-4	Burger, Stewart, Blackmun, Rehnquist

Part Two

CONSTITUTIONAL SAFEGUARDS OF AN ACCUSED: FOURTH, FIFTH, AND SIXTH AMENDMENT PROBLEMS

6

FIFTH AMENDMENT PROBLEMS: DOUBLE JEOPARDY, SELF-INCRIMINATION, AND THE GRAND JURY

6.02 The Guarantee Against Double Jeopardy

A. PRIOR CONVICTIONS

Felony Murder and Double Jeopardy

HARRIS v. OKLAHOMA

Supreme Court of the United States, 1977
433 U.S. ___, 97 S. Ct. 2912, 53 L. Ed. 2d 1054

The facts are stated in the opinion.

PER CURIAM.

A clerk in a Tulsa, Okla., grocery store was shot and killed by a companion of petitioner in the course of a robbery of the store by the two men. Petitioner was convicted of felony murder in Oklahoma state court. The opinion of the Oklahoma Court of Criminal Appeals in this case states that "In a felony murder case, the proof of the underlying felony [here robbery with firearms] is needed to prove the intent necessary for a felony murder conviction." Harris v. State, 555 P.2d 76, 80–81 (1976). Petitioner nevertheless was thereafter brought to trial and convicted on a separate information charging the robbery with firearms, after denial of his motion to dismiss on the ground that this prosecution violated the Double Jeopardy Clause of the Fifth Amendment because he had been already convicted of the offense in the felony murder trial. The Oklahoma Court of Criminal Appeals affirmed. 555 P.2d 76, supra.

When, as here, conviction for a greater crime, murder, cannot be had without conviction for the lesser crime, robbery with firearms the Double Jeopardy Clause bars prosecution for the lesser crime after conviction for the greater one. In re Hans

Nielsen, 131 U.S. 176 (1889); cf. Brown v. Ohio, 432 U.S. 161 (1977). "... [A] person [who] has been tried and convicted for a crime which has various incidents included in it ... cannot be a second time tried for one of those incidents without being twice put in jeopardy for the same offense." 131 U.S., at 188. See also Waller v. Florida, 397 U.S. 387 (1970); Grafton v. United States, 206 U.S. 333, 352 (1907).

The motion for leave to proceed in forma pauperis is granted, the petition for writ of certiorari is granted, and the judgment of the Court of Criminal Appeals is Reversed.

Mr. Justice BRENNAN, with whom Mr. Justice MARSHALL joins.

I join the Court's opinion but in any event would reverse on a ground not addressed by the Court, namely that the State did not prosecute the two informations in one proceeding. I adhere to the view that the Double Jeopardy Clause of the Fifth Amendment, applied to the States through the Fourteenth Amendment, requires the prosecution in one proceeding, except in extremely limited circumstances not present here, of "all the charges against a defendant that grow out of a single criminal act, occurrence, episode, or transaction." Ashe v. Swenson, 397 U.S. 436, 453–454 (1970) (BRENNAN, J., concurring). See Thompson v. Oklahoma, 429 U.S. 1053 (1977) (BRENNAN, J., dissenting), and cases collected therein.

E. GOVERNMENT APPEALS IN CRIMINAL CASES—U.S.C. § 3731

Judgments of Acquittal and Governmental Appeals

ORAL ARGUMENTS BEFORE THE
U.S. SUPREME COURT*

United States v. Martin Linen Supply Co., No. 76-120; argued 2/23/77

In a trilogy of cases decided two Terms ago, the Court undertook to provide guidance for the lower courts on the limits of the Fifth Amendment's protection against double jeopardy, *U.S.* v. *Wilson,* 420 U.S. 332 (1975), *U.S.* v. *Jenkins,* 420 U.S. 358 (1975), and *Serfass* v. *U.S.,* 420 U.S. 377 (1975). But the principles expressed in these cases have not been uniformly applied by the federal courts of appeal, and the Court has already found it necessary to undo what it saw as misreadings of the trilogy. See *U.S.* v. *Sanford,* [429 US. 14] (1976); *U.S.* v. *Morrison,* [429 U.S. 1] (1976); *U.S.* v. *Rose,* [429 U.S. 5] (1976); and *U.S.* v. *Kopp,* [429 U.S. 121] (1976).

The Court heard argument recently in yet another case involving the issues discussed in the 1975 trilogy. Two corporate defendants were charged with contempt for allegedly violating a consent decree. The first trial ended in a hung jury, with one juror holding out for acquittal. A mistrial was declared, but the defendants also filed motions for judgments of acquittal within the seven-day period mandated by F. R. Crim. P. 29(c). After more than 20 months, the district court granted the motion, and the Fifth Circuit held that this ruling was unappealable under 18 U.S.C. §3731 and the Double Jeopardy Clause.

The government's argument was presented by Frank H. Easterbrook, Assistant to the Solicitor General. There are two issues lurking in this case that need not be addressed, he said. First, we do not raise the question here whether corporations enjoy the benefit of the Double Jeopardy Clause; this question is raised, however, by our petition in *U.S.* v. *Security National Bank,* [97 S. Ct. 1591(1977), cert. denied]. Second, this case does not involve a mid-trial termin-

---

*From 21 Crim. L. Rptr. 4181–4183. Reprinted by permission of the Bureau of National Affairs. Inc.

ation of a prosecution. We would argue that there is no absolute bar to reprosecution except an acquittal by the jury. This problem has recently been the subject of a thoughtful analysis of the First Circuit in *U.S. v. Sanabria* [20 Cr. L. 2419, petition for certiorari filed 20 Cr. L. 4167].

Once the mistrial is declared because of manifest necessity, there is no double jeopardy bar to reprosecution, Easterbrook continued. This principle is simple and has been accepted ever since *U.S. v. Perez,* 22 U.S. (9 Wheat.) 579 (1824). If the trial court can set the case for a second trial, then the court of appeals can order it to do so. The recent decision in *Sanford* makes this clear.

Mr. Justice Stevens asked Easterbrook for the statutory authority for this position.

Admittedly § 3731 does not speak in terms of appeals from judgments of acquittal, counsel said. [The section permits a government appeal "from a decision, judgment, or order of a district court dismissing an indictment or information as to any one or more courts, except that no appeal shall lie where the Double Jeopardy Clause of the United States Constitution prohibits further prosecution."] But § 3731 has been held, in *U.S. v. Wilson.,* to contemplate the broadest scope for government appeals consistent with double jeopardy principles.

Mr. Justice Stevens: "But in *Wilson* the district court dismissed the indictment—isn't that different than the acquittal here?"

The *Wilson* Court indicated that it didn't really matter what the disposition is called, Easterbrook replied.

Importance of Jorn

U.S. v. Jorn, 400 U.S. 470 (1971), is also important to this case, counsel continued. If a mistrial is properly declared, then a second trial is permitted. A mistrial declaration, the *Jorn* plurality noted, contemplates a second trial.

Mr. Justice Stevens: "In *Jorn* the judge dismissed the information because he thought reprosecution was barred by the Double Jeopardy Clause. But in this case the termination was an acquittal, and the judge took his action because of the merits of the prosecution's case. [The judge observed that he "almost instructed a verdict for all defendants" before the case went to the jury.

He also said, "I have seen some contempt cases, but this is without a doubt the weakest I've ever seen."—ed.]

Easterbrook: "I use *Jorn* to show that the mere fact that a new trial would follow a successful government appeal isn't an independent double jeopardy prior."

Mr. Justice Marshall: "What is the effect of the finding of prior acquittal?"

Just as in *Sanford,* the defendant would go free, counsel replied.

Mr. Justice Marshall: "But what is the purpose of Rule 29(c)? [The Rule read as follows: "If the jury returns a verdict of guilty or is discharged without having returned a verdict, a motion for judgment of acquittal may be made or renewed within 7 days after the jury is discharged or within such further time as the court may fix during the 7-day period. If a verdict of guilty is returned the court may on such motion set aside the verdict and enter judgment of acquittal. If no verdict is returned the court may enter judgment of acquittal. It shall not be necessary to the making of such a motion that a similar motion has been made prior to the submission of the case to the jury."]

The Rule's purpose is to bring the proceedings to a close if the government does not have a case, Easterbrook replied. We don't argue that there should always be a new trial after a mistrial, he added.

The Chief Justice asked at what point the judge could enter an acquittal.

He has power to do so at any time, counsel answered. The order here, as well as that in *Sanford,* was within the trial court's power. The question is not one of power; rather it is whether the judge was correct and whether the ruling can be appealed.

Mr. Justice White: "Would you make the same argument if the judge had not declared a mistrial?"

Easterbrook: "Yes. Once the jury deadlocks, manifest necessity is created. It doesn't matter whether the judge says 'mistrial.'"

Mr. Justice Marshall: "Suppose a judge enters an acquittal before the case goes to the jury, and the defendant has not requested it?"

We probably could not appeal in that case, counsel said. But in this case, the jury went out and returned; moreover, the defendants got what they asked for. If one asks for something that takes the case away from the jury, then he gives up his right to have the jury return a verdict.

Mr. Justice Stevens again referred to *Wilson,* saying that where *Wilson* involved what was functionally a dismissal, the trial court's action here was functionally an acquittal. I see no basis in *Wilson,* the Justice added, for your conclusion that the type of action taken isn't important.

Counsel referred to *Sanford,* which he said controls this case. [In *Sanford,* a mistrial was declared because of a jury deadlock. Four months later, while the government was preparing for retrial, the defendant moved to dismiss the indictment. The court granted dismissal on a legal ground, not material here, and the Ninth Circuit dismissed the government's appeal from that dismissal on double jeopardy grounds. The Supreme Court reversed in a per curiam decision, noting that as in *Serfass* v. *U.S.,* the dismissal order came "prior to a trial (the scheduled retrial) that the government had a right to prosecute and that the defendant was required to defend."—ed.]

A possible reason for § 3731 not mentioning appeals from acquittals, Mr. Justice Stewart suggested, is that Congress thought that such appeals were barred by the Double Jeopardy Clause. Counsel had no answer to this suggestion.

Judge's Power

J. Burleson Smith, of San Antonio, Texas, presented the argument for the defendants. The proper focus in this case, he said, is on the question of the trial judge's power. Mr. Justice Harlan's opinion in *U.S.* v. *Sisson,* 399 U.S. 267 (1970), makes clear that judges can cause defendants to be acquitted. And *Illinois* v. *Somerville,* 410 U.S. 458 (1976), emphasizes that the trial judge has broad discretion to declare a mistrial.

A Second Circuit case, *U.S.* v. *Suarez,* 505 F.2d 166 (1974), is on all fours with this case in terms of procedure, counsel said. The appeals court there held the government's appeal was barred by double jeopardy. The Sixth Circuit came to the same conclusion in *U.S.* v. *Robbins,* 510 F.2d 301 (1975). *Robbins* involved a Rule 29(a) motion, but we submit that there is no difference between acquittals under 29(a) and 29(c).

Mr. Justice White: "Suppose the jury comes back with a guilty verdict, and then the judge enters an acquittal?"

Counsel did not go so far as to say that the government could not appeal in that situation. There is no talismanic quality to an acquittal, he said.

The controlling case here, Smith continued, is *U.S.* v. *Jenkins.* Footnote 7 in *Jenkins* is especially important; there the Court said "it is of critical importance whether the proceedings in the trial court terminate in a mistrial as they did in the *Somerville* line of cases, or in the defendant's favor, as they did [in *Jenkins*]." *Serfass* and *Sanford* involved pretrial dismissals. In contrast "the trial here was long gone."

Policy

Smith then argued that policy considerations support his position. As in any double jeopardy case, the defendants' interest in avoiding the burdens of a second prosecution is involved. The Second Circuit's decision in *Security National Bank* shows that corporations face the same dangers in this context as individuals do. Counsel outlined the trial proceedings and adverted to the judge's comments about the government's case.

Even if the judge was wrong on the merits, Mr. Justice Stewart remarked, you say there can be no appeal.

Yes, counsel said, citing *Fong Foo* v. *U.S.,* 369 U.S. 141 (1962).

If the judgment here is not affirmed, Smith concluded, how are we to describe the trial judge's function? For practical purposes, he would be "sterilized to the position of an impotent umpire at a tennis match."

UNITED STATES v. MARTIN LINEN SUPPLY CO.

Supreme Court of the United States, 1977
430 U.S. 564, 97 S. Ct. 1349, 51 L. Ed. 2d 642

The facts are stated in the opinion.

Mr. Justice BRENNAN delivered the opinion of the Court.

A "hopelessly deadlocked" jury was discharged when unable to agree upon a verdict at the criminal contempt trial of respondent corporations in the District Court for the Western District of Texas. Rule 29(c) of the Federal Rules of Criminal Procedure provides that in such case "a motion for judgment of acquittal may be made . . . within seven days after the jury is discharged [and] . . . the court may enter judgment of acquittal. . . ." Timely motions for judgments of acquittal under the Rule made by respondents six days after the discharge of the jury resulted two months later in the entry by the District Court of judgments of acquittal. The sole question presented for our decision is whether these judgments of acquittal under Rule 29(c) are appealable by the United States pursuant to 18 U.S.C. § 3731. Section 3731 provides that an appeal by the United States in a criminal case "shall lie to a court of appeals from a . . . judgment . . . of a district court dismissing an indictment . . ., except that no appeal shall lie where the double jeopardy clause of the United States Constitution prohibits further prosecution." The Court of Appeals for the Fifth Circuit held that no appeal lay under § 3731 from the judgments of acquittal entered by the District Court under Rule 29(c). 534 F.2d 585 (1976). The Court of Appeals reasoned that, since reversal of the acquittals would enable the United States to try respondents a second time, the bar of the Double Jeopardy Clause "leads inescapably to the conclusion that no appeal lies from the directed verdict ordered by the court below." Id., at 589. We granted certiorari. 429 U.S. ___ (1976). We affirm.

I

It has long been established that the United States cannot appeal in a criminal case without express congressional authorization. United States v. Wilson, 420 U.S. 332, 336 (1975); United States v. Sanges, 144 U.S. 310 (1892). Only two Terms ago Wilson traced the uneven course of such statutory authority until 1970 when the Congress amended the Criminal Appeals Act, 420 U.S., at 336–339, and that history need not be repeated here. See also United States v. Sisson, 399 U.S. 267, 307–308 (1970). It suffices for present purposes that this Court in Wilson found that in enacting § 3731 as Title III of the Omnibus Crime Control Act of 1970, Pub. L. No. 91-644, 84 Stat. 1890, "Congress intended to remove all statutory barriers to Government appeals and to allow appeals whenever the Constitution would permit." Id., at 337. Therefore unless barred by the Double Jeopardy Clause of the Constitution, appeals by the Government from the judgments of acquittal entered by the District Court under Rule 29(c) are authorized by § 3731.

* * *

"The development of the Double Jeopardy Clause from its common-law origins . . . suggests that it was directed at the threat of multiple prosecutions, not at Government appeals, at least where those appeals would not require a new trial." Id., at 342. Thus Wilson held that the "controlling constitutional principle" focuses on prohibitions against multiple trials. Id., at 346. At the heart of this policy is the concern that permitting the sovereign freely to subject the citizen to a second trial for the same offense would arm government with a potent instrument of oppression. The Clause, therefore, guarantees that the State shall not be permitted to make repeated attempts to convict the accused, "thereby subjecting him to embarrassment, expense and ordeal and compelling him to live in a continuing state of anxiety and insecurity as well as enhancing the possibility that even though innocent he may be found guilty." Green v. United States, 355 U.S. 184, 187–188 (1957); see also Downum v. United States, 372 U.S. 734, 736 (1963)....

In animating this prohibition against multiple prosecutions, the Double Jeopardy Clause rests upon two threshold conditions. The protections afforded by the Clause are implicated only when the accused has actually been placed in jeopardy. Serfass v. United States, 420 U.S. 377 (1975). This state of jeopardy attaches when a jury is empaneled and sworn, or, in a bench trial, when the judge begins to receive evidence. Illinois v. Somerville, 410 U.S. 458, 471 (1973) (WHITE, J., dissenting); Downum v. United States, supra. Further, where a government appeal presents no threat of successive prosecutions, the Double Jeopardy Clause is not offended. Thus a post-verdict dismissal of an indictment after a jury rendered a guilty verdict has been held to be appealable by the United States because restoration of the guilty verdict, and not a new trial, would necessarily result if the Government prevailed. United States v. Wilson, supra.

II

None of the considerations favoring appealability is present in the case of a government appeal from the District Court's judgment of acquittal under Rule 29(c) where the jury failed to agree on a verdict. The normal policy granting the Government the right to retry a defendant after a mistrial that does not determine the outcome of a trial, United States v. Perez, 9 Wheat. 579, 580 (1824), is not applicable since valid judgments of acquittal were entered on the express authority of, and strictly in compliance with, Rule 29(c). Those judgments, according to the very wording of the Rule, act to terminate a trial in which jeopardy has long since attached. And a successful governmental appeal reversing the judgments of acquittal would necessitate another trial, or, at least, "further proceedings of some sort, devoted to the resolution of factual issues going to the elements of the offense charged. ..." United States v. Jenkins, 420 U.S. 358, 370 (1975). Therefore, the present case is not one where the double jeopardy bar to appealability is automatically averted. Rather, we must inquire further into the constitutional significance of a Rule 29(c) acquittal.

Perhaps the most fundamental rule in the history of double jeopardy jurisprudence has been that "[a] verdict of acquittal ... could not be reviewed, on error or otherwise, without putting [a defendant] twice in jeopardy, and thereby violating the Constitution." United States v. Ball, 163 U.S. 662, 671 (1896). In Fong Foo v. United States, [369 U.S. 141 (1962)], supra, for example, a District Court directed jury verdicts of acquittal and subsequently entered formal judgments of acquittal. The Court of Appeals entertained the appeal of the United States and reversed the District Court's ruling on the ground that the trial judge was without power to direct acquittals under the circumstances disclosed by the record. We reversed, holding that, although the Court of Appeals may correctly have believed "that the acquittal was based upon an egregiously erroneous foundation, ... [n]evertheless, 'the verdict of acquittal was final, and could not be reviewed ... without putting [the defendant] twice in jeopardy, and thereby violating the Constitution' ...." 369 U.S., at 143.... In applying this teaching of Ball, Fong Foo, and like cases, we have emphasized that what constitutes an "acquittal" is not to be controlled by the form of the judge's action.... Rather, we must determine whether the ruling of the judge, whatever its label, actually represents a resolution, correct or not, of some or all of the factual elements of the offense charged.

There can be no question that the judgments of acquittal entered here by the District Court were "acquittals" in substance as well as form. The District Court plainly granted the Rule 29(c) motion on the view that the Government had not proved facts constituting criminal contempt. The Court made only too clear its belief that the prosecution was "the weakest [contempt case that] I've ever seen." In entering the judgments of acquittal, the Court also recorded its view that "the Government has failed to prove the material allegations beyond a reasonable doubt" and that "defendant should be found 'not guilty.'"

Thus, it is plain that the District Court in this case evaluated the government's evidence and determined that it was legally insufficient to sustain a conviction. The Court of Appeals concluded that this determination of insufficiency of the evidence triggered double jeopardy protection. The Government, however, disputes the constitutional significance of the District Court's action. It submits that only a verdict of acquittal formally returned by the jury should absolutely bar further proceedings and that "[o]nce the district court declared a mistrial and dismissed the jury, any double jeopardy bar to a second trial dissolved." Petitioner's Brief, at 21. We cannot agree.

Of course, as the Government argues, in a jury trial the primary finders of fact are the jurors. Their overriding responsibility is to stand between the accused and a potentially arbitrary or abusive government that is in command of the criminal sanction. For this reason, a trial judge is forbidden from entering a judgment of conviction or directing the jury to come forward with such a verdict, see Sparf & Hansen v. United States, 156 U.S. 51, 105 (1895); United Bd. Carpenters v. United States, 330 U.S. 395, 408 (1947), regardless of how overwhelmingly the evidence may point in that direction. The trial judge is thereby barred from attempting to override or interfere with the jurors' independent judgment in a manner contrary to the interests of the accused.

Such a limitation on the role of a trial judge, however, has never inhibited his ruling in favor of a criminal defendant. Fong Foo v. United States, supra, establishing the binding nature of a directed verdict, is dispositive on that point. Since Rule 29 merely replaces the directed-verdict mechanism employed in Fong Foo, and accords the federal trial judge greater flexibility in timing his judgment of acquittal, no persuasive basis exists for construing the rule as weakening the trial court's binding authority for purposes of double jeopardy. Rather, the Notes of the Advisory Committee have confirmed that Rule 29 intends no substantive alteration in the role of judge or jury, but creates a purely formal modification of the directed verdict device in order "to make the nomenclature accord with the realities." Cited in 18 U.S.C.A. Fed. Rule Crim. Proc. 18–31, at 183. Accordingly, United States v. Sisson, supra, at 290, held that Rule 29 recognizes no "legal distinction" between judge and jury with respect to the invocation of the protection of the Double Jeopardy Clause.

The Government, however, would read Fong Foo and, by implication, Rule 29 differently. It argues that the judge's directed verdict in Fong Foo was binding for double jeopardy purposes because the formal verdict of acquittal, though on direction, was rendered not by the judge but by the jury, which then was discharged. This in effect turns the constitutional significance of a Rule 29 judgment of acquittal on a matter of timing. Thus, if the judge orders entry of judgment of acquittal on his own or on defendant's motion prior to submission of the case to the jury, as he may under Rule 29(a), or after submission but prior to the jury's return of a verdict, as authorized by Rule 29(b) — and the jury thereafter is discharged — the Government's argument necessarily concedes that the Double Jeopardy Clause would preclude both appeal and retrial. If, however, the judge chooses to await the outcome of the jury's deliberations, and upon its failure to reach a verdict, acts on a timely motion for acquittal filed under Rule 29(c) within seven days of its discharge, the Government submits that the Double Jeopardy Clause should not bar an appeal.

We are not persuaded. Rule 29 contemplated no such artificial distinctions. Rather, the differentiations in timing were intentionally incorporated into the Rule to afford a trial judge the maximum opportunity to consider with care a pending acquittal motion. Insofar as the Government desires an appeal to correct error, irrational behavior, or prejudice on the part of the trial judge, its interest is not dependent on the point of trial when the judge enters his Rule 29 judgment, and suffers no special prejudice by a judge's acquittal after the jury disagrees and is discharged. And to the extent that the judge's authority under Rule 29 is designed to provide additional protection to a defendant by filtering out deficient prosecutions, the defendant's interest in such protection is essentially identical both before the jury is allowed to come to a verdict and after the jury is unable to reach a verdict. In either case, the defendant has neither been condemned nor exculpated by a panel of his peers and, in the absence of intervention by the trial judge, his vindication must await further action by a jury.

We thus conclude that judgments under Rule 29 are to be treated uniformly and, accordingly, the Double Jeopardy Clause bars appeal from an acquittal entered under

29(c) after a jury mistrial no less than under 29(a) or (b). United States v. Sanford, [429 U.S. 14] (1976), does not dictate a contrary result. In Sanford a jury trial ended in the declaration of a mistrial. A judgment of acquittal was never entered. Some four months later, with the second trial well into the preparatory stage, the trial court dismissed the prosecution's indictment. Because the dismissal "occurred several months after the first trial had ended in a mistrial, but before the retrial of respondents had begun," id., at 21, the Court characterized the judge's dismissal as a "pretrial order" and concluded that its appealability was governed by Serfass v. United States, supra. The Court's linking of Sanford and Serfass highlights the distinctiveness of an acquittal under Rule 29(c). In Serfass the Court carefully distinguished between appeal of a pretrial order and appeal of "a legal determination on the basis of facts adduced at the trial relating to the general issue of the case." 420 U.S., at 393, quoting United States v. Sisson, supra, at 290 n.19. A Rule 29 acquittal, however, falls squarely within the latter category: By the very language of the Rule, such a judgment of acquittal plainly concludes a pending prosecution in which jeopardy has attached, following the introduction at trial of evidence on the general issue. In that circumstance we hold that "although retrial is sometimes permissible after a mistrial is declared but no verdict or judgment has been entered, the verdict of acquittal foreclosed retrial and thus barred appellate review." United States v. Wilson, supra, at 348.

Affirmed.

Mr. Justice STEVENS, concurring in the judgment.

There is no statutory authority for a government appeal from a judgment of acquittal in a criminal case. The plain language of 18 U.S.C. § 3731, together with its unambiguous legislative history, makes it perfectly clear that Congress did not authorize—and did not intend to authorize—appeals from acquittals.

* * *

Since I am satisfied that Congress has not authorized the Government to appeal from a judgment of acquittal, the only question presented is whether such a judgment was entered in this case. The answer to that question, as the Court demonstrates, is perfectly clear. By virtue of Rule 29(c) of the Federal Rules of Criminal Procedure, the mistrial did not terminate the judge's power to make a decision on the merits. His ruling, in substance as well as form, was therefore an acquittal. For this reason, I concur in the Court's judgment.

Mr. Chief Justice BURGER, dissenting.

The order of acquittal in favor of respondents was entered by the District Judge after a mistrial had been declared due to jury deadlock. Once the jury was dismissed, respondents ceased to be in jeopardy in that proceeding; they could no longer be convicted except after undergoing a new trial. For a century and a half it has been accepted that a defendant may properly be reprosecuted after the declaration of such a mistrial, United States v. Perez, 9 Wheat. 579 (1824). Therefore the District Judge's ruling here was made "prior to a trial that the Government had a right to prosecute and that the defendant was required to defend." United States v. Sanford, 45 U.S.L.W. 3278, 3279 (Oct. 12, 1976).[1]

The present case cannot be distinguished from Sanford in constitutionally material respects. It is true that the District Judge here phrased his order as an acquittal rather than as a dismissal, and that the order was entered pursuant to a timely Rule 29(c)

---

[1] Fong Foo v. United States, 369 U.S. 141 (1962), on which the Court relies so heavily, is not in point. There the District Judge directed a verdict while the original trial was still in progress. Unlike the case before us, the jury there was still properly empaneled, and had not yet even begun to deliberate. Where the District Judge interrupts the trial process, important rights of the defendant may be jeopardized. The opportunity to try the case is frustrated so that the possibility of an acquittal from the originally empaneled jury is lost. No such rights are implicated where, as here, the original trial has ended when the jury cannot agree; at that point the defendant is already subject to a second trial. Thus, the timing of the District Court's order is not, as the Court suggests, an irrelevant technicality. A mid-trial judgment of acquittal interrupts the trial process at a time when the defendant is constitutionally entitled to have it proceed to verdict.

motion. However, such mechanical niceties are not dispositive of whether retrial would expose respondents to double jeopardy; our Fifth Amendment inquiry should focus on the substance, not the form of the proceedings below. In ruling on a motion for acquittal the District Judge must pass on the sufficiency, *not* on the weight, of the Government's case, United States v. Isaaks, 516 F.2d 409, 410 (5th Cir.), cert. denied, 423 U.S. 936 (1975), United States v. Wotten, 503 F.2d 65, 66 (4th Cir. 1974); "the applicable standard is whether [the District Judge as a trier of fact] *could,* not whether he *would,* find the accused guilty on the Government's evidence." United States v. Consolidated Laundries Corp., 291 F.2d 563, 574 (2d Cir. 1961) (emphasis original).

The District Judge's ruling is thus plainly one of law, not of fact; it could only exonerate, not convict, the defendant. No legitimate interest of the defendant requires that this ruling be insulated from appellate review. On the other hand, barring the appeal jeopardizes the Government's substantial interest in presenting a legally sufficient case to the jury. The Court's holding today is thus wholly inconsistent with the intent of Rule 29(c) as described by the drafters in the Advisory Committee Notes. In explaining the 1966 amendments to the Rule, the Notes expressly state: "No legitimate interest of the government is intended to be prejudiced by permitting the court to direct an acquittal on a post-conviction motion." Surely the well recognized right to reprosecute is such a "legitimate interest of the government" and should remain unaffected by the District Judge's order of acquittal.

Nor will the interest of clarity and consistency in the administration of the criminal justice system be served by today's holding. By hinging the outcome of this case on the timing of the post-trial motion and the label on the order, the Court is elevating form over substance and undermining the theoretical framework established by the Wilson-Jenkins-Serfass trilogy of two Terms ago and the Sanford and Morrison decisions earlier this Term. All litigants in our criminal courts — government and defendants alike — are harmed by the uncertainty thus created. For these reasons, I cannot join the Court's holding and I respectfully dissent.

[Mr. Justice REHNQUIST took no part in the consideration or decision of this case.]

When the Trial Court Dismisses the Charges
FINCH v. UNITED STATES

SUPREME COURT OF THE UNITED STATES, 1977
431 U.S. 407, 97 S. Ct. 2909, 53 L. Ed. 2d 1048

The facts are stated in the opinion.

PER CURIAM.

In an information filed in the United States District Court for the District of Montana, petitioner was charged with knowingly fishing on a portion of the Big Horn River in Montana reserved for use by the Crow Indians, in violation of 18 U.S.C. § 1165. The case was submitted to the District Court on an agreed statement of facts, which showed that petitioner had cast his lure into the river while standing on land owned by the State of Montana within the exterior boundaries of the Crow Reservation. After considering the stipulated facts and reviewing the applicable treaties, the court dismissed the information for failure to state an offense, 395 F. Supp. 205 (1975).

On the Government's appeal, the Court of Appeals for the Ninth Circuit reversed. 548 F. 2d 822 (1976). The court held that the appeal was permissible under 18 U.S.C. § 3731 and the Double Jeopardy Clause because, as in United States v. Wilson, 420 U.S. 332 (1975), no further factual proceedings would be required in the District Court in the event that its legal conclusions were found to be erroneous:

"Here, as in Wilson, it is easy to separate factual resolutions from determinations of law. No additional facts must be found to determine whether the stipulation supports the conviction of the defendant. The only determination to be made is a legal one." Id., at 827.

On the merits, the court viewed the pertinent treaties differently from the District Court and held that petitioner had violated 18 U.S.C. § 1165 "by willfully and knowingly fishing without lawful authority or permission of the tribe." Id., at 835. The court directed entry of a judgment of conviction.

We think that the Court of Appeals was without jurisdiction to entertain the appeal. When the District Court dismissed the information, jeopardy had attached, see Serfass v. United States, 420 U.S. 377, 388 (1975), but no formal finding of guilt or innocence had been entered, see Jenkins v. United States, 420 U.S. 358 (1975); Lee v. United States, No. 76-5187. Slip op., at 4 n. 4, and 6 n. 7. In these circumstances, the holding of United States v. Wilson is inapposite. A successful Government appeal "would not justify a reversal with instructions to reinstate the general finding of guilt: there was no such finding, in form or substance, to reinstate." United States v. Jenkins, supra, at 368. Absent a plea of guilty or nolo contendere, see Fed. Rule Crim. Proc. 11, a verdict or general finding of guilt by the trial court is a necessary predicate to conviction. Id. 23. Because the dismissal was granted prior to any declaration of guilt or innocence, "on the ground, correct or not, that the defendant simply cannot be convicted of the offense charged." Lee, supra, at 7, we hold that the Government's appeal was barred by the Double Jeopardy Clause.

We grant the petition for certiorari, vacate the judgment of the Court of Appeals, and remand to that court with directions that the appeal be dismissed.

[Mr. Justice STEVENS would have granted certiorari and set the case for oral argument.]

Mr. Justice REHNQUIST, with whom the CHIEF JUSTICE [BURGER] joins, dissenting.

I dissent from the summary disposition of this case for two reasons. The first is that the factual assumption, made both by the Court of Appeals for the Ninth Circuit and by this Court, that petitioner and respondent had agreed to submit the issue of guilt to the District Court on the "agreed statement of facts" is by no means clear from Judge Battin's principal opinion in this case. United States v. Finch, 395 F. Supp. 205. My second reason for disagreeing with summary disposition is that this Court has never passed on any claim of double jeopardy where the issues were submitted on an agreed statement of facts, rather than to a jury for its verdict or to the court for a finding of guilt or innocence after hearing witnesses. While I am not prepared to say that the Court's decision on the legal issue involved here is wrong, I am not sufficiently convinced that it is right so as to justify summary disposition without either argument or briefing on the merits.

The Court states that "the case was submitted to the District Court on an agreed statement of facts," and "after considering the stipulated facts and reviewing the applicable treaties, the court dismissed the information for failure to state an offense." The Court of Appeals for the Ninth Circuit put the matter much the same way. Implicit in this statement is that the submission involved a waiver of petitioner's right to jury trial and both his and the government's consent that the District Court decide the issue of guilt or innocence. The District Court's opinion in the case, however, is by no means clear on these points. That court put the matter this way:

"On June 14, 1974, the defendant filed a motion to dismiss said information. The parties submitted extensive and well-considered memoranda of law. On September 4, 1974, an order was filed wherein I denied the motion to dismiss and noted that the information was sufficient on its face. An agreed Statement of Facts and additional memoranda of law have been filed. Additionally, counsel for the Crow Tribe of Indians and the State of Montana, Department of

Fish and Game, have appeared herein as amici curiae.

"After a thorough review of the file, I am compelled to reconsider my order dated September 4, 1974, wherein I denied defendant's motion to dismiss. I conclude that the information is not sufficient on its face for several reasons." 395 F. Supp. 205, 207.

While this statement is by no means inconsistent with an agreement by the parties to submit the issue of guilt or innocence to the District Court, neither is it inconsistent with an agreement by the parties to submit on an agreed statement of facts a motion for reconsideration of the motion to dismiss the information, which the District Court had previously denied. This factual uncertainty, unless somehow clarified, would lead me to deny certiorari in this case in order that this Court not render an advisory opinion on what may be an important double jeopardy question.

The Court of Appeals, proceeding on the hypothesis that the case had been submitted to the District Court for a determination of guilt or innocence, as well as the sufficiency of the information, decided that jeopardy *had* attached. It therefore proceeded to inquire whether a reversal of the District Court's dismissal of the information would require further factual determinations, and therefore constitute double jeopardy under United States v. Jenkins, 420 U.S. 358 (1975), or would instead be governed by United States v. Wilson, 420 U.S. 332 (1975).

I agree with the Court that the Court of Appeals' alignment of this case with Wilson rather than with Jenkins was conclusory and gave too little attention to the ways in which this case differs from Wilson. But I do not think the opposite result is so obvious as to warrant summary reversal. In deciding the question of law which this case poses, I do not think we can ignore three double jeopardy decisions which have intervened since the Jenkins-Wilson-Serfass trilogy of two years ago. United States v. Dinitz, 424 U.S. 600 (1976), qualified the "manifest necessity" requirement of Perez v. United States, 9 Wheat. 579 (1824), where a mistrial was granted at the request of the defendant. Its stress on the absence of prosecutorial overreaching or misconduct, while in no way inconsistent with that trilogy, nonetheless emphasized more of a balancing and fairness test than the sort of "bright line" distinction set forth in Wilson and Jenkins. United States v. Martin Linen Supply Co., [430 U.S. 564] (1976), and Lee v. United States, 432 U.S. 23 (1977), likewise read more in terms of balancing and of "double jeopardy values" than in terms of the strict Wilson-Jenkins distinction.

If there has been some shift in emphasis in the Court's case this Term, it seems to me that the submission of the issue of guilt or innocence on an agreed statement of facts not only factually distinguishes this case from Jenkins, but is a factor to be weighed in any balancing test against a finding of double jeopardy. We have held that the Double Jeopardy Clause bars repeated prosecutions not only to reduce the possibility that an innocent man will finally be convicted, but to avoid subjecting defendants "to embarrassment, expense and ordeal and compelling [them] to live in a continuing state of anxiety and insecurity...." Green v. United States, 355 U.S. 184, 187–188 (1957). See United States v. Jorn, 400 U.S. 470, 479 (1971). Since if the Court's factual hypothesis is right, the facts of this case are not in issue, not only is some of the embarrassment and ordeal absent, but the expense that would normally be involved in a full scale retrial with its calling of witnesses for both sides is likewise avoided.

The factual uncertainties in this case are not entirely unrelated to the double jeopardy questions involved. Because we have never decided a case involving double jeopardy claims where the issue of guilt or innocence was submitted to the Court on an agreed statement of facts without the calling of any witness, we have never had occasion to pass on when jeopardy attaches in such a situation. Assuming that the factual uncertainties in the procedural history of the case can be clarified, and that the issue of guilt or innocence was submitted to the trial judge, I do not believe this case is controlled by Jenkins. The double jeopardy issues which it raises are not as straightforward as suggested in the Court's summary disposition. If the Court feels this case should be decided on the merits, I would therefore grant certiorari and have it briefed and argued.

F. OTHER DECISIONS OF INTEREST INVOLVING DOUBLE JEOPARDY

During the 1976–1977 Term, the Supreme Court decided a number of cases involving the Double Jeopardy Clause of the Fifth Amendment. See *United States* v. *Morrison*, 429 U.S. 1 (1976); *United States* v. *Rose*, 429 U.S. 5 (1976); *United States* v. *Sanford*, 429 U.S. 14 (1976); *United States* v. *Kopp*, 429 U.S. 121 (1976); and *Finch* v. *United States*, 431 U.S. 407 (1977) (supra) —all per curiam opinions involving governmental appeals under 18 U.S.C. § 3731. See also *Harris* v. *Oklahoma*, 433 U.S. ___ (1977) (per curiam); and *Brown* v. *Ohio*, 432 U.S. 161 (1977), which appears in Chapter Six, § 6.02, of the principal text.

In *Abney* v. *United States*, 431 U.S. 615 (1977), the Supreme Court granted certiorari to decide whether a pretrial order denying a motion to dismiss an indictment on double jeopardy grounds is a "final decision" within the meaning of 28 U.S.C. § 1291. Section 1291 provides in pertinent part: "The courts of appeals shall have jurisdiction of appeals from all final decisions of the district courts of the United States ... except where a direct review may be had in the Supreme Court." Petitioners, Donald Abney and others, were charged in a single-count indictment with conspiracy and attempted obstruction of interstate commerce by means of extortion in violation of the Hobbs Act, 18 U.S.C. § 1951. Petitioners challenged the indictment on the ground that the single count improperly charged both a conspiracy and an attempt to violate the Hobbs Act. The district court refused to dismiss the indictment and required the prosecution to prove all the elements of both offenses charged. The jury returned a verdict of guilty against each petitioner. On appeal, the Court of Appeals (3d Cir.) reversed petitioners' convictions and remanded for a new trial. On remand, the court agreed with the petitioners that the indictment was duplicitous and ordered the prosecution to elect between the conspiracy and the attempt charges. When the government elected to proceed on the conspiracy charge, petitioners moved to dismiss the indictment, arguing that the retrial would expose them to double jeopardy. The district court denied the motion to dismiss and the petitioners appealed to the Court of Appeals (3d Cir.). The court of appeals affirmed, but did not address the government's argument that the court lacked jurisdiction to hear the appeal because of the denial of petitioners' motion to dismiss was not a "final decision" within the meaning of 28 U.S.C. § 1291. The United States Supreme Court granted certiorari.

The Supreme Court affirmed in a unanimous decision (White, J., concurring.) In an opinion written by Chief Justice Burger, the Court held that:

1. The district court's pretrial order denying the motion to dismiss was a "final decision" within the meaning of § 1291.

2. Although lacking the finality traditionally required for appellate review, the pretrial order was within the "collateral exception" because it constituted a complete, formal, and final rejection of the petitioners' double jeopardy claim, the principal issue being the accused's guilt or innocence of the offense charged. *Cohen* v. *Beneficial Industrial Loan Corp.*, 337 U.S. 541 (1949).

3. A defendant may seek immediate appellate review of a district court's rejection of his double jeopardy claim because the Fifth Amendment is a guarantee against being twice put to trial for the same offense.

4. The court of appeals lacked jurisdiction under § 1291 to pass on the merits of the petitioners' challenge to the sufficiency of the indictment. The district court's rejection of that claim was not "collateral" since it went to the heart of the issues to be resolved at the trial.

5. The court had instructed the jury that the government would have to establish the elements of both crimes before it could return a verdict of guilty against the petitioners. Therefore, the petitioners' retrial on the conspiracy charge would not violate the Double Jeopardy Clause because it appeared that the jury, while convicting petitioners on the attempt charge, had not acquitted them on the conspiracy charge.

In *Lee* v. *United States*, 432 U.S. 23 (1977), the Supreme Court granted certiorari to decide whether the Double Jeopardy Clause prohibits the retrial of a federal defendant whose first trial ended with a dismissal, following the prosecution's presentation of its evidence, because of a defective indictment. After the prosecutor's opening statement in petitioner's bench trial for theft, petitioner's counsel moved to dismiss the information on the ground that it did not allege the specific intent required under the statute. The court tentatively denied the motion subject to further study, and petitioner's counsel did not object to going forward with the trial. At the close of the evidence, the court granted petitioner's motion to dismiss. Thereafter, petitioner, over his claim that the Double Jeopardy Clause barred the second trial, was indicted for the same offense and convicted. The Court of Appeals (7th Cir.) affirmed, and the United States Supreme Court granted certiorari.

The Supreme Court, by an 8-1 majority, held that the second trial did not run afoul of the Double Jeopardy Clause. Mr. Justice Powell, writing for the Court, held that:

1. The dismissal was "functionally indistinguishable" from a mistrial that contemplates a retrial.

2. The judge's order in no way resolved the question of the defendant's guilt or innocence, and the trial judge stressed that the only obstacle to the defendant's conviction was the defective indictment.

3. Double jeopardy principles bar only a retrial after a dismissal that terminates a proceeding in a defendant's favor, not a reprosecution when the defendant chooses to terminate his trial by requesting a mistrial. Only if the underlying error was "motivated by bad faith or undertaken to harass or prejudice" would a retrial be barred. *United States* v. *Dinitz,* 424 U.S. 600, 611 (1976).

4. The trial court's decision to delay the ruling was reasonable in light of the failure of defense counsel to request a continuance or otherwise stress the importance to the defendant of not being placed in jeopardy on a defective charge.

Justices Brennan and Rehnquist each wrote concurring opinions. Justice Marshall dissented, stating that most of the responsibility for the error-prone first trial rested on the prosecution because it made no effort to defend or to correct the faulty information.

In *Jeffers* v. *United States,* 432 U.S. 137 (1977), the Supreme Court granted certiorari to decide whether granting of defendant's demand for separate trials on two indictments deprived him of any rights under the Double Jeopardy Clause, which protects against successive prosecutions on lesser and greater offenses. A federal grand jury indicted the petitioner on two indictments, one for conspiracy to distribute heroin and cocaine (21 U.S.C. § 846) and the other for operating a continuing criminal enterprise "in concert" with five or more other persons (21 U.S.C. § 848). The petitioner opposed a motion by the prosecution to consolidate the indictments for trial, and the trial court denied the government's motion. Petitioner was tried and convicted on the § 846 indictment, which was affirmed on appeal. Petitioner then moved to dismiss the § 848 indictment because he had already been placed in jeopardy for the same offense owing to the fact that a § 846 conspiracy is a lesser included offense of a § 848 continuing criminal enterprise. The trial court held that §§ 846 and 848 described separate offenses, and petitioner was tried and convicted of the § 848 offense. The Court of Appeals (7th Cir.) affirmed, although it concluded that § 846 involved a lesser included offense under § 848. The court noted that *Iannelli* v. *United States,* 420 U.S. 770 (1975), created a new double jeopardy rule applicable to complex statutory crimes whereby greater and lesser included offenses could be separately punished if Congress so intended. The United States Supreme Court granted certiorari.

Writing for a four-Justice plurality, Mr. Justice Blackmun concluded that:

1. The defendant's opposition to the prosecution's motion to consolidate the indictments for trial waived any right he might have had against consecutive trials, and the government was entitled to prosecute him for the § 848 offense.

2. Even though conspiracy under § 846 is a lesser included offense under § 848, the defendant's opposition to the consolidation motion is an exception to the rule established in *Brown* v. *Ohio,* 432 U.S. 161 (1977) (Chapter Six, § 6.02, principal text), that the Double Jeopardy Clause prohibits the trial of a defendant for a greater offense after he has been convicted of a lesser offense.

3. Because the defendant could have been tried in one proceeding but chose not to, he was solely responsible for the separate prosecutions.

Justice White wrote a concurring opinion, stating that the case is governed by *Iannelli* v. *United States,* 420 U.S. 770 (1975). Mr. Justice Stevens, joined by Justices Brennan, Stewart, and Marshall, dissented, stating that a defendant should not be required to advise the prosecution that a double jeopardy problem exists.

6.04 THE GRAND JURY

C. RACIAL DISCRIMINATION AND THE SELECTION OF GRAND JURORS

The "Substantial Under-representation" Test

ORAL ARGUMENTS BEFORE THE
U.S. SUPREME COURT*

Castaneda v. Partida, No. 74-1552; argued 11/9/76

The court considered a grand jury discrimination case on oral argument that focused to a large extent on the meaning of population figures and who has to prove what to establish discrimination. The sheriff of Hidalgo County, Texas, asked the Court to overturn a Fifth Circuit decision, 524 F. 2d 481 (1975), holding that county officials had failed to rebut a Mexican-American defendant's claim that the grand jury which indicted him was selected under a system that discriminates against Mexican-Americans.

The figures presented by the defendant established that Mexican-Americans constitute 79.2 percent of the county's population but comprised only 39 percent of the grand jurors over a 10-year period.

Thomas Parker Beery, Assistant Criminal District Attorney for Hidalgo County, began his argument by explaining the selection system. Texas, he noted, uses the commissioner system under which a district judge selects three to five commissioners prior to the beginning of each term of court. These commissioners then select 15–20 potential grand jurors who meet the statutory qualifications. After these persons are examined the judge impanels the grand jury.

Mr. Justice Rehnquist: "Is there a fixed size for grand juries?"

"Yes, sir. Twelve."

"Is there a minimum number which must vote to indict?"

"Nine."

---

*From 20 Crim. L. Rptr. 4077–4078. Reprinted by permission from the Bureau of National Affairs, Inc.

The Chief Justice: "You don't challenge the 79.2 percent figure, do you?"

"No sir. We don't."

"Are you aware that this figure is at odds with those of the Census Bureau?"

Counsel replied that he had not been aware of that disparity. The petitioner here, he said, had relied on the exhibits presented below.

Mr. Justice Marshall: "Why didn't the jury commissioners testify below?"

"I don't know, sir. I did not handle the hearing for the state."

"How can we know the reasons for the disparity between population figures and grand jury representation without their testimony?"

Counsel thought the information in the record would provide a basis to discuss issues.

Waiver

At this point in the argument the possible applicability of *Francis* v. *Henderson* [425 U.S. 536] (1976) was raised by Mr. Justice Marshall. [*Francis* held that a state prisoner's failure to comply with a Louisiana statute providing that defects in the indictment must be raised prior to trial or be deemed waived precluded federal habeas corpus relief on his claim that Negroes had been excluded from the grand jury which indicted him. — ed.].

Mr. Justice Marshall asked whether *Francis* v. *Henderson* helped the petitioner's case here since this issue was raised for the first time on a post-trial motion. He also wondered why the question was not raised in his brief.

Beery replied that he was unaware of the *Francis* decision at the time he prepared his brief. At any rate, he was unsure whether it would apply because the federal courts passed over the waiver issue and reached the merits.

Mr. Justice Stewart observed that he didn't think counsel could rely on *Francis* for that reason.

Mr. Justice Stewart then inquired whether Beery agreed that a prima facie case of discrimination had been made.

Counsel said he would accept the existence of a prima facie case in view of the disparity shown on the record. At any rate, he argued, even assuming that the respondent had made out a prima facie case, the state has established that there was no purposeful discrimination.

There is another important point here, he said. The fact that 79.2 percent of the population is Mexican-American makes them a governing majority. This is a point discussed by both the district court and the court of appeals while reaching different conclusions.

Mr. Justice Blackmun wondered whether this governing majority theory assumes that members of one ethnic group which constitutes the governing majority will not discriminate against members of their own group.

Beery thought that it did.

"Do you think that assumption is valid?"

"Yes, sir, I do."

"Is there any evidence to support this governing majority argument?"

Counsel replied that he believed the record in this case, coupled with human experience, would support it.

"Do you think it's possible that a state judge might discriminate in favor of the non-Mexican minority?"

Beery thought it possible but not likely.

The Chief Justice: "Do you want us to take judicial notice of this assumption?"

"Yes, sir."

Mr. Justice Marshall: "I can't take judicial notice of something that is in dispute."

Beery concluded by arguing that the state judge's testimony below effectively rebutted the respondent's claim and that to uphold the Court of Appeals' decision here would condemn Texas' grand jury selection system.

Important Fact

The single most important fact in this case is the disparity between population and grand jury participation, David G. Hall, of Welasco, Texas, said as he opened his argument for the defendant-respondent. While it's true that this figure represents the total population and may not reflect the percentage of people eligible for grand jury service, none of the other jury discrimination cases have talked in terms of the percentage eligible to serve. Rather, he said, they have focused on the disparity between population and grand jury make-up.

Mr. Justice Rehnquist inquired whether there was evidence in any of these cases of a requirement that prospective grand jurors be citizens.

Counsel said he was not aware of any state that did not have a citizenship requirement.

This case comes down to a question of who bears the burden of proof, Hall said. It is the respondent's position that once a disparity between population and grand jury participation is shown, the county officials must then prove that the disparity was not the result of discrimination.

Asked if the most logical and relevant figure would be the total number of citizens rather than simply the total population, Hall agreed it would be. However none of the other jury discrimination cases discussed this point. They focused on the population.

Mr. Justice Stewart: "Isn't that because most of the other cases presented no likelihood that there was a large alien population in the area involved?" [Hidalgo County borders on Mexico. — ed.]

That may be true, Hall replied, but then it becomes necessary to speculate as to the number of legal aliens, illegal aliens, and persons not qualified for jury service for other reasons such as language.

"What do you have to show in order to shift the burden to the state?"

Hall noted that the state here has relied on pure conjecture and speculation as to the number of persons eligible for grand jury service. He reiterated his argument that once a disparity between the total population and the number of Mexican-Americans on grand jury service is shown, it becomes incumbent on the state to show that the disparity was not the result of discrimination.

The Chief Justice: "Don't you have some obligation to show how many of these people were qualified for grand jury service?"

"If the state is going to rely on a claim that the alleged victims of discrimination were unqualified, it must prove that."

Mr. Justice White: "The state argues that just showing a disparity won't make your case. What else do you have?"

Hall argued that he can still rely on the system itself which is subjective in nature.

Mr. Justice Stewart: "What constitutes a prima facie case here?"

"Simply a showing that there is a significant disparity."

Mr. Justice White interjected that the jury discrimination cases only go so far as to say that a criminal defendant has a right to a grand jury that was selected without racial or ethnic discrimination.

The Chief Justice: "You base your argument on the assumption that all Mexican-Americans were eligible, is that correct?"

Not exactly, Hall responded. This case involved a 40-percent-plus disparity. Only one of the other cases involved a disparity greater than this.

"You think that your showing of a 79.2 percent Mexican-American population shifted the burden to the state to show that some of these people were not citizens or didn't speak English or were not otherwise eligible?"

"Yes, that is right."

CASTENEDA v. PARTIDA

United States Supreme Court, 1977
430 U.S. 482, 97 S. Ct. 1272, 51 L. Ed. 2d 498

The facts are stated in the opinion.

Mr. Justice BLACKMUN delivered the opinion of the Court.

I

The sole issue presented in this case is whether the State of Texas, in the person of petitioner, the Sheriff of Hidalgo County, successfully rebutted respondent-prisoner's prima facie showing of discrimination against Mexican-Americans in the state grand jury selection process. . . .

Texas employs the "key man" system, which relies on jury commissioners to select prospective grand jurors from the community at large. The procedure begins with the state district judge's appointment of from three to five persons to serve as jury commissioners. Tex. Code Crim. Proc. Art. 19.01 (1966). The commissioners then "shall select not less than 15 nor more than 20 persons from the citizens of different portions of the county" to comprise the list from which the actual grand jury will be drawn. Art. 19.06. When at least 12 of the persons on the list appear in court pursuant to summons, the district judge proceeds to "test their qualifications." Art. 19.21. The qualifications themselves are set out in Art. 19.08: a grand juror must be a citizen of Texas and of the county, be a qualified voter in the county, be "of sound mind and good moral character," be literate, have no prior felony conviction, and be under no pending indictment "or other legal accusation for theft or of any felony." Interrogation under oath is the method specified for testing the prospective juror's qualifications. Art. 19.22. The precise questions to be asked are set out in Art. 19.23, which, for the most part, tracks the language of Art. 19.08. After the court finds 12 jurors who meet the statutory qualifications, they are impaneled as the grand jury. Art. 19.26.

II

Respondent, Rodrigo Partida, was indicted in March 1972 by the grand jury of the 92d District Court of Hidalgo County for the crime of burglary of a private residence at night with intent to rape. Hidalgo is one of the border counties of southern Texas. After a trial before a petit jury, respondent was convicted and sentenced to eight years in the custody of the Texas Department of Corrections. He first raised his claim of discrimination in the grand jury selection process on a motion for new trial in the state district court. In support of his motion, respondent testified about the general existence of discrimination against Mexican-Americans in that area of Texas and introduced statistics from the 1970 Census and the Hidalgo County grand jury records. The census figures show that in 1970, the population of Hidalgo County was 181,535. . . . Persons of Spanish language or Spanish surname totaled 143,611. . . . On the assumption that all persons of Spanish language or Spanish surname were Mexican-Americans, these figures show that 79.1% of the county's population was Mexican-American.

Respondent's data compiled from the Hidalgo County grand jury records from 1962 to 1972 showed that over that period, the average percentage of Spanish-surnamed grand jurors was 39.0%. In the two and one-half year period during which the district judge who impanelled the jury that indicted respondent was in charge, the average percentage was 45.5%. On the first from which the grand jury that indicted respondent was selected, 50% were Spanish-surnamed. The last set of data that respondent introduced, again from the 1970 Census, illustrated a number of ways in which Mexican-Americans tend to be underprivileged, including poverty level incomes, less desirable jobs, substandard housing and lower levels of education. The State offered no evidence at all either attacking respondent's allegations of discrimination or demonstrating that his statistics were unreliable in any way. The state district court, nevertheless, denied the motion for a new trial.

On appeal, the Texas Court of Criminal Appeals affirmed the conviction. Partida v. State, 506 S.W.2d 209 (1974). Reaching the merits of the claim of grand jury discrimination, the court held that respondent had failed to make out a prima facie case. In the court's view, he should have shown how many of the females who served on the grand juries were Mexican-Americans married to men with Anglo-American surnames, how many Mexican-Americans were excused for reasons of age, health, or other legal reasons, and how many of those listed by the Census would not have met the statutory qualifications of citizenship, literacy, sound mind, moral character, and lack of criminal record or accusation. Id., at 210–211. Quite beyond the uncertainties in the statistics, the court found it impossible to believe that discrimination could have been directed against a Mexican-American, in light of the many elective positions held by Mexican-Americans in the county and the substantial representation of Mexican-Americans on recent grand juries. Id., at 211. In essence, the court refused to presume that Mexican-Americans would discriminate against their own kind.

After exhausting his state remedies, respondent filed his petition for habeas corpus in the Federal District Court, alleging a denial of due process and equal protection, guaranteed by the Fourteenth Amendment, because of gross under-representation of Mexican-Americans on the Hidalgo County grand juries. . . .

On the basis of the evidence before it, the court concluded that respondent had made out a *"bare prima facie case"* of invidious discrimination with his proof of "a long continued disproportion in the composition of the grand juries in Hidalgo County." 384 F. Supp. 79, 90 (S.D. Tex. 1974) (emphasis in original). Based on an examination of the reliability of the statistics offered by respondent, however, despite the lack of evidence in the record justifying such an inquiry, the court stated that the prima facie case was weak. The court believed that the census statistics did not reflect the true situation accurately, because of recent changes in the Hidalgo County area and the court's own impression of the demographic characteristics of the Mexican-American community. On the other hand, the court recognized that the Texas key man system of grand jury selection was highly subjective, and was "archaic and inefficient," id., at 91, and that this was a factor arguing for less tolerance in the percentage differences. On balance, the court's doubts about the reliability of the statistics, coupled with its opinion that Mexican-Americans constituted a "governing majority" in the county, caused it to conclude that the prima facie case was rebutted. The "governing majority" theory distinguished respondent's case from all preceding cases involving similar disparities. On the basis of those findings, the court dismissed the petition.

The United States Court of Appeals for the Fifth Circuit reversed. 524 F.2d 481 (1975). It agreed with the District Court that respondent had succeeded in making out a prima facie case. It found, however, that the State had failed to rebut that showing. The "governing majority" theory contributed little to the State's case in the absence of specific proof to explain the disparity. In light of the State's abdication of its responsibility to introduce controverting evidence, the court held that respondent was entitled to prevail.

We granted certiorari to consider whether the existence of a "governing majority" in itself can rebut a prima facie case of discrimination in grand jury selection, and, if not, whether the State otherwise met its burden of proof. 426 U.S. 934 (1976).

III

A

This Court has long recognized that "it is a denial of the equal protection of the laws to try a defendant of a particular race or color under an indictment issued by a grand jury ... from which all persons of his race or color have, solely because of that race or color, been excluded by the State...." While the earlier cases involved absolute exclusion of an identifiable group, later cases established the principle that substantial under-representation of the group constitutes a constitutional violation as well, if it results from purposeful discrimination. Recent cases have established the fact that an official act is not unconstitutional *solely* because it has a racially disproportionate impact. Washington v. Davis, 426 U.S. 229, 239 (1976); see Arlington Heights v. Metropolitan Housing Corp., [429 U.S. 252, 260] (1977). Nevertheless, as the Court recognized in Arlington Heights, "[s]ometimes a clear pattern, unexplainable on grounds other than race, emerges from the effect of the state action even when the governing legislation appears neutral on its face." Id., at 260. In Washington v. Davis, the application of these principles to the jury cases was considered:

"It is also clear from the cases dealing with racial discrimination in the selection of juries that the systematic exclusion of Negroes is itself such an 'unequal application of the law ... as to show intentional discrimination.' ... A prima facie case of discriminatory purpose may be proved as well by the absence of Negroes on a particular jury combined with the failure of the jury commissioners to be informed of eligible Negro jurors in a community ... or with racially non-neutral selection procedures. ... With a prima facie case made out, 'the burden of proof shifts to the State to rebut the presumption of unconstitutional action by showing that permissible racially neutral selection criteria and procedures have produced the monochromatic result.' Alexander [v. Louisiana, 405 U.S.,] at 632." 426 U.S., at 241.

Thus, in order to show that an equal protection violation has occurred in the context of grand jury selection, the defendant must show that the procedure employed resulted in substantial under-representation of his race or of the identifiable group to which he belongs. The first step is to establish that the group is one that is a recognizable, distinct class, singled out for different treatment under the laws, as written or as applied. Hernandez v. Texas, 347 U.S., at 478-479 (1954). Next, the degree of under-representation must be proved, by comparing the proportion of the group in the total population to the proportion called to serve as grand jurors, over a significant period of time. Id., at 480. See Norris v. Alabama, 294 U.S. 587 (1935). This method of proof, sometimes called the "rule of exclusion," has been held to be available as a method of proving discrimination in jury selection against a delineated class. Hernandez v. Texas, 347 U.S., at 480. Finally, as noted above, a selection procedure that is susceptible to abuse or not racially neutral supports the presumption of discrimination raised by the statistical showing. Washington v. Davis, 426 U.S., at 241; Alexander v. Louisiana, 405 U.S., at 630 (1972). Once the defendant has shown substantial under-representation of his group, he has made out a prima facie case of discriminatory purpose, and the burden then shifts to the State to rebut that case.

B

In this case, it is no longer open to dispute that Mexican-Americans are a clearly identifiable class. The statistics introduced by respondent from the 1970 Census illustrate disadvantages to which the group has been subject. Additionally, as in Alexander v. Louisiana, the selection procedure is not racially neutral with respect to Mexican-Americans; Spanish surnames are just as easily identifiable as race was from the questionnaires in Alexander or the notations and card colors in Whitus v. Georgia, 385 U.S. 545 (1967), and in Avery v. Georgia, 345 U.S. 559 (1953).

The disparity proved by the 1970 Census statistics showed that the population of the county was 79.1% Mexican-American, but that, over an 11-year period, only 39% of the persons summoned for grand jury service were Mexican-American. This difference of 40% is greater than that found significant in Turner v. Fouche, [396 U.S. 346 (1970)], (60% Negroes in the general population, 37% on the grand jury lists). Since the State presented no evidence showing why the 11-year period was not reliable, we take it as the relevant base for comparison. The mathematical disparities that have been accepted by this Court as adequate for a prima facie case have all been within the range presented here. For example, in Whitus v. Georgia, supra, the number of Negroes listed on the tax digest amounted to 27.1% of the population, but only 9.1% of those on the grand jury venire. The disparity was held to be sufficient to make out a prima facie case of discrimination. See Sims v. Georgia, 389 U.S. 404 (1967) (24.4% on tax lists, 4.7% on grand jury lists); *Jones* v. *Georgia,* 389 U.S. 24 (1967) (19.4% on tax lists, 5.0% on jury list). We agree with the District Court and the Court of Appeals that the proof in this case was enough to establish a prima facie case of discrimination against the Mexican-Americans in the Hidalgo County grand jury selection.

* * *

The showing made by respondent therefore shifted the burden of proof to the State to dispel the inference of intentional discrimination. Inexplicably, the State introduced practically no evidence. The testimony of the State district judge dealt principally with the selection of the jury commissioners and the instructions given to them. The commissioners themselves were not called to testify.

[T]he census figures showed that only a small part of the population reported for Hidalgo County was not native born. Without some testimony from the grand jury commissioners about the method by which they determined the other qualifications for grand jurors prior to the statutory time for testing qualifications, it is impossible to draw any inference about literacy, sound mind and moral character, and criminal record from the statistics about the population as a whole. These are questions of disputed fact that present problems not amenable to resolution by an appellate court. We emphasize, however, that we are not saying that the statistical disparities proved here could never be explained in another case; we are simply saying that the State did not do so in this case.

C

In light of our holding that respondent proved a prima facie case of discrimination that was not rebutted by any of the evidence presently in the record, we have only to consider whether the District Court's "governing majority" theory filled the evidentiary gap. In our view, it did not dispel the presumption of purposeful discrimination in the circumstances of this case. Because of the many facets of human motivation, it would be unwise to presume as a matter of law that human beings of one definable group will not discriminate against other members of their group. The problem is a complex one, about which widely differing views can be held, and, as such, it would be somewhat precipitous to take judicial notice of one view over another on the basis of a record as barren as this.

Furthermore, the relevance of a governing majority of elected officials to the grand jury selection process is questionable. The fact that certain elected officials are Mexican-American demonstrates nothing about the motivations and methods of the grand jury commissioners who select persons for grand jury lists. The only arguably relevant fact in this record on the issue is that three of the five jury commissioners in respondent's case were Mexican-American. Knowing only this, we would be forced to rely on the reasoning that we have rejected—that human beings would not discriminate against their own kind—in order to find that the presumption of purposeful discrimination was rebutted. Without the benefit of this simple behavioral presumption, discriminatory intent can be rebutted only with evidence in the record about the way in which the commissioners operated and their reasons for doing so. It was the State's burden to supply such evidence, once respondent established his prima facie case. The State's failure in this regard leaves unchallenged respondent's proof of purposeful discrimination.

Finally, even if a "governing majority" theory has general applicability in cases of this kind, the inadequacy of the record in this case does not permit such an approach. Among the evidentiary deficiencies are the lack of any indication of how long the Mexican-Americans have enjoyed "governing majority" status, the absence of information about the relative power inherent in the elective offices held by Mexican-Americans, and the uncertain relevance of the general political power to the specific issue in this case. Even for the most recent time period, when presumably the political power of Mexican-Americans was at its greatest, the discrepancy between the number of Mexican-Americans in the total population and the number on the grand jury lists was substantial. Thus, under the facts presented in this case, the "governing majority" theory is not developed fully enough to satisfy the State's burden of rebuttal.

IV

Rather than relying on an approach to the jury discrimination question that is as faintly defined as the "governing majority" theory is on this record, we prefer to look at all the facts that bear on the issue, such as the statistical disparities, the method of selection, and any other relevant testimony as to the manner in which the selection process was implemented. Under this standard, the proof offered by respondent was sufficient to demonstrate a prima facie case of discrimination in grand jury selection. Since the State failed to rebut the presumption of purposeful discrimination by competent testimony, despite two opportunities to do so, we affirm the Court of Appeals' holding of a denial of equal protection of the law in the grand jury selection process in respondent's case.

Affirmed.

[Mr. Justice MARSHALL wrote a concurring opinion.]

Mr. CHIEF JUSTICE BURGER, with whom Mr. Justice POWELL and Mr. Justice REHNQUIST join, dissenting.

... What the majority characterizes as a prima facie case of discrimination simply will not wash. The decisions of this Court suggest, and common sense demands, that the *eligible* population statistics, not gross population figures, provide the relevant starting point. In Alexander v. Louisiana, 405 U.S. 625, 630 (1972), for example, the Court in an opinion by Mr. Justice WHITE looked to the "population of blacks in the *eligible* population...." (Emphasis supplied.)

The failure to produce evidence relating to the eligible population in Hidalgo County undermines respondent's claim that any statistical "disparity" existed in the first instance. Particularly where, as here, substantial numbers of members of the identifiable class actually served on grand jury panels, the burden rightly rests upon the challenger to show a meaningful statistical disparity. After all, the presumption of constitutionality attaching to all state procedures has even greater force under the circumstances presented here, where exactly one-half the members of the grand jury list now challenged by respondent were members of the allegedly excluded class of Mexican-Americans.

The Court has not previously been called upon to deal at length with the sort of statistics required of persons challenging a grand jury selection system. The reason is that in our prior cases there was little doubt that members of identifiable minority groups had been excluded in large numbers. The case before us, in contrast, involves neither tokenism nor absolute exclusion; rather, the State has used a selection system resulting in the inclusion of large numbers of Spanish-surnamed citizens on grand jury lists. In this situation, it is particularly incumbent on respondent to adduce precise statistics demonstrating a significant disparity. To do that, respondent was obligated to demonstrate that disproportionately large numbers of eligible individuals were excluded systematically from grand jury service.

Respondent offered no evidence whatever in this respect. He therefore could not have established any meaningful case of discrimination, prima facie or otherwise. In contrast to respondent's approach, which the Court's opinion accepts without analysis, the Census Bureau's statistics for 1970 demonstrate that of the *adults* in Hidalgo County, 72%, not 79.1% as respondent implies, are Spanish-surnamed. At the outset, therefore, respondent's gross population figures are manifestly overinclusive.

But that is only the beginning. Respondent offered no evidence whatever with respect to other basic qualifications for grand jury service. The statistics relied on in the Court's opinion suggest that 22.9% of Spanish-surnamed persons over age 25 in Hidalgo County have had no schooling at all. Since one requirement of grand jurors in Texas is literacy in the English language, approximately 20% of adult-age Mexican-Americans are very likely disqualified on that ground alone.

The Court's reliance on respondent's overbroad statistics is not the sole defect. As previously noted, one-half of the members of respondent's grand jury list bore Mexican-American surnames. Other grand jury lists at about the same time as respondent's indictment in March 1972 were *predominantly Mexican-American.* Thus, with respect to the September 1971 grand jury list, 70% of the prospective grand jurors were Mexican-American. In the January 1972 Term, 55% were Mexican-American. Since respondent was indicted in 1972, by what appears to have been a truly representative grand jury, the mechanical use of Hidalgo County's practices some 10 years earlier seems to me entirely indefensible. We do not know, and on this record we cannot know, whether respondent's 1970 gross population figures, which served as the basis for establishing the "disparity" complained of in this case, had any applicability at all to the period prior to 1970. Accordingly, for all we know, the 1970 figures may be totally inaccurate as to prior years; if so, the apparent disparity alleged by respondent would be increased improperly.

Therefore, I disagree both with the Court's assumption that respondent established a prima facie case and with the Court's implicit approval of respondent's method for showing an allegedly disproportionate impact of Hidalgo County's election system upon Mexican-Americans.

Mr. Justice STEWART, dissenting.

In my view, the findings of the District Court in this case cannot be said to be "clearly erroneous." Fed. Rule Cov. Proc. 52(a); United States v. United States Gypsum Co., 333 U.S. 364, 394–395 [1948]. Given those findings, there was no constitutional violation in the selection of the grand jury that indicted the respondent. Upon that basis, I would reverse the judgment of the Court of Appeals. I add only that I am in substantial agreement with the dissenting opinions of the CHIEF JUSTICE and Mr. Justice POWELL.

Mr. Justice POWELL, with whom the CHIEF JUSTICE [BURGER] and Mr. Justice REHNQUIST join, dissenting.

* * *

The Court holds that a criminal defendant may demonstrate a violation of the Equal Protection Clause merely by showing that the procedure for selecting grand jurors "resulted in substantial under-representation of his race or the identifiable group to which he belongs." By so holding, the Court blurs the traditional constitutional distinctions between the grand and petit juries, and misapplies the equal protection analysis mandated by our most recent decisions.

The Fifth Amendment right to a grand jury does not apply to a state prosecution. Hurtado v. California, 110 U.S. 516 (1884). A state defendant cannot complain if the State foregoes the institution of the grand jury and proceeds against him instead through prosecutorial information, as many States prefer to do. See Gerstein v. Pugh, 420 U.S. 103, 116–119 (1975). Nevertheless, if a State chooses to proceed by grand jury it must proceed within the constraints imposed by the Equal Protection Clause of the Fourteenth Amendment. Thus in a line of cases beginning with Strauder v. West Virginia, 100 U.S. 303 (1880), this Court has held that a criminal defendant is denied equal protection of the law if, as a result of *purposeful* discrimination, members of his own race are excluded from jury service. See, e.g., Alexander v. Louisiana, 405 U.S. 625, 6248–629 (1972); Carter v. Jury Comm'n, 396 U.S. 320, 335–337, 339 (1970); Cassell v. Texas, 339 U.S. 282, 287 (1950); Akins v. Texas, 325 U.S. 398, 403–404 (1945). As the Court points out, this right is applicable where purposeful discrimination results only in substantial rather than total exclusion of members of the defendant's class, see, e.g., Turner v. Fouche, 396 U.S. 346 (1970).

But a state defendant has no right to a

grand jury that reflects a fair cross-section of the community.² The right to a "representative" grand jury is a federal right that derives not from the requirement of equal protection but from the Fifth Amendment's explicit requirement of a grand jury. That right is similar to the right—applicable to state proceedings—to a representative petit jury under the Sixth Amendment. See Taylor v. Louisiana, 419 U.S. 522 (1975). To the extent that the Fifth and Sixth Amendments are applicable, a defendant need only show that the jury selection procedure "systematically exclude[s] distinctive groups in the community and thereby fail[s] to be reasonably representative thereof." Id., at 538. But in a state case in which the challenge is to the grand jury, only the Fourteenth Amendment applies, and the defendant has the burden of proving a violation of the Equal Protection Clause.

Proof of discriminatory intent in such a case was explicitly mandated in our recent decisions in Washington v. Davis, 426 U.S. 229 (1976), and Arlington Heights v. Metropolitan Housing Development Corp., [429 U.S. 252] (1977). In Arlington Heights we said:

"Our decision last Term in Washington v. Davis, 426 U.S. 229 (1976), made it clear that official action will not be held unconstitutional solely because it results in a racially disproportionate impact. 'Disproportionate impact is not irrelevant, but it is not the sole touchstone of an invidious racial discrimination.' Id., at 242. Proof of racially discriminatory intent or purpose is required to show a violation of the Equal Protection Clause...." [429 U.S., at 560].

We also identified the following standards for resolving issues of discriminatory intent or purpose:

"Determining whether invidious discriminatory purpose was a motivating factor demands a sensitive inquiry into such circumstantial and direct evidence of intent as may be available. The impact of the official action—whether it "bears more heavily on one race than another," Washington v. Davis, 426 U.S., at 242—may provide an important starting point. Sometimes a clear pattern, unexplainable on grounds other than race, emerges from the effect of the state action even when the governing legislation appears neutral on its face. Yick Wo v. Hopkins, 118 U.S. 356 (1886); Guinn v. United States, 238 U.S. 347 (1915); Lane v. Wilson, 307 U.S. 268 (1939); Gomillion v. Lightfoot, 364 U.S. 339 (1960). The evidentiary inquiry is then relatively easy. But such cases are rare. Absent a pattern as stark as that in Gomillion or Yick Wo, impact alone is not determinative, and the Court must look to other evidence." [429 U.S., at 261] (footnotes omitted).

The analysis is essentially the same where the alleged discrimination is in the selection of a state grand jury.

* * *

Considered together, [our cases] make clear that statistical evidence showing under-representation of a population group on the grand jury lists should be considered in light of "such [other] circumstantial and direct evidence of intent as may be available." Arlington Heights, [97 S. Ct., at 564].

In this case, the following critical facts are beyond dispute: the judge who appointed the jury commissioners and later presided over respondent's trial was Mexican-American; three of the five jury commissioners were Mexican-American; 10 of the 20 members of the grand jury array were Mexican-American; five of the 12 grand jurors who returned the indictment, including the foreman, were Mexican-American, and seven of the 12 petit jurors who returned the verdict of guilt were Mexican-American. In the year in which respondent was indicted, 52.5% of the persons on the grand jury list were Mexican-American. In addition, a majority of the elected officials in Hidalgo County were Mexican-American, as were a majority of

---

²It may be that nondiscriminatory methods of selection will, over time, result in a representative grand jury. See Carter v. Jury Comm'n, 396 U.S., at 330 [1970]. But the Fourteenth Amendment does not mandate that result. Nothing would prevent a State for example, from seeking to assure informed decisionmaking by requiring that all grand jurors be lawyers familiar with the criminal law; and if that requirement should result in substantial under-representation on grand juries of some segments of the community in some areas of the State, the Fourteenth Amendment would not render the selection process unconstitutional.

the judges. That these positions of power and influence were so held is not surprising in a community where 80% of the population is Mexican-American. As was emphasized by District Judge Garza, the able Mexican-American jurist who presided over the habeas proceedings in the District Court, this case *is* unique. Every other jury discrimination case reaching this Court has involved a situation where the governing majority, and the resulting power over the jury selection process, was held by a white electorate and white officials.

The most significant fact in this case, all but ignored in the Court's opinion, is that a majority of the jury commissioners were Mexican-American. The jury commission is the body vested by Texas law with the authority to select grand jurors. Under the Texas selection system, as noted by the Court, ... the jury commission has the opportunity to identify in advance those potential jurors who have Spanish surnames. In these circumstances, where Mexican-Americans control both the selection of jurors and the political process, rational inferences from the most basic facts in a democratic society render improbable respondent's claim of an intent to discriminate against him and other Mexican-Americans. As Judge Garza observed, "If people in charge can choose whom they want, it is unlikely they will discriminate against themselves." 384 F. Supp. 79, 90.

That individuals are more likely to discriminate in favor of, than against, those who share their own identifiable attributes is the premise that underlies the cases recognizing that the criminal defendant has a personal right under the Fourteenth Amendment not to have members of his own class excluded from jury service. . . .

* * *

With all respect, I am compelled to say that the Court today has "lightly" concluded that the grand jury commissioners of this county have disregarded not only their sworn duty but also their likely inclination to assure fairness to Mexican-Americans.

* * *

There is for me a sense of unreality when Justices here in Washington decide solely on the basis of inferences from statistics that the Mexican-Americans who control the levers of power in this remote border county are manipulating them to discriminate "against themselves." In contrast, the judges on the scene, the state judge who appointed the jury commissioners and presided over the respondent's trial and the United States District Judge—both Mexican-Americans and familiar with the community—perceived no basis for respondent's claim of invidious discrimination.

It seems to me that the Court today, in rejecting the District Court's finding that no such discrimination took place, has erred grievously. I would reinstate the judgment of the District Court.

TABLE 6.1 Double Jeopardy Cases Decided by the Supreme Court: 1976–1977 Term

Case	Holding	Vote	Dissenting Opinions
United States v. Sanford, 429 U.S. 14 (1976) (per curiam)	When jury trial ended in hung jury and district court declared a mistrial, government appeal under 18 U.S.C. §3731 permitted following court's dismissal of indictment; government not barred by Double Jeopardy Clause from retrying defendants.	7–2	Brennan, Marshall (would set the case for oral argument)
United States v. Morrison, 429 U.S. 1 (1976) (per curiam); *United States v. Rose*, 429 U.S. 5 (1976) (per curiam)	When district court found the defendant guilty following a bench trial, but prior to sentencing ordered certain evidence suppressed, a governmental appeal under 18 U.S.C. §3731 challenging the suppression order is permitted and is not barred by the Double Jeopardy Clause.	9–0	—
United States v. Kopp, 429 U.S. 121 (1976) (per curiam)	Government appeal under 18 U.S.C. §3731 permitted when defendant was found guilty following bench trial and trial court dismissed the indictment.	9–0	—
Abney v. United States 431 U.S. 615 (1977)	A defendant may seek immediate appellate review of a district court's denial of motion to dismiss indictment on double jeopardy grounds.	9–0	—
Lee v. United States, 97 S. Ct. 2141 (1977)	Double Jeopardy Clause is not violated by the retrial of a defendant whose first trial ended when a district court granted, after jeopardy had attached, his motion to dismiss because of a defective indictment.	8–1	Marshall

Case	Holding	Vote	Dissenters
Jeffers v. United States, 432 U.S. ___ (1977)	Defendant's demand for separate trials on two indictments waived his rights under the Double Jeopardy Clause to be protected from successive prosecutions on lesser and greater offenses.	5–4	Stevens, Brennan, Stewart, Marshall
Brown v. Ohio, 432 U.S. ___ (1977)	The Double Jeopardy Clause prohibits a prosecution for a greater offense following a conviction for a lesser included one.	6–3	Burger, Blackmun, Rehnquist
United States v. Dieter, 429 U.S. 6 (1976) (per curiam)	The 30-day limitation period for a governmental appeal (18 U.S.C. §3731) from an order dismissing an indictment runs from the denial in the district court of a timely petition for rehearing.	9–0	—
United States v. Martin Linen Supply Co., 430 U.S. 564 (1977)	Double Jeopardy Clause bars appeal by the government following a judgment of acquittal under Fed. R. Crim. P. 29(c) after the jury has been discharged because it could not reach a verdict.	8–1	Burger
Harris v. Oklahoma, 433 U.S. ___ (1977) (per curiam)	The Double Jeopardy Clause bars prosecution for a lesser included offense after conviction for the greater one.	9–0	—
Finch v. United States, 431 U.S. 407 (1977) (per curiam)	Governmental appeal under 18 U.S.C. §3731 not permitted when district court dismissed bill of information based on stipulated facts after jeopardy had attached, even though no formal finding of guilt or innocence had been entered.	7–2	Rehnquist, Burger

*The Criminal Appeals Act, 18 U.S.C. §3731 (1970), provides in part: "In a criminal case an appeal by the United States shall lie to a court of appeals from a decision, judgment, or order of a district court dismissing an indictment or information as to any one or more counts, except that no appeal shall lie where the double jeopardy clause of the United States Constitution prohibits further prosecution."

7

SIXTH AMENDMENT PROBLEMS: THE RIGHT TO COUNSEL, JURY TRIALS, SPEEDY TRIALS, THE CONFRONTATION CLAUSE, DEFENSE WITNESSES, AND PUBLIC TRIALS

7.02 THE RIGHT TO COUNSEL

Informers and the Effective Assistance of Counsel

ORAL ARGUMENTS BEFORE THE
U.S. SUPREME COURT*

Weatherford v. Bursey, No. 75-1510; argued 12/12/76

The turbulence of the 1960's has disappeared, but litigation spawned by student protests and police surveillance of Vietnam-era dissidents still surfaces from time to time. In a case arising from one war protest, South Carolina recently asked the Court to overturn a Fourth Circuit holding that an undercover agent's intrusion, however inadvertent, into a state defendant's relationship with his attorney violated the Sixth Amendment and gave rise to a 42 U.S.C. § 1983 action.

J. C. Coleman, Deputy Attorney General of South Carolina, began his argument by noting that the events which gave rise to this § 1983 suit occurred near the end of several years of student dissension on this country's campuses. Jack M. Weatherford, a South Carolina Law Enforcement Division undercover agent, met Bursey, a student activist, at the University of South Carolina. They developed a close relationship and, in fact,

---

*From 20 Crim. L. Rptr. 4111–4113. Reprinted by permission from the Bureau of National Affairs, Inc.

Weatherford later married a friend of Bursey's wife.

On March 19, 1970, Bursey and Weatherford were both arrested for malicious destruction of property during a late night raid at the Richland County (South Carolina) Selective Service Board. Early the next morning Weatherford advised SLED agents of the raid on the Selective Service Board. Both Bursey and Weatherford were arrested, booked and charged with malicious destruction of property. Weatherford's arrest was a "sham"; SLED was not yet ready to "blow Weatherford's cover" by disclosing his identity as a state agent. State Solicitor Foard surreptitiously arranged for a local attorney to "pose" as Weatherford's lawyer. Bursey was represented by another attorney.

Protecting His Cover

Mr. Justice Stewart: "Is the Solicitor a state or county official?"

Coleman explained that a solicitor represents several counties. He again stressed that the arrangement with the local attorney was merely to protect Weatherford's cover. At any rate, both Bursey and Weatherford were released and returned to their "normal lives." On two occasions, Weatherford met with Bursey and his attorney to discuss the upcoming trial.

Mr. Justice Stewart: "Bursey was then out on bail pending trial?"

"Yes, sir."

Mr. Justice Stewart: "Was Weatherford also 'purportedly' out on bail?"

"Yes, sir."

At no time did Weatherford seek these meetings; he engaged in the discussions at Bursey's invitation merely to protect his cover. On neither occasion did Weatherford solicit information or pass on information about the discussion to either co-petitioner Chief Strom or any other SLED agent. However, Weatherford intimated at one of these meetings, which took place during a social gathering, that he would not testify for or against Bursey.

Not until the morning of their trial, did Bursey learn Weatherford's true identity. At trial, Solicitor Foard called Weatherford as a prosecution witness.

There is no basis for the Fourth Circuit's holding that the mere presence of Weatherford at the attorney-client discussions constituted a violation of the Sixth Amendment, counsel argued. His presence at these meetings was necessitated by the state's interest in maintaining his cover. He could not shrug off Bursey's invitations without undermining that cover.

The state disagrees with the Fourth Circuit's observation that *Black* v. *U.S.*, 385 U.S. 26 (1966), and *O'Brien* v. *U.S.*, 386 U.S. 345 (1967), establish support for a per se rule, that the attorney-client relationship is violated by a nondeliberate intrusion, counsel noted.

Black and *O'Brien* require that the fact of an intrusion mandates a full examination into the question whether the state has denied a defendant effective assistance of counsel. "We submit further that the facts in *O'Brien* and *Black* are so different from those here as to render them inapplicable." In *Black* and *O'Brien*, the intrusion into the attorney-client relationship was deliberate, Coleman maintained.

In response to questioning from Mr. Justice Marshall, counsel again stressed that Weatherford's intrusion was not deliberate, but was necessary to maintain his cover—a legitimate state interest.

Mr. Justice Marshall: "And that [protecting Weatherford's cover] was sufficient to override a federal constitutional right?"

This inadvertent intrusion did not amount to a Sixth Amendment violation in light of the state's interest.

But Mr. Justice Marshall suggested that there might have been other ways to protect Weatherford's cover without intruding on the attorney-client relationship. Weatherford could have picked a "fight with Bursey and told Bursey that he didn't want to talk with him."

Mr. Justice Marshall: "He [Weatherford] is not the only agent they have in South Carolina, right?"

"No, your honor." But Weatherford was the only SLED agent at the University of South Carolina.

Mr Justice Marshall: "You admit that it [the intrusion] was wrong?"

"I admit only that I wouldn't have done it."

Mr. Justice Marshall: "Was it [the intrusion] immoral, . . . dirty pool?"

Counsel thought not under these circumstances. However unfortunate, the intrusion was necessary. But "it wasn't a deliberate effort. . . ."

The Chief Justice asked whether Bursey had challenged his state court conviction.

Bursey who fled the state soon after his conviction took no appeal, Coleman answered.

Mr Justice Stewart: "But he did come back and serve his sentence?"

"Yes, sir."

Liability of Chief

The Fourth Circuit erred in holding Chief Strom liable to Bursey under the respondeat superior doctrine, counsel maintained. The district court's judgment that Strom played no part in the intrusion should not have been disturbed. The Fourth Circuit ties Strom's liability to his decisions to maintain Weatherford's cover, to allow Solicitor Foard to work out the details for protecting Weatherford's cover, and to allow Weatherford to testify. But these decisions simply do not lead to the conclusion that he approved Weatherford's intrusions.

Andrew L. Frey, Deputy U.S. Solicitor General, joined in the state's request that the Court overturn the Fourth Circuit holding. Appearing as amicus curiae, he pointed out that the government's position is based on the district court's finding of fact.

The district court, Frey explained, concluded that the state expected to make out its case without Weatherford's testimony; that Weatherford's role in the attorney-client meeting was limited, and that Weatherford conveyed no information learned during the "intrusions" to the prosecution. The Fourth Circuit accepted all these facts, but merely provided a different legal analysis, Frey stated.

Mr. Justice White: "When does a Sixth Amendment violation occur?"

Not until the fruits of the violation are utilized, Frey answered.

Frey further argued that *Black* and *O'Brien* do not support the Fourth Circuit's per se rule. The Fourth Circuit also should have distinguished between an agent's intrusion and prosecutorial intrusion and went too far in adopting a prophylactic rule that all "intrusions" into the attorney-client relationship violate the Sixth Amendment. The Sixth Amendment prohibits deliberate intrusions or governmental action directed at learning defense strategy. But that was not Weatherford's aim—he only wanted to maintain his cover. A broad-based per se rule serves no useful societal purposes here.

Mr. Justice White asked whether the state could have asked Weatherford to testify about information he learned that bore on Bursey's guilt or innocence.

Such testimony would probably be inadmissible, Frey said.

When the prosecution acquires defense strategy, the remedy is to order a new trial. On the other hand, where information learned during an intrusion does not reach the prosecution, there should be an inquiry as to prejudice. That should have been followed here.

Preventive Measure

Laughlin McDonald, of Atlanta, told the Court that the state could have warded off this suit by ending Weatherford's assignment as a SLED agent immediately after the Selective Service arrests.

Chief Strom conceded at the federal trial that he was "unconcerned about Weatherford's cover [after the arrests]." By that time, Weatherford's effectiveness had ended, counsel added. At trial, Strom testified that Weatherford's cover was not needed for anything he was working on at the University. Furthermore, Strom conceded that "what happened here was unethical and unconstitutional," McDonald said.

The Chief Justice: "How did the testimony of Weatherford cause actionable damage?"

There was an interference with Bursey's Sixth Amendment rights.

The Chief Justice: "To what did Weatherford testify?"

He testified about the Selective Service Board incident. Counsel also pointed out that Weatherford's testimony took the defense by surprise in light of his earlier intimation that he would not testify at all.

Mr. Justice Stevens: "I have trouble with your surprise theory. What difference would it have made if you had known [of his expected testimony] earlier?"

Counsel thought defense strategies could have been better planned.

In response to a question from Mr. Justice Marshall, McDonald stressed that the question whether an informer's identity must be disclosed before trial is not involved here.

Mr. Justice Marshall: "Did he set up any of the meetings?"

"No, sir."

McDonald also urged the Court not to upset the Fourth Circuit's holding with respect to Strom's liability. Weatherford was hired by Strom to infiltrate university groups. For the purposes of § 1983, Strom must be held responsible for the reasonably foreseeable consequences of Weatherford's actions. The Chief knew that Weatherford was continuing his investigation of Bursey and that a sham attorney had been appointed. It is difficult to believe that Strom did not know that Weatherford was participating in defense meetings, McDonald asserted.

Mr. Justice Marshall: "What evidence do you have in the record that the Chief did not tell the truth [about his knowledge of Weatherford's meetings with the defense]?"

The continuous contacts between the Chief and Weatherford lead to the conclusion that he knew of the meetings

Mr. Justice Marshall: "Is there any testimony from Weatherford that he talked to the Chief about this?"

"No, sir."

Mr. Justice Stevens asked if it was crucial to the respondent that some use was made of information gained from the meetings.

Counsel did not think so.

Mr. Justice Stevens: "What triggers the Sixth Amendment violation?"

"We think that a defendant has a right not to have an agent sit in on counsel meetings."

Mr. Justice Stevens: "Even if the defendant asks him to sit in?"

"Yes, sir. Weatherford was there because of his assignment."

Mr. Justice Powell: "In your brief, you say the prosecution was able to discover the defense strategy."

"Yes, sir."

Mr. Justice Stevens: "What was the defense strategy?"

The strategy was to put the state to its proof.

WEATHERFORD v. BURSEY

Supreme Court of the United States, 1977
429 U.S. 545, 97 S. Ct. 837, 51 L. Ed. 2d 30

In 1970, Brett Bursey (respondent), a student activist, and Jack Weatherford (petitioner), an undercover agent, were arrested for vandalizing a county selective service office in Columbia, South Carolina, a state criminal offense. Thereafter each retained separate counsel. At Bursey's invitation, Weatherford attended two pretrial meetings between Bursey and his counsel, Wise, at which the defense strategy for the upcoming trial was discussed. Weatherford did not discuss Bursey's trial strategy or the pending criminal action with either his superiors or the prosecution. After telling Bursey that he would not be a prosecution witness, Weatherford did, in fact, testify for the prosecution, which on the morning of the trial decided to call him as a witness because he had lost his effectiveness as an undercover agent. Bursey was convicted and served an 18-month sentence. Thereafter, he brought an action against Weatherford and Strom, the head of the South Carolina State Law Enforcement Division, under 42 U.S.C. § 1983, alleging that Weatherford's participation in the two defense meetings had deprived him of the effective assistance of counsel as well as the right to a fair trial guaranteed by the Due Process Clause of the Fourteenth Amendment. The district court found for Weatherford and Strom in all respects, but the Court of Appeals (4th Cir.) reversed, holding that "whenever the prosecution knowingly arranges and permits intrusion into the attorney-client relationship," a new trial is required. The court further held that Bursey had been denied a fair trial under *Brady* v. *Maryland*, 373 U.S. 83 (1963), because Weatherford's statement that he would not be a prosecution witness had lulled Bursey into a false sense of security and interfered with his preparations for trial. The United States Supreme Court granted certiorari.

Mr. Justice WHITE delivered the opinion of the Court.

The issue here is whether in the circumstances present in this case the conduct of an undercover agent for a state law enforcement agency deprived respondent Bursey of his right to the effective assistance of counsel guaranteed him by the Sixth and Fourteenth Amendments of the United States Constitution or deprived him of due process of law in violation of the Fourteenth Amendment.

* * *

The exact contours of the Court of Appeals' per se right-to-counsel rule are difficult to discern; but as the Court of Appeals applied the rule in this case, it would appear that if an undercover agent meets with a criminal defendant who is awaiting trial and the defense's trial strategy is discussed without the agent revealing his identity, a violation of the defendant's constitutional rights has occurred, whatever was the purpose of the agent in attending the meeting, whether or not he reported on the meeting to his superiors, and whether or not any specific prejudice to the defendant's preparation for or conduct of the trial is demonstrated or otherwise threatened. The Court of Appeals was of the view . . . that this Court "establish[ed] such a per se rule" in Black v. United States, 385 U.S. 26 (1966), and O'Brien v. United States, 386 U.S. 345 (1967). The Court of Appeals also relied on Hoffa v. United States, 385 U.S. 293 (1966).

We cannot agree that these cases, individually or together, either require or suggest the rule announced by the Court of Appeals and now urged by Bursey. Both Black and O'Brien involved surreptitious electronic surveillance by the Government, which was discovered after trial and conviction and which was plainly illegal under the Fourth Amendment. In each case, some, but not all, of the conversations overheard were between the criminal defendant and his counsel during trial preparation. The conviction in each case was set aside and a new trial ordered. The explanatory per curiam in Black, although referring to the overheard conversations with counsel, did not rule that whenever conversations with counsel are overheard the Sixth Amendment is violated and a new trial must be had. Indeed, neither the Sixth Amendment nor the right to counsel was even mentioned in the short opinion. . . . In O'Brien, the Court wrote nothing further, merely citing Black per curiam. . . .

It is difficult to believe that the Court in Black and O'Brien was evolving a definitive construction of the Sixth Amendment without identifying the amendment it was interpreting, especially in view of the well-established Fourth Amendment grounds for excluding the fruits of the illegal surveillance. If anything is to be inferred from these two cases with respect to the right to counsel, it is that when conversations with counsel have been overheard, the constitutionality of the conviction depends on whether the overheard conversations have produced, directly or indirectly, any of the evidence offered at trial. This is a far cry from the per se rule announced by the Court of Appeals below, for under that rule trial prejudice to the defendant is deemed irrelevant. Here, the courts below have already conducted the "judicial determination," lacking in Black and O'Brien, of the effect of the overheard conversations on the defendant's conviction, and there is nothing in their findings nor in the record to indicate any "use of evidence that might otherwise be inadmissible."

Neither does the Court's decision in Hoffa v. United States, supra, support the proposition urged by respondents. There, an informer sat in on conversations that defendant Hoffa had with his lawyers and with others during the course of Hoffa's trial on a charge of violating the Taft-Hartley Act. The jury at that trial hung. Hoffa was then tried for tampering with that jury. The informer testified at the latter trial with respect to conversations he had overheard in Hoffa's hotel suite during the prior trial, not including, however, the conversations Hoffa had with counsel. Hoffa's jury tampering conviction was sustained over his claim, among others, that his Sixth Amendment counsel right had been violated.

In doing so, the Court did not hold that the Sixth Amendment right to counsel subsumes a right to be free from intrusion by informers into counsel-client consultations. Nor did it purport to describe the contours of any such right. The Court merely *assumed*, without deciding, that two cases in the Court of Appeals for the District of Columbia dealing with the right to counsel, Caldwell v. United

States, 92 U.S. App. D.C. 355, 205 F.2d 879 (1953), and Coplon v. United States, 89 U.S. App. D.C. 103, 191 F.2d 749 (1951), were correctly decided; *assumed* without deciding, that had Hoffa been convicted at his first trial, the conviction would have been set aside because the informer had overheard Hoffa and his lawyers conversing and had reported to the authorities the substance of at least some of those conversations; and then held that Hoffa's *assumed* Sixth Amendment rights had not been violated because the informer's testimony at the jury tampering trial did not touch upon the overheard conversations with counsel but dealt only with conversations between Hoffa and third parties when his lawyers were not present. 385 U.S., at 307-308. Neither Black, O'Brien, Hoffa, nor any other case in this Court to which we have been cited furnishes grounds for the interpretation and application of the Sixth and Fourteenth Amendments appearing in the Court of Appeals' opinion and judgment.

At the same time, we need not agree with petitioners that whenever a defendant converses with his counsel in the presence of a third party thought to be a confederate and ally, the defendant assumes the risk and cannot complain if the third party turns out to be an informer for the Government who has reported on the conversations to the prosecution and who testifies about them at the defendant's trial. Had Weatherford testified at Bursey's trial as to the conversations between Bursey and Wise; had any of the Government's evidence originated in these conversations; had those overheard conversations been used in any other way to the substantial detriment of Bursey; or even had the prosecution learned from Weatherford, an undercover agent, the details of the Bursey-Wise conversations about trial preparations, Bursey would have a much stronger case.

None of these elements is present here, however. Weatherford's testimony for the prosecution about the events of April 1970 revealed nothing said or done at the meetings between Bursey and Wise that he attended. None of the Government's evidence was obtained as a consequence of Weatherford's participation in those meetings. . . .

. . . If the fact was as found by the District Court, that Weatherford communicated nothing about the two meetings to anyone else, we are quite unconvinced that a constitutional claim under the Sixth and Fourteenth Amendments was made out.

. . . As long as the information possessed by Weatherford remained uncommunicated, he posed no substantial threat to Bursey's Sixth Amendment rights. Nor do we believe that federal or state prosecutors will be so prone to lie or the difficulties of proof so great that we must always assume not only that an informant communicates what he learns from an encounter with the defendant and his counsel but also that what he communicates has the potential for detriment to the defendant or benefit to the prosecutor's case.

Moreover, this is not a situation where the State's purpose was to learn what it could about the defendant's defense plans and the informant was instructed to intrude on the lawyer-client relationship or where the informant has assumed for himself that task and acted accordingly. . . . Weatherford went, not to spy, but because he was asked and because the State was interested in retaining his undercover services on other matters and it was therefore necessary to avoid raising the suspicion that he was in fact the informant whose existence Bursey and Wise already suspected.

That the per se rule adopted by the Court of Appeals would operate prophylactically and effectively is very likely true; but it would require the informant to refuse to participate in attorney-client meetings, even though invited, and thus for all practical purposes to unmask himself. Our cases, however, have recognized the unfortunate necessity of undercover work and the value it often is to effective law enforcement. E.g., United States v. Russell, 411 U.S. 423, 432 (1973); Lewis v. United States, 385 U.S. 206, 208-209 (1966). We have also recognized the desirability and legality of continued secrecy even after arrest. Roviaro v. United States, 353 U.S. 53, 59, 62 (1957). We have no general oversight authority with respect to state police investigations. We may disapprove an investigatory practice only if it violates the Constitution; and judged in this light, the Court of Appeals' per se rule cuts much too broadly. . . . [U]nless Weatherford communicated the substance of the Bursey-Wise conversations and thereby created at least a realistic possibility of injury to Bursey or benefit to the Government, there can be no Sixth Amendment violation. Yet under the Court of Appeals' rule, Bursey's conviction would have been set aside on appeal.

There being no tainted evidence in this case, no communication of defense strategy to the prosecution, and no purposeful intrusion by Weatherford, there was no violation of the Sixth Amendment insofar as it is applicable to the States by virtue of the Fourteenth Amendment. The proof in this case thus fell short of making out a § 1983 claim....

It is also apparent that neither Weatherford's trial testimony nor the fact of his testifying added anything to the Sixth Amendment claim. Weatherford's testimony for the prosecution related only to events prior to the meetings with Wise and Bursey and referred to nothing that was said at those meetings. There is no indication that any of this testimony was prompted by or was the product of those meetings. Weatherford's testimony was surely very damaging, but the mere fact that he had met with Bursey and his lawyer prior to trial did not violate Bursey's right to counsel....

Because under Brady v. Maryland, supra, the prosecution has the "duty under the due process clause to insure that 'criminal trials are fair' by disclosing evidence favorable to the defendant upon request," the Court of Appeals also held that the State was constitutionally forbidden to "conceal the identity of an informant from a defendant during his trial preparation," to permit the informant to "deny up through the day before his appearance at trial that he will testify against the defendant," and then to have the informant "testify with devastating effect." 528 F.2d. at 487. This conduct, the Court of Appeals thought, lulled the defendant into a false sense of security and denied him "the opportunity (1) to consider whether plea bargaining might be the best course, (2) to do a background check on Weatherford for purposes of cross-examination, and (3) to attempt to counter the devastating impact of eyewitness identity." Ibid. The Court of Appeals apparently would have arrived at this conclusion whether or not Weatherford had ever met with Wise.

Again we are in disagreement. Brady does not warrant the Court of Appeals' holding. It does not follow from the prohibition against concealing evidence favorable to the accused that the prosecution must reveal before trial the names of all witnesses who will testify unfavorably. There is no general constitutional right to discovery in a criminal case, and Brady did not create one; as the Court wrote recently, "the Due Process Clause has little to say regarding the amount of discovery which the parties must be afforded...." Wardius v. Oregon, 412 U.S. 470, 474 (1973). Brady is not implicated here where the only claim is that the government should have revealed that it would present the eyewitness testimony of a particular agent against the defendant at trial.

In terms of the defendant's right to a fair trial, the situation is not changed materially by the additional element relied upon by the Court of Appeals, namely, that Weatherford not only concealed his identity but represented he would not be a witness for the prosecution, an assertion that proved to be inaccurate. There are several answers to the contention that the claim of misrepresentation is of crucial importance. The first is that there was no deliberate misrepresentation in this regard: the trial court found that until the day of trial Weatherford did not expect to be called as a witness; until then he did not know that he would testify. Second, as we understand the argument, it is that once the undercover agent has successfully caused an arrest, he risks causing an unfair trial if he denies his identity when accused or asked. We would hesitate so to construe the Due Process Clause. We are not at all convinced that there is a constitutional difference between the situation where the informer is sufficiently trusted that he is never suspected and never asked about the possibility of his testifying but nevertheless surprises the defendant by giving devastating testimony, and the situation we have here, where the defendant is suspicious enough to ask and the informer denies that he will testify but nevertheless does so. Moreover, if the informer must confess his identity when confronted by an arrested defendant, in many cases the agent in order to protect himself will simply disappear pending trial, before the confrontation occurs. In the last analysis, however, the undercover agent who stays in place and continues his deception merely retains the capacity to surprise; and unless the surprise witness or unexpected evidence is without more a denial of constitutional rights, Bursey was not denied a fair trial.

The Court of Appeals suggested that Weatherford's continued duplicity lost Bursey the opportunity to plea bargain. But there is no constitutional right to plea bargain; the prosecutor need not do so if he prefers to go to trial. It is a novel argument that constitutional rights are infringed by trying the defendant rather than accepting his plea of guilty. Moreover, Wise could have approached the prosecutor before trial and surely was under no misapprehension about Bursey's plight during trial. It was also suggested by the Court of Appeals that Bursey was deprived of the opportunity to investigate Weatherford in preparation for possible impeachment on cross-examination. But there was no objection at trial to Weatherford's testimony, no request for a continuance, and even now no indication of substantial prejudice from this occurrence. As for Bursey's claimed disability to counter Weatherford's "devastating" testimony, the disadvantage was no more than exists in any case where the Government presents very damaging evidence that was not anticipated. Wise and Bursey must have realized that in going to trial the Government was sufficiently confident of conviction and that if there were any exculpatory evidence or possible defenses it would be extremely wise to have them available. Prudence would have counseled at least as much.

The judgment of the Court of Appeals is Reversed.

[Mr. Justice MARSHALL, joined by Mr. Justice BRENNAN, dissented.]

Part Three

JUVENILE JUSTICE, LEGAL RIGHTS OF THE CONVICTED FELON, THE CIVIL RIGHTS ACT OF 1964, AND THE CONSTITUTIONAL RIGHTS OF LAW ENFORCEMENT AUTHORITIES

9
LEGAL RIGHTS OF CONVICTED FELONS

9.05 OTHER DECISIONS OF INTEREST: LEGAL RIGHTS OF CONVICTED FELONS— 1976–1977 TERM OF COURT

During the 1976–1977 Term, the Supreme Court decided a number of cases involving the constitutional rights of inmates, including *Estelle* v. *Gamble,* 429 U.S. 97 (1976) (medical malpractice in prisons), *Bounds* v. *Smith,* 430 U.S. 817 (1977) (prison law libraries), and *Jones* v. *North Carolina Prisoners' Union, Inc.,* 433 U.S. 119 (1977) (inmate unions). These cases are found in Chapter Nine, § 9.03, of the principal text.

Parole Hearings and Due Process

In *Scott* v. *Kentucky Parole Board,* 429 U.S. 60 (1976), the Supreme Court granted certiorari to decide whether any constitutionally mandated procedural safeguards apply to parole release proceedings On July 26, 1974, the petitioner, Ewell Scott, filed a complaint in federal district court contending that the Kentucky Parole Board had denied him parole, and that by doing so, it had denied him liberty without due process because no procedural safeguards had attended the parole proceeding. The district court dismissed the complaint, and the Court of Appeals (6th Cir.) affirmed. On November 26, 1975, shortly before the Supreme Court granted certiorari, the petitioner was paroled. In a 6–3 per curiam order, and without reaching the merits, the Supreme Court vacated the case and remanded it to the court of appeals "for consideration of the question of mootness." Mr. Justice Stevens, joined by Justices Brennan and Powell, dissented, stating that (1) the case should be decided because of the conflict in the circuits on the question presented—compare *Brown* v. *Lundgren,* 528 F.2d 1050 (5th Cir. 1976) (due process guarantees do not apply), with *United States ex rel. Richerson* v. *Wolff,* 525 F.2d 797 (7th Cir. 1975) (written statement of reasons must be given for denial of parole); (2) the petitioner is under "close parole supervision," which "imposes a significant restraint on his liberty"; and (3) the issue is "capable of repetition yet review is repeatedly denied"—the most common exception to the mootness doctrine.

Parole Revocation Hearings

In *Moody* v. *Daggett,* 429 U.S. 78 (1976), the Supreme Court granted certiorari to decide "whether a federal parolee imprisoned for a crime committed while on parole is constitutionally entitled to a prompt parole revocation hearing when a parole violator warrant is issued and lodged with the institution of his confinement but not served on him." In 1962, Minor Moody, the petitioner, was convicted in federal court of committing rape on a government reservation. He received a 10-year sentence but was paroled in 1966. While on parole, he shot and killed two persons on an Indian reservation. He pleaded guilty and was convicted of manslaughter and second-degree murder and received concurrent 10-year sentences for the two offenses. In committing these crimes, Moody violated the terms of his 1966 parole. Following his reimprisonment the United States Board of Parole issued, but did not execute, a parole violator warrant which was lodged with prison officials as a detainer (a writ or instrument authorizing the continued detention of a prisoner). Moody requested the board to execute the warrant immediately so that any term of imprisonment imposed for violation of his 1966 parole could run concurrently with his 1971 homicide sentences. The board refused to execute the warrant until petitioner had completed his current homicide sentence. Moody filed a federal habeas corpus action in January, 1975, seeking dismissal of the parole violator warrant on the ground that he had been denied a prompt hearing at which the parole revocation issues could have been resolved. The district court dismissed the petition, and the Court of Appeals (9th Cir.) affirmed.

The United States Supreme Court, in a 7-2 decision, affirmed. Writing for the Court, Chief Justice Burger held that

(1) There is no constitutional right to an immediate parole revocation hearing when a parole violator warrant has been issued but not executed.

(2) Petitioner's incarceration and loss of liberty resulted not from the parole violator warrant but from his convictions for crimes committed while on parole.

(3) Deferral of the parole revocation decision until execution of the warrant does not deny the petitioner the opportunity to serve any sentence imposed for parole violation concurrently with the sentences imposed for the crimes committed while on parole because the parole commission has the power to grant unconditional or conditional release upon completion of the sentences.

Mr. Justice Stevens, joined by Mr. Justice Brennan, wrote a dissenting opinion in which he stated, "If unlimited delay is permitted, the procedural safeguards which were fashioned in Morrissey [v. Brewer, 408 U.S. 471 (1972)] to assure the parolee a fair opportunity to present facts in mitigation and to challenge the government's assertions will have become meaningless."

10

THE CIVIL RIGHTS ACT OF 1964 AND THE CONSTITUTIONAL RIGHTS OF LAW ENFORCEMENT AUTHORITIES

10.04 OTHER DECISIONS OF INTEREST: THE CIVIL RIGHTS ACT AND THE CONSTITUTIONAL RIGHTS OF LAW ENFORCEMENT AUTHORITIES—1976–1977 TERM OF COURT

The 1976–1977 Term produced few opinions involving § 1983 actions under the Civil Rights Act relevant to the criminal process. The most significant decision in this area was *Dothard* v. *Rawlinson*, 433 U.S. 321 (1977) (prison guards' height and weight requirements and gender-based discrimination), which is presented in Chapter Ten, § 10.02, of the principal text.

§ 1983 Actions Involving Off-Duty Policemen

In *Belcher* v. *Stengel*, 429 U.S. 118 (1976), the Supreme Court granted certiorari to consider the previously undecided question of whether the fact that an off-duty, out-of-uniform police officer is required by police department regulations to carry a weapon at all times establishes that any use of that weapon against the person bringing suit or another is an act 'under color of law' within the meaning of 42 U.S.C. § 1983 even though the officer is engaged in purely private conduct at the time. This case grew out of a barroom affray in Columbus, Ohio, in which Raymond Belcher, an off-duty police officer, shot and killed two persons and injured a third. The injured victim and the relatives of the deceased victims brought an action against the petitioner in federal district court under 42 U.S.C. § 1983. A jury awarded them monetary damages, and the Court of Appeals (6th Cir.) affirmed. In a unanimous per curiam opinion, the Supreme Court dismissed the writ as improvidently granted because it was subsequently brought to light that "(1) the petitioner had been awarded Workmen's Compensation benefits for injuries that he received in the affray; (2) the petitioner, after the affray, had been granted official leave on account of injuries received 'in line of duty under circumstances relating to police duties'; (3) a Board of Inquiry convened to investigate the barroom episode had determined that the petitioner's 'actions were in the line of duty.'" Chief Justice Burger wrote a brief concurring opinion.

The Measure of Damages under § 1983 Actions

In *Jones* v. *Hildebrant,* 432 U.S. 183 (1977), the Supreme Court granted certiorari to decide the following question: "Where the black mother of a 15-year-old child who was intentionally shot and killed by a white policeman acting under the color of state law brings suit in a state court pursuant to 42 U.S.C. § 1983, what is the measure of damages? Particularly, can the state measure of damages cancel and displace an action brought pursuant to 42 U.S.C. § 1983"?

Respondent, Douglas Hildebrant, a Denver police officer, defended on the ground that he had used reasonable force in stopping a fleeing felon. The mother's lawsuit asserted three causes of action: (1) battery, (2) negligence, and (3) intentional deprivation of federal constitutional rights. The first two claims were based on the Colorado wrongful death statute, and the third on 42 U.S.C. § 1983 (1970). Although petitioner alleged damages of $1,500,000, she stipulated to a reduction of her prayer for relief on the first two claims because the Colorado wrongful death statute limited her recovery to $45,000. The trial judge ruled that her § 1983 claim was merged into the battery claim and dismissed the § 1983 action. The jury returned a damage award of $1,500. On appeal, the Colorado Supreme Court affirmed, 550 P.2d 339 (1976), and the United States Supreme Court granted certiorari. During oral arguments, counsel for petitioner asserted that the petitioner's sole claim of constitutional deprivation was based not on the pecuniary loss resulting from her son's wrongful death but rather on her constitutional right to raise her son without state interference.

In a 6–3 per curiam opinion, the Supreme Court dismissed the petition for certiorari as improvidently granted because (1) petitioner's claim of personal liberty was not set forth in the original complaint, (2) the claim was not included in the briefs to the Colorado Supreme Court, (3) the claim was only casually referred to in the opinion of the Colorado Supreme Court, and (4) the claim was not presented in the petition for certiorari to the United States Supreme Court or fairly subsumed in the question that was presented.

Mr. Justice White, joined by Justices Brennan and Marshall, wrote a dissenting opinion accusing the majority of being "hypertechnical" in dismissing the petition and stressing that the Court "is not bound by concessions of counsel in oral argument as to whether a legal issue is open in this Court."

Thus, the questions remain open whether an off-duty policeman can act "under color of law" for the purposes of § 1983 actions and whether such actions are separate and independent from any remedies afforded under state law. However, most federal courts of appeals permit survivor suits under § 1983.

Part Four

SPECIAL PROBLEMS IN THE ADMINISTRATION OF JUSTICE

13

GUILTY PLEAS AND THE PLEA BARGAINING PROCESS

13.01 INTRODUCTION

PLEA BARGAINING AND THE TRANSFORMATION OF THE CRIMINAL PROCESS*

The American criminal justice system has been transformed by plea bargaining. The traditional model of the criminal process provides for an impartial trier of fact to determine guilt after a formal adversarial trial and then for a judge to select a penalty appropriate for the offender from a range specified by the legislature. In practice, however, the locus of the criminal process has shifted largely from trial to plea bargaining. In the vast majority of cases, guilt and the applicable range of sentences are determined through informal negotiations between the prosecutor and the defense attorney. While it has been argued that plea bargaining burdens the defendant's constitutional right to a trial by imposing heavier sentences on those who are convicted after trial, the Supreme Court repeatedly has rejected this argument and upheld plea bargaining. The Court has accepted guilty pleas induced in part by prosecutorial concessions as long as the pleas are voluntarily and intelligently rendered upon the advice of reasonably competent defense counsel.

Plea bargaining has provoked almost universal criticism among commentators. Some have urged its abolition, while others, recognizing the inevitability of a low-cost bargaining system, have proposed reforms to ameliorate plea bargaining's deviations from the traditional model. Specifically, commentators have addressed such problems as the sentencing irrationalities of plea bargaining, the coercive impact of plea concessions upon the defendant, the need to regulate abuses of prosecutorial discretion, and the risk that innocent defendants will plead guilty. Commentators, however, generally have not recognized that, despite these defects, plea bargaining has several potential advantages, in addition to lower costs, over the traditional model—greater accuracy, reduction of sentencing disparities, and increased self-determination by the defendant, who is given more control over sentencing. In devising structural reforms of plea bargaining, then, it is essential not only to remedy the problems associated with plea bargaining, but also to build upon its theoretical advantages over the traditional model. . . .

1. BREAKDOWN OF THE TRADITIONAL MODEL

In the American criminal justice system, guilt traditionally is determined through a formal adversarial process in which the

---

*From Note, 90 Harv. L. Rev. 564–582 (1977). Copyright 1977 by the Harvard Law Review Association. Reprinted by permission. The references have been omitted.

prosecutor and the defense attorney have independent responsibilities for investigating the facts and for presenting arguments to an impartial trier of fact. To secure conviction, the state must prove the defendant guilty beyond a reasonable doubt, unless the defendant voluntarily and intelligently pleads guilty. The state must satisfy this burden solely on the basis of constitutionally admissible evidence. The defendant has the right to cross-examine the state's witnesses and to present witnesses and arguments on his own behalf. If the defendant is found guilty, the judge then fashions a punishment within bounds specified by the legislature.

This process reflects the American concern for protecting the individual from governmental oppression. The system compromises the simple, efficient enforcement of the substantive criminal laws to the perceived need to preserve individual autonomy. While the procedures of the traditional model reflect important value choices, they nevertheless have provoked significant criticism.

A. Criticisms of the Traditional Model

1. High Systems Costs. The first problem with the traditional model of the American criminal process is that it is over-proceduralized and, thus, expensive and time-consuming. Proving guilt beyond a reasonable doubt in a formal adversarial trial before a jury consumes valuable police, prosecutorial, and judicial resources. The large volume of criminal cases in metropolitan areas increases these burdens. Despite the fact that most defendants either plead guilty or waive their right to a jury trial, court dockets are clogged and trials delayed. This delay increases the burden of pretrial detention on those defendants unable to afford bail and exposes the public to the risk of additional criminal acts by those able to secure release pending trial. Finally, the substantial time gap between the criminal act and the imposition of punishment undermines, to some extent, the deterrent and rehabilitative functions of the sanction.

2. Inaccurate Guilt Determinations. Another criticism frequently directed at the traditional model is that its inaccuracy favors the defendant and that, as a result, it acquits at least some guilty persons. Of course, the beyond-a-reasonable-doubt standard is premised on the belief that it is necessary to minimize the risk of wrongful conviction. Moreover, the exclusion of evidence secured in violation of the defendant's fourth amendment rights reflects the belief that the public interest in deterring unlawful police conduct outweighs the importance of convicting individual defendants. While both the heavy presumption of innocence and the constitutional exclusionary rule promote significant public policies, they do so at the cost of acquitting some individuals who in fact committed the crimes with which they are charged.

Accuracy is further threatened by the adversary system itself and the privilege against self-incrimination at trial. Both are designed to protect the defendant's autonomy. They produce, however, a theory of justice which is often ill-suited to the accurate and efficient determination of guilt. While the prosecution has an obligation to ensure accurate determinations of guilt, no such obligation is placed upon the defense. The defendant may deny charges that he knows to be true and compel the prosecution to shoulder the entire burden of proof. Unlike the prosecution, the defense generally has no duty either to disclose evidence or to correct errors in the state's case. Indeed, the defense counsel is ethically obliged to advance his client's interests as far as the law will permit, even at the cost of truth. While these contrasting duties are designed to safeguard the innocent defendant from an unjust conviction, their effect is to create a systematic inaccuracy in favor of acquittal.

3. Unpredictability. In addition to producing occasionally inaccurate results, the traditional model suffers from unpredictability, both at trial and during sentencing. Due to a variety of factors—limited pretrial discovery, indeterminate questions of credibility, and the uncertainties of jury decisions—neither the prosecution nor the defense can be confident of the outcome of trial.

This problem is exacerbated at sentencing. Modern penological theory generally favors the individualization of punishment to fit the circumstances of the case and the rehabilitative needs of the particular offender. Accordingly, most criminal statutes grant the judge a wide and largely uncontrolled latitude of sentencing discretion. There are no uniform, determinate tests of rehabilitative potential. Moreover, judges are not required to articulate reasons to support their sentence decisions, and sentences falling within the statutory range normally are not subject to appellate review. As a result, judicial discretion in sentencing has led to broad and somewhat arbitrary variations in punishment.

The uncertainty of this process creates an unstable environment from the perspectives of both the prosecution and the defense. In addition, the seemingly random imposition of the criminal sanction undermines the predictability of punishment and the deterrence dependent on such predictability. Those defendants who are more severely punished become cynical, question the legitimacy of the sanction, and thus are less receptive to rehabilitation. For those who receive inordinately lenient sentences, the criminal justice system loses credibility and is less likely to deter them from future offenses. Both situations impair the effectiveness and moral legitimacy of the criminal sanction.

B. Outgrowth of Plea Bargaining

The problems identified with the traditional model have contributed to the breakdown of that system and to the growth of plea bargaining as an alternative criminal process. Plea bargaining is relied upon by prosecutors, and to some extent by defense attorneys, to correct certain perceived defects in the traditional model. But plea bargaining exacerbates other inadequacies of the traditional model and creates new problems of its own.

1..Cost Savings. The primary advantage of plea bargaining is that it reduces systemic costs by avoiding expensive trials. Plea bargaining enables courts to process cases more expeditiously than under the traditional model. This acceleration mitigates the hardships of pretrial detention, decreases the period in which those defendants who can afford bail may commit crimes while awaiting trial, and brings the sanction closer to the time that the criminal act itself was committed. In addition, since a guilty plea operates as a waiver of all nonjurisdictional objections, plea bargaining enhances the finality of criminal dispositions and thus conserves valuable appellate resources.

Although plea bargaining processes cases more quickly than the traditional model, it has not eliminated all unnecessary delays. Because prosecutors and defense attorneys have limited pretrial contact and because the imminence of trial is often needed to spur negotiations, plea bargains in many cases are not struck until shortly before the commencement of trial. In addition, delay frequently is used as a tactical weapon. For instance, prosecutors may postpone bargaining in order to wear down those defendants who are in jail pending trial. Similarly, those defense attorneys whose clients are out on bail might file motions and seek continuances to backlog dockets further, harass the prosecution, and thus secure better deals for their clients.

2. Guilt Determinations in Plea Bargaining. Prosecutors also use plea bargaining to convict many defendants who, although guilty in fact, would have been acquitted at trial. First, plea bargaining diminishes the impact of the fourth amendment exclusionary rule, since prosecutors frequently reduce charges in exchange for waivers of arguable constitutional objections. The policies behind the exclusionary rule thus are expressed in the forms of sentencing discounts in numerous uncertain cases rather than in total acquittal in only a few cases. This practice seems to preserve some element of deterrence to police misconduct while guaranteeing at least some degree of punishment for those who break the law.

In addition, plea bargaining replaces the beyond-a-reasonable-doubt standard with a more indeterminate standard based on the defense's assessment of both the likelihood of conviction and the value of the concessions offered by the prosecution. The greater the concession that is offered, the smaller the risk of conviction that a defendant will be willing to accept, and thus the greater the incentive to plead guilty that the defendant will have.

Limited pretrial discovery further eases the burden of securing convictions, since judgments in plea bargaining are made on the basis of less information than would be available at trial. Because cross-examination of witnesses is impossible in plea bargaining, imperfections in the state's case might go undiscovered. The effect of this reduction in the burden of proof is that the state is able to convict through plea bargaining some defendants who are guilty in fact, but who would not be convicted at trial or whose convictions at trial would necessitate drastically increased expenditures for the investigation and preparation of evidence.

While plea bargaining thus reduces the inaccuracies and costs of the traditional model, it also presents a danger that innocent defendants will be tempted to plead guilty. Courts have attempted to minimize this risk by inquiring into the factual basis for the guilty plea before accepting it. This remedy is insufficient, though, because defense counsel might advise their clients to admit involvement in the crime in order not to jeopardize the bargain that has already been struck.

The Supreme Court also has attempted to solve this problem by insisting that defense counsel be adequate and that the defendant understand the nature of the offense. Implicit in these responses are the assumptions that no competent attorney will advise an innocent defendant to plead guilty and that no defendant who understands the charges against him will admit having committed a crime which he in fact did not commit. There is no reason, according to this logic, to enact a formal barrier of convictability in plea bargaining since only guilty defendants engage in the practice.... Nevertheless, given the pressures on defense counsel to encourage pleas and the direct correlation between the weakness of the prosecution's case and the size of the offered concessions, some formal burden should be imposed on the state's case in order to ensure that no innocent defendants plead guilty and to maintain the dignity of the individual that is implicit in such a burden.

3. Reduction of Uncertainty. Just as prosecutors use plea bargaining to diminish the unpredictability and inaccuracy of trial, so defendants use plea bargaining to minimize the uncertainty and rigor of sentencing. By pleading guilty in return for a plea concession, the defendant can eliminate the risk of a heavier sentence following conviction at trial. This practice has the process value of allowing the defendant to exert some control over the sentencing process. It has the substantive value of ameliorating sentencing disparities by reducing the possible range of punishment.

(a) Potential Process Value. The notion of participation is basic to American criminal jurisprudence. Indeed, in recently upholding the defendant's right to waive counsel and proceed pro se in *Faretta* v. *California,* the Supreme Court made clear that the right to participate in the trial process inheres in the defendant himself, who retains the option of exercising the right directly or participating vicariously through an attorney. If the defendant chooses the latter course, he retains the right under the traditional model to be present during the guilt determination process in order to oversee the presentation of his case. In practice, however, the defendant's participation in the trial may be more illusory than real. The typical defendant, lacking legal training, is unable to supervise his attorney intelligently. As a result, the defendant may passively permit his attorney to control the case. Moreover, the unilateral nature of sentencing under the traditional model impairs any participation rights that the defendant might have at this stage of the proceedings.

In theory, plea bargaining has the potential of alleviating these problems of the traditional model. Sentencing is less unilateral than it is in the traditional model, since the state must secure the defendant's assent before it can impose punishment. The defendant has the opportunity to bargain with the prosecution in a less technical, legalized setting, to negotiate the terms of his assent, and thus to become a co-decisionmaker in the sentence determination. Direct participation of this sort not only promotes individual dignity, but also has an instrumental value. Because the defendant may feel morally obliged to honor the compromise that he has struck—that is, to respect the product of the process in which he has participated—he is more likely to feel reconciled to his punishment. Finally, by making the bargaining process appear less arbitrary, the defendant's participation serves the broader function of promoting the political legitimacy of the criminal justice system.

The process value of plea bargaining, then, depends upon the voluntary and intelligent participation of the defendant—his right to negotiate with the prosecutor and his right to accept or reject the proposed bargain. Unfortunately, because these rights are attenuated in practice, the potential process value of plea bargaining seldom is attained.

The right to negotiate inheres more in the defense attorney than it does in the defendant. The primacy of defense counsel stems initially from the Supreme Court's emphasis on the advice of counsel in ensuring the voluntariness and intelligence of guilty pleas. In addition, while lower federal courts have forbidden prosecutors from negotiating with the defendant in the absence of defense counsel, they have not forbidden bilateral negotiations between the prosecutor and the defense attorney. Because prosecutors find three-way bargaining cumbersome and because, in any case, prosecutors have greater rapport with defense attorneys than they do with defendants, virtually all prosecutors negotiate solely with defense counsel. Plea bargaining in practice thus accentuates, rather than alleviates, the traditional model's isolation of the defendant from the criminal process and makes the defendant's direct participation in plea negotiations impossible.

The frequent inadequacy of defense counsel's representation and the defendant's suspicion of such inadequacy make even vicarious participation unlikely. Many defense attorneys prefer to settle cases expeditiously through guilty pleas and consequently fail to press for the best possible plea bargain for their clients. Public defenders, by persuading their clients to plead guilty, can relieve the burden of heavy caseloads and maintain rapport with prosecutors with whom they work repeatedly. Those criminal defense practitioners and appointed counsel who are paid by the case rather than by the hour have a financial incentive to dispose of cases quickly by encouraging their clients to plead guilty. Moreover, countervailing pressures, characteristic of the traditional model and designed to ensure zealous advocacy, are absent in plea bargaining. Stripped of the formal trappings of the adversary system, defense counsel may feel less psychological adherence to ethical rules developed in that context to guarantee vigorous representation. Because plea bargaining takes place in private, neither the judge nor the defendant is present to ensure the attorney's undivided loyalty to his client. In any case, the collaborative nature of plea bargaining creates the appearance, if not the reality, of disloyalty. The defendant's absence from the plea negotiations prevents him from participating vicariously through his attorney and thus from satisfying himself as to the legitimacy of the process.

The right to reject the proposed plea bargain is largely chimerical. Fear of heavier sentence after trial and deference to advice of defense counsel might lead defendants to accept virtually all plea agreements, thereby impairing, at least in a pragmatic sense, the voluntariness of the guilty plea. Moreover, the lack of full pretrial discovery disturbs the intelligence with which the defendant can gauge both his chances at trial and the personal benefits of the plea bargain.

Finally, the defendant's presence at the plea-taking proceeding is insufficient to promote the values inherent in voluntary and intelligent participation in a bargaining process. As noted earlier, questioning the defendant at plea-taking after a bargain has already been struck might not guarantee the voluntariness of the guilty plea. Moreover, although the judge generally informs the defendant of the nature of the offense and its maximum punishment, the defendant often remains unsure of the exact sanction that will be imposed if he pleads guilty or if he goes to trial. Frustrating the intelligence of the defendant's decision distorts the self-determination component of plea bargaining. In addition, plea bargaining's failure to accord defendants adequate participation rights threatens the individual dignity which is crucial to the American criminal justice system.

(b) Substantive Value. By exchanging plea concessions for guilty pleas, prosecutors effectively limit the range of judges' sentencing discretion, thus reducing sentencing disparities and mitigating the substantive harshness of numerous criminal statutes. On the other hand, by introducing factors extrinsic to the purposes of the criminal sanction into the sentencing calculation, plea bargaining creates sentencing disparities of its own.

First, plea bargaining creates sentencing inequalities between those defendants who plead guilty and those convicted after trial. In addition, there are inequalities among those who plead guilty. Defendants who promise to testify against others often receive greater plea concessions than those who either refuse to testify or have no evidence to offer. Moreover, prosecutors regularly grant substantial concessions to defendants against whom the state's case is weak. Within this category, some defense attorneys, instead of bringing suppression motions, use possible constitutional objections as bargaining chips to induce larger concessions from prosecutors. Consequently, sentences vary not on the basis of the relative culpability of the particular defendant, but on the basis of the relative strength of the prosecution's case. While these concessions might be necessary both to conserve investigative and prosecutorial resources and to secure convictions in certain cases, they should be regulated in order to minimize and indeed to justify the concomitant sentencing inequalities.

The informality and low visibility of plea bargaining exacerbate this problem of inequitable sentencing. Subjective factors such as the prosecutor's desire to enhance his status within his department and his instinctive like or dislike for a particular defendant may enter into the calculation of plea concessions. These irrational considerations often produce unnecessarily lenient or unnecessarily severe sentences in individual cases. Either result frustrates the goal of uniform penalties for equally culpable defendants

The tremendous variation in the quality of defense representation further undermines the objective of equitable sentencing. Some defense attorneys spend enough time and energy preparing a defense to make credible their threats of going to trial. Prosecutors faced with such adversaries are likely to make substantial plea concessions in order to avert litigation. Other defense attorneys, however, lack the resources or even the inclination to prepare their cases for trial. These lawyers may discard their normal adversarial roles and act primarily as mediators between the prosecutor and the defendant—trying to arrive at a mutually acceptable deal as quickly and as inexpensively as possible. Defendants represented by the latter type of counsel generally do much worse than those represented by more vigorous advocates.

This inequality of defense representation weighs most heavily against poor and unsophisticated defendants. The indigent defendant is usually represented by a low-cost private attorney eager to collect his paycheck, a public defender burdened by a heavy caseload, or a randomly appointed private attorney wanting to return to his practice as soon as possible. These attorneys all have less incentive to prepare for trial than does the affluent defendant's lawyer who is compensated at a standard, hourly rate. Among the less affluent defendants, inadequate representation most seriously handicaps those who are unfamiliar with the plea bargaining system. Such unsophisticated defendants are more likely to defer to their attorneys and thus to accept poor bargains. While the interests of poor and unsophisticated defendants are less protected under the traditional model as well, the absence of formal scrutiny inherent in plea bargaining increases the threat of differential treatment.

As in the traditional model, these inequities undermine the legitimacy of the criminal justice system. When defendants similarly situated with respect to the purposes of the criminal sanction are sentenced differently, the system appears capricious or even discriminatory. The absence of equitable, uniform sentencing, then, upsets the moral justification for the punishment and impairs the underlying functions of the criminal sanction....

13.02 PROBLEMS IN PLEADING

Collateral Attacks on Guilty Pleas

ORAL ARGUMENTS BEFORE THE
U.S. SUPREME COURT*

Blackledge v. Allison, No. 75-1693; argued 2/2/77

The Court was recently asked to decide whether a federal district judge abused his discretion in denying a habeas hearing for a North Carolina inmate who sought to repudiate a 1969 guilty plea made in open court which he claims was induced by an unkept plea bargain between the defense and prosecution.

Richard N. League, Assistant Attorney General of North Carolina, began his argument by noting that respondent Allison

---

*From 20 Crim. L. Rptr. 4179–4181 (1977). Reprinted by permission from the Bureau of National Affairs, Inc.

told a state trial judge in open court that his guilty plea was not induced by any "promise or threat." This question was one of 14 that the judge asked to determine whether the plea was knowing, intelligent, and voluntary. On the basis of this inquiry, the state judge concluded that the plea was voluntary and sentenced Allison to 17 to 20 years on a safecracking charge.

Allison took no appeal from this conviction, League pointed out, but attacked his plea through state post-conviction procedures.

After exhausting his state remedies, Allison turned to the federal courts for habeas relief. Initially, a federal district judge dismissed the petition without an evidentiary hearing—impliedly accepting the state trial judge's finding. The district judge construed the petition to allege no more than a lawyer's erroneous sentencing prediction. On reconsideration, the district judge, however, concluded that Allison had not supported his allegations of an unkept plea bargain through proper affidavits naming the person who had allegedly witnessed his attorney's promise.

The Fourth Circuit reversed on appeal. 537 F.2d 894 (1976). It found that North Carolina guilty-plea procedures existing at the time of Allison's plea were unreliable, and held that the district court should have granted an evidentiary hearing.

However, League maintained that the district judge acted properly in accepting the state court's finding that Allison's plea was not induced by threats or promises. Allison received a full and fair state hearing within the sense of *Townsend* v. *Sain,* 372 U.S. 293 (1967), on the voluntariness of his plea.

Undercutting Boykin

The Fourth Circuit's decision undercut *Boykin* v. *Alabama,* 395 U.S. 238 (1969), and *McCarthy* v. *U.S.,* 394 U.S. 459 (1969), League argued. North Carolina required an in-court colloquy for determining the voluntariness of a plea, he said.

Other federal courts of appeals have indicated such claims as those now advanced by Allison would not ordinarily be given a hearing.

Mr. Justice Stevens: "Is it your position that if the record shows that the defendant answered no to a question concerning threats or promises, that's the end of the matter?"

Counsel thought so. But he would permit a hearing on the point if there were substantial evidence indicating that the plea was flawed.

Mr. Justice Marshall: "Is an affidavit necessary to support a federal habeas petitioner's claim?"

League answered that the district judge did not err in requiring an affidavit here. He also reiterated his claim that the district judge properly relied on the state court's findings.

The Chief Justice: "In the federal courts, a habeas proceeding is a civil case governed by the Federal Rules of Civil Procedure. Could a federal court order a pretrial hearing to explore the claims of a plaintiff in a civil case before trial?"

"Yes, sir."

The Chief Justice: "Are you analogizing what the district court did here to an ordinary civil case?"

"That would be an acceptable analogy," League responded.

The Chief Justice: "Are you suggesting that this case is comparable to the district judge's authority to order production of civil documents before trial? But in a criminal case, the judge would have no right to require the plaintiff to make a prima facie showing before trial?"

Counsel answered affirmatively to both questions. The court could require this habeas petitioner to submit affidavits before he would be entitled to a hearing.

Mr. Justice Marshall: "But he did [submit] such an affidavit."

The statement submitted by Allison failed to comply with the district court's order, League answered.

The federal judge had practiced with some of the state judges; he was well aware of their abilities and he was convinced that they had conducted reliable proceedings.

Mr. Justice Stevens: "As I understood it, there was no appeal to the state courts."

"Yes, sir," League said. But Allison did collaterally attack his conviction through state post-conviction procedures.

Mr. Justice Stevens: "How did the transcript of Allison's plea get into the record?"

It was filed with the state's answer, League said.

C. Frank Goldsmith, Jr., of Marion, North Carolina began his arguments by asking the Court to affirm the Fourth Circuit's holding. Having stated a claim for which relief could have been granted, Allison was entitled to an evidentiary hearing to prove the truth of his allegation.

Imprisonment that stems from a guilty plea induced by an unkept promise can be collaterally attacked, Goldsmith asserted, and Allison alleges that his plea resulted from an unkept bargain between the prosecution and the defense.

Mr. Justice Marshall: "How did the guilty plea get into the habeas record?"

Goldsmith's explanation was the same as League's; he replied that the plea was filed with the state's answer in the habeas proceedings. However, Goldsmith went on to say the habeas record was insufficient in light of the district court's disposition. The only record here of the state trial court's proceeding is a sheet of paper containing Allison's answers at the guilty plea colloquy.

The circumstances of Allison's particular case renders unreliable his pro forma denial of threats or promises, Goldsmith asserted. The record that the state seeks to have the Court find conclusive consists of only "yes" or "no" answers to form questions. This record is not a verbatim account of what actually occurred; hence it is impossible to determine what any of the parties said during the pauses between the questions at the colloquy.

Many an unlearned defendant has been told that a sentencing understanding or agreement is not a "promise or threat" made to influence him to plead guilty, or at least that disclosure of such an agreement is not contemplated by the plea inquiry, counsel continued.

The Chief Justice: "In a civil case, after judgment, a new trial may be sought on the basis of newly discovered evidence. Would it be appropriate in that situation to require the movant to state what the new evidence is before any other proceeding begins?"

"Yes, sir."

The Chief Justice: "I take it that your friend [opposing counsel] is analogizing that situation to the one here."

That might be true, Goldsmith said, but the situation here is slightly different.

The Chief Justice: "How could the trial judge accept the guilty plea without making a determination of its voluntariness?"

Counsel reiterated his position that the then-existing North Carolina procedures were inadequate for making a determination of voluntariness. The petitioners here simply ignore the realities of former North Carolina trial practices, he said.

The Chief Justice: "What if any impact did then-existing North Carolina statutes have on this case?"

None, counsel thought.

Allison's position finds support in *Townsend v. Sain,* Goldsmith submitted. There simply was no fair and adequate determination of the voluntariness of the plea in the state courts. Thus Allison is entitled to a hearing in the federal habeas courts.

"Could there ever be an adequate inquiry at the state trial level in your view?" Mr. Justice White asked. Can you envision the kind of inquiry at the state trial level at the time of the plea's acceptance that would insulate the plea from habeas attack? Does your argument expand *Townsend v. Sain?*

The statutes incorporate the *Townsend* requirements at the very least.

Mr. Justice Stevens: "Did the state file anything comparable to summary judgment on the basis of affidavits in the federal district court?"

"No," counsel answered.

Mr. Justice Stevens: "By filing affidavits, the state could have put the burden on the petitioner to come forward with his own affidavits in support of his claims."

The Chief Justice: "Taking the federal habeas statutes literally, would you say that on this record, the petitioner is entitled to release?"

The record does not conclusively show that the defendant is entitled to relief, Goldsmith replied. But that points up the need for further proceedings.

Mr. Justice White: "As I understand your position, you can always plead yourself into a hearing?"

"Yes, sir, in many circumstances."

Perjury Indictment

The Chief Justice: "Suppose you had a hearing; would false statements to the state trial court subject Allison to any kind of penalty for contempt of court, or for perjury?"

Counsel was uncertain on this point.

The Chief Justice: "As I understand it, your client may have deliberately misled the state trial judge?"

Goldsmith disagreed on this point.

Mr. Justice Stevens: "Will you tell me if it is now appropriate in North Carolina to make an inquiry of defense counsel as to the voluntariness of the plea?"

At the time Allison entered his plea no such inquiry was required, but it apparently is now, Goldsmith stated. Had such a procedure existed at the time Allison entered his plea, arguably this case would not now be before the Court, counsel added. The fact that North Carolina has expanded its plea inquiry lends credence to the view that the former procedures were inadequate to forestall later claims of an undisclosed plea bargain.

Unless this Court can say that the North Carolina trial court conducted a full and fair inquiry on the plea bargain point, the Fourth Circuit's opinion should be affirmed. Goldsmith submitted.

BLACKLEDGE v. ALLISON

Supreme Court of the United States, 1977
431 U.S. 63, 97 S. Ct. 1621, 52 L.Ed. 2d 136

Gary Allison, the respondent, was indicted in North Carolina for breaking and entering, attempted safe robbery, and possession of burglary tools. At his arraignment, where he was represented by court-appointed counsel, he entered a guilty plea to a single count of attempted safe robbery. The judge in open court read from a printed form 14 questions generally concerning the defendant's understanding of the charge and its consequences and the voluntariness of his plea. Without further questioning, the judge accepted the plea. At a sentencing hearing three days later, Allison was sentenced to 17 to 21 years' imprisonment. After unsuccessfully exhausting a state collateral remedy, Allison sought a writ of habeas corpus in a federal district court, claiming that his guilty plea had been induced by the promise of his attorney, who had consulted with the judge, that he would receive only a 10-year sentence. He also stated that he had been instructed to answer the questions by the judge in such a way that the court could accept his guilty plea. The district court dismissed the petition on the ground that the printed form conclusively showed that Allison had pleaded guilty knowingly, voluntarily, and with full awareness of the consequences. The Court of Appeals (4th Cir.) reversed, holding that Allison's allegation of a broken promise was not foreclosed by his responses to the form questions and that he was at least entitled to an evidentiary hearing. The United States Supreme Court granted certiorari.

Mr. Justice STEWART delivered the opinion of the Court.

* * *

II

Whatever might be the situation in an ideal world, the fact is that the guilty plea and the often concomitant plea bargain are important components of this country's criminal justice system. Properly administered, they can benefit all concerned. The defendant avoids extended pretrial incarceration and the anxieties and uncertainties of a trial; he gains a speedy disposition of his case, the chance to acknowledge his guilt, and a prompt start in realizing whatever potential there may be for rehabilitation. Judges and prosecutors conserve vital and scarce resources. The public is protected from the risks posed by those charged with criminal offenses who are at large on bail while awaiting completion of criminal proceedings.

These advantages can be secured, however, only if dispositions by guilty plea are accorded a great measure of finality. To allow indiscriminate hearings in federal postconviction proceedings, whether for federal prisoners under 28 U.S.C. § 2255 or state prisoners under 28 U.S.C. §§ 2241-2254, would eliminate the chief virtues of the plea system—speed, economy, and finality. And there is reason for concern about that prospect. More often than not a prisoner has everything to gain and nothing to lose from filing a collateral attack upon his guilty plea. If he succeeds in vacating the judgment of conviction, retrial may be difficult. If he convinces a court that his plea was induced by an advantageous plea agreement that was violated, he may obtain the benefit of its terms. A collateral attack may also be inspired by "a mere desire to be freed temporarily from the confines of the prison." Price v. Johnston, 334 U.S. 266, 284-285, 68 S. Ct. 1049, 1059, 92 L. Ed. 1356; accord, Machibroda v. United States, 368 U.S. 487, 497, 82 S. Ct. 510, 515, 7 L. Ed. 2d 473 (Clark, J., dissenting).

Yet arrayed against the interest in finality is the very purpose of the writ of habeas corpus—to safeguard a person's freedom from detention in violation of constitutional guarantees. Harris v. Nelson, 394 U.S. 286, 290-291, 89 S. Ct. 1082, 1086, 22 L. Ed. 2d 281. "The writ of *habeas corpus* has played a great role in the history of human freedom. It has been the judicial method of lifting undue restraints upon personal liberty." Price v. Johnston, 334 U.S. 266, 269, 68 S. Ct. 1049, 1052, 92 L. Ed. 1356 (emphasis in original). And a prisoner in custody after pleading guilty, no less than one tried and convicted by a jury, is entitled to avail himself of the writ in challenging the constitutionality of his custody.

* * *

... [T]he barrier of the plea or sentencing proceeding record, although imposing, is not invariably insurmountable. In administering the writ of habeas corpus and its § 2255 counterpart, the federal courts cannot fairly adopt a per se rule excluding all possibility that a defendant's representations at the time his guilty plea was accepted were so much the product of such factors as misunderstanding, duress, or misrepresentation by others as to make the guilty plea a constitutionally inadequate basis for imprisonment.

III

The allegations in this case were not in themselves so "vague [or] conclusory,"... as to warrant dismissal for that reason alone. Allison alleged as a ground for relief that his plea was induced by an unkept promise.[8] But he did not stop there. He proceeded to elaborate upon this claim with specific factual allegations. The petition indicated exactly what the terms of the promise were; when, where, and by whom the promise had been made; and the identity of one witness to its communication. The critical question is whether these allegations, when viewed against the record of the plea hearing were so "palpably incredible," ibid., so "patently frivolous or false", Pennsylvania ex rel. Herman v. Claudy, 350 U.S. 116, 119, 76 S. Ct. 223, 225, 100 L. Ed. 126, as to warrant summary dismissal. In the light of the nature of the record of the proceeding at which the guilty plea was accepted, and of the ambiguous status of the process of plea bargaining at the time the guilty plea was made, we conclude that Allison's petition should not have been summarily dismissed.

Only recently has plea bargaining become a visible practice accepted as a legitimate component in the administration of criminal justice. For decades it was a sub rosa process shrouded in secrecy and deliberately concealed by participating defendants, defense lawyers, prosecutors, and even judges. Indeed, it was not until our decision in Santobello v. New York, 404 U.S. 257, 92 S. Ct. 495, 30 L. Ed. 2d 427,

---

[8]Allison's petition stated that his lawyer, "who had consulted presumably with the Judge and Solicitor," had promised that the maximum sentence to be imposed was 10 years. This allegation, in light of the other circumstances of this case, raised the serious constitutional question whether his guilty plea was knowingly and voluntarily made. See Santobello v. New York, 404 U.S. 257, 92 S. Ct., 495, 30 L. Ed. 2d 427; Brady v. United States, 397 U.S. 742, 755, 90 S. Ct. 1463, 1472, 25 L. Ed. 2d 747.

that lingering doubts about the legitimacy of the practice were finally dispelled.

* * *

The litany of form questions followed by the trial judge at arraignment nowhere indicated to Allison (or indeed to the lawyers involved) that plea bargaining was a legitimate practice that could be freely disclosed in open court. Neither lawyer was asked to disclose any agreement that had been reached, or sentencing recommendation that had been promised. The process thus did nothing to dispel a defendant's belief that any bargain struck must remain concealed — a belief here allegedly reinforced by the admonition of Allison's lawyer himself that disclosure could jeopardize the agreement. Rather than challenging counsel's contention at oral argument in this Court that "at that time in North Carolina plea bargains were never disclosed in response to such a question on such a form," counsel for the State conceded at oral argument that "[t]he form was a minimal inquiry."

* * *

North Carolina has recently undertaken major revisions of its plea bargaining procedures in part to prevent the very kind of problem now before us. Plea bargaining is expressly legitimate. N.C. Gen. Stat. 15A-1021, and Official Commentary (1975). The judge is directed to advise the defendant that courts have approved plea bargaining and he may thus admit to any promises without fear of jeopardizing an advantageous agreement or prejudicing himself in the judge's eyes. See Brief for Respondent, App. D. Specific inquiry about whether a plea bargain has been struck is then made not only of the defendant, but also of his counsel and the prosecutor. N.C. Gen. Stat. 15A-1023(a), (c) (1975). Finally, the entire proceeding is to be transcribed verbatim. Id., 15A-1026, as amended, ibid. (Int.Supp. 1976).

Had these commendable procedures been followed in the present case, Allison's petition would have been cast in a very different light. The careful explication of the legitimacy of plea bargaining, the questioning of both lawyers, and the verbatim record of their answers at the guilty plea proceedings would almost surely have shown whether any bargain did exist and, if so, insured that it was not ignored. But the salutary reforms recently implemented by North Carolina highlight even more sharply the deficiencies in the record before the District Court in the present case.

This is not to say that every set of allegations not on its face without merit entitles a habeas corpus petitioner to an evidentiary hearing. As in civil cases generally, there exists a procedure whose purpose is to test whether facially adequate allegations have sufficient basis in fact to warrant plenary presentation of evidence. That procedure is, of course, the motion for summary judgment. Upon remand the Warden will be free to make such a motion, supporting it with whatever proof he wishes to attach. If he chooses to do so, Allison will then be required either to produce some contrary proof indicating that there is a genuine issue of fact to be resolved by the District Court or to explain his inability to provide such proof. Fed. Rule Civ. Proc. 56(e), (f).

* * *

Affirmed.

Chief Justice BURGER concurred in the judgment.

Mr. Justice POWELL, concurring.

I join the opinion of the Court, and write briefly only to emphasize the importance of finality to a system of justice. Our traditional concern for "persons whom society has grievously wronged and for whom belated liberation is little enough compensation," Fay v. Noia, 372 U.S. 391, 441, 83 S. Ct. 822, 850, 9 L. Ed. 2d 837 (1963), has resulted in a uniquely elaborate system of appeals and collateral review, even in cases in which the issue presented has little or nothing to do with innocence of the accused. The substantial societal interest in both innocence and finality of judgment is subordinated in many instances to formalisms.

The case before us today is not necessarily an example of abuse of the system. It is an example, however, of how finality can be frustrated by failure to adhere to proper procedures at the trial court level. I do not prejudge the ultimate result in this case by saying that respondent's guilty plea may well have been made knowingly and voluntarily. The case is here, five years after respondent's conviction, and following review by the North Carolina courts, the United States District Court and the Fourth Circuit Court of Appeals, primarily because the record before us leaves room for some doubt as to the reliability of the procedure followed with respect to the guilty plea. All that we have in the record, as a basis for testing the possible merit of respondent's petition, are answers to a printed form certified by the trial judge. We do not know whether anything was said by the judge, the prosecutor or counsel for respondent, other than the questions read from the form and the monosyllabic answers by respondent. There was no transcript of the proceedings.

* * *

Mr. Justice REHNQUIST took no part in the consideration or decision of this case.

The Plea Bargaining System and Confessions

HUTTO v. ROSS

Supreme Court of the United States, 1977
429 U.S. 28, 97 S. Ct. 202, 50 L. Ed. 2d 194

The facts are stated in the opinion.

PER CURIAM.

In March, 1972, in Johnson County, Ark., respondent was charged by information with the crime of embezzlement. With the assistance of counsel, respondent entered into plea negotiations with the prosecuting attorney, and the parties reached an agreement that respondent would enter a plea of guilty on the understanding that the prosecutor would recommend a 15-year prison sentence, with 10 years suspended. Approximately two weeks later, the prosecuting attorney asked respondent's counsel whether respondent would be willing to make a statement concerning the crimes. Although counsel advised respondent of his Fifth Amendment privilege and informed him that the terms of the negotiated plea bargain were available regardless of his willingness to comply with the prosecuting attorney's request, the respondent agreed to make a statement confessing to the crime charged. The record discloses that the statement was made under oath in the office of respondent's counsel, with counsel present, and after respondent had been advised of his rights under Miranda v. Arizona, 384 U.S. 436, 86 S. Ct. 1602, 16 L. Ed. 2d 694 (1966).

Respondent subsequently withdrew from the plea bargain, retained new counsel, and demanded a jury trial. The trial court ruled, after hearing evidence outside the presence of the jury, that respondent had confessed voluntarily. The statement was admitted at trial, and respondent was convicted and sentenced to 21-years' imprisonment. On appeal, the Arkansas Supreme Court affirmed. Ross v. State, 257 Ark. 44., 514 S.W. 2d 409 (1974). This Court denied certiorari. 421 U.S. 931, 95 S. Ct. 1658, 44 L. Ed. 2d 88 (1975).

Respondent then filed a petition for a writ of habeas corpus in the United States District Court for the Western District of Arkansas challenging the state court's finding of voluntariness. 28 U.S.C. § 2254. The District Court held an evidentiary hearing, and on May 23, 1975, denied the petition, agreeing with the state court that the confession was voluntary and therefore admissible. Mobley ex rel. Ross v. Meek, 394 F. Supp. 1219.

The Court of Appeals for the Eighth Circuit reversed, finding the statement inadmissible because "it ... was made in connection with an offer to plead guilty and after a [plea] bargain had been agreed upon." 531 F.2d 924, 926. It made no difference, in the court's view, that the confession was not an express precondition of the plea bargain; the confession became "part and parcel" of the plea bargain because "[the] confession would [not] have been made at the request of the prosecution *but for* the plea bargain." Id., at 926 (emphasis added). Since the plea bargain had not been executed, the court found the confession involuntary and therefore inadmissible.

The only question in this case is whether a confession is per se inadmissible in a criminal trial because it was made subsequent to an agreed upon plea bargain that did not call for such a confession.[3] We conclude that the Court of Appeals erred when it held that any statement made as a result of a plea bargain is inadmissible.

The Court of Appeals reasoned that respondent's confession was involuntary because it was made "as a result of the plea bargain" and would not have been made "but for the plea bargain." Id., at 926, 927. But causation in that sense has never been the test of voluntariness. See Brady v. United States, 397 U.S. 742, 749–750, 90 S. Ct. 1463, 1469, 25 L. Ed. 2d 747 (1970). The test is whether the confession was "extracted by any sort of threats or violence, [or] obtained by any direct or implied promises, however slight, [or] by the exertion of any improper influence." Bram v. United States, 168 U.S. 532, 542–543, 18 S. Ct. 183, 187, 42 L. Ed. 568 (1897); see Brady v. United States, supra, 397 U.S. at 753, 90 S. Ct. at 1471. The existence of the bargain may well have entered into respondent's decision to give a statement, but counsel made it clear to respondent that he could enforce the terms of the plea bargain whether or not he confessed. The confession thus does not appear to have been the result of "any direct or implied promises" or any coercion on the part of the prosecution, and was not involuntary. Bram. v. United States, supra, 168 U.S. at 542–543, 18 S. Ct. at 186–187.

The petition for a writ of certiorari is granted, the judgment of the Court of Appeals is reversed, and the case is remanded for further proceedings consistent with this opinion.

Mr. Justice STEWART dissents. Agreeing with the reasoning of the Court of Appeals, he would affirm its judgment.

---

[3]This case does not involve the admissibility at trial of a guilty plea subsequently withdrawn by leave of court. That issue was settled in Kerchevai v. United States, 274 U.S. 220, 47 S. Ct. 582, 71 L. Ed. 1009 (1927), which held that such pleas could not be used as evidence of guilt at a subsequent trial. Nor does this case involve the admissibility in criminal trials of statements made during the plea negotiation process. See Fed. Rule Crim. Proc. 11(e)(6); Moulder v. State, 154 Ind. App. 248, 289 N.E.2d 522 (Ct. App. 1972); ABA Minimum Standards for Criminal Justice, Standards Relating to Pleas of Guilty, §3.4.

15

THE FIRST AMENDMENT IN ITS CRIMINAL CONTEXT: FREEDOM OF THE PRESS, SPEECH, RELIGION, AND ASSEMBLY

15.03 FREEDOM OF THE PRESS

Retroactivity of Miller v. California

ORAL ARGUMENTS BEFORE THE
U.S. SUPREME COURT*

Marks v. United States, No. 75-708; argued 11/12/76

In a case involving a federal obscenity prosecution, the Court was faced with an unusual situation, as counsel for both sides agreed on the proper solution of two of the three issues presented in the certiorari petition. This situation arose because of the government's decision to confess error on two points. The Solicitor General showed up in person to explain the government's position, and if he had anticipated an adverse reaction from the Court, his expectations were fulfilled. The Court made it abundantly clear that it did not enjoy the spectacle of the government confessing error as to issues over which lower courts have divided.

Despite the Solicitor General's confession, the defendant's counsel, Robert Eugene Smith, of Atlanta, Georgia, addressed all three issues in his presentation. He began by noting that the conduct in question began in 1970 and continued until February, 1973, shortly before the Court announced its decision in *Miller* v. *California*, 413 U.S. 15. Yet the jury was instructed under the *Miller* standards, instead of the test derived from *Roth* v. *U.S.*, 354 U.S. 476 (1957), and *Memoirs* v. *Massa-*

---

*From 20 Crim. L. Rptr. 4073–4075 (1976). Reprinted by permission from the Bureau of National Affairs, Inc.

chusetts, 383 U.S. 413 (1966). The *Roth-Memoirs* standard was the law at that time, Smith said. "It had been, we suggest, the law in practice and generally understood—although this Court had not articulated it—that there were three elements," including the "utterly without redeeming social value" test. Smith noted that Mr. Justice Rehnquist took this view when, as a Justice Department official, he testified before a House Committee.

Thus *Miller* represented "an expansion, a judicial gloss, a change, a detriment" from the defendants' view, and ex post facto considerations preclude the application to them of the stricter standard.

Distasteful Duty

Smith's second point was the failure of the Sixth Circuit to view the movies in question. The two judges who made up the majority used the description contained in the search warrant affidavits to reach the conclusion that the movies were hardcore pornography.

"Unfortunately," Smith said, "hardcore pornography is not a talisman that says anything that is hardcore pornography is, in and of itself, obscene. Elsewise it would not have been necessary for this Court through Chief Justice Burger's [*Miller*] decision to enunciate three definitive aspects of what is to be used to define material that can be considered as obscene."

Smith was asked whether he considered an appellate court viewing to be constitutionally required.

He replied in the affirmative, noting that the question of obscenity is a mixed question of law and fact. Mr. Justice Clark took the view, in *Memoirs,* that obscenity is merely a question of fact, Smith remarked, but the other members of the Court did not agree.

This is a requirement that arises from a penumbra of the First Amendment, Smith said. The requirement is necessary to avoid a "chilling that may occur in a particular region ... or in a particular jurisdiction because a court in that jurisdiction may be conservative, perhaps, more narrow in its point of view." And persons other than the defendants here may be chilled.

The question then arose whether the Supreme Court ought to view the films. Individual Justices have made it amply clear that they strongly dislike this job.

But Smith assured the Court that it could avoid looking at these films, which included "Deep Throat." Asked why, he pointed out that the case reached the Court under its discretionary review power.

But now that we have granted review, a Justice asked, do we have to view them?

"I don't think it necessary for the resolution of the arguments in this case, because I think these are legal arguments."

"And they weren't legal arguments in the court of appeals?"

The problem below, Smith answered, is that the court refused to view the films. But viewing by this Court isn't necessary to the resolution of the three issues here.

Suppose a judge is blind, Smith was asked. Can his inability to see be compensated by having an explicit description of the materials?

Yes, Smith said, but not a description prepared by an FBI agent who is trying to get a search warrant and who may not discuss the potential serious literary and artistic values that may exist. Something in the nature of a translator would be required.

Definition of Community

The defendants' final point—and the one issue on which the Solicitor General did not confess error—involved the concept of contemporary community standards. The theatre here is located in Newport, Kentucky, part of the Cincinnati metropolitan area. The jury was instructed to apply the community standards of the Eastern District of Kentucky. But the defendants, Smith said, wanted a standard based on the contemporary community standards of the Cincinnati area. Half the jurors either worked in Cincinnati or had spouses or "significant" relatives who did. The venire itself was drawn from the Covington area, not the entire Eastern District. Smith found support for his argument in Mr. Justice Rehnquist's opinion for the Court in *Jenkins* v. *Georgia,* 418 U.S. 153 (1974).

This is the only adult theatre in the Eastern District, Smith continued, but there were others in Cincinnati. "And if you're going to talk about the level of tolerance and the community standards, we certainly are opting to have the larger community, that is to say, the metropolitan community, included to make it meaningful." Most of the Eastern District is Appalachia; a standard based on that community is not meaningful in terms of these defendants and this case.

Confession of Error

The Solicitor General, Robert H. Bork, began by saying "it has become apparent by now the government has confessed error on two of the three issues in this case. And we think that it is clear that we are required to do so." *Miller* clearly represented a break away from *Memoirs* and a swing back towards the original understanding of *Roth,* Bork continued. "And it seems clear, therefore, that the petitioners were tried under a standard that gave the prosecution less of a burden—considerably less of a burden—than the law provided at the time they acted."

There is nothing in the argument that the three-Justice plurality test in *Memoirs* never became the law, that Roth was still the law, and that since *Miller* is like *Roth,* the defendants got a jury instruction at least close to the one to which they were entitled. If *Memoirs* wasn't the law, then either there was no law or *Roth* remained the law. The second cannot be true because any conviction under *Roth* would have been reversed—by the three-Justice *Memoirs* plurality joined by Justices Black and Douglas. *Redrup* v. *New York,* 386 U.S. 767 (1967), and *Hamling* v. *U.S.,* 418 U.S. 87 (1974), also show that *Roth-Memoirs* was the law at this time.

"Now, even though it is Court-made law, it is effectively read into the statute. And I don't think there is any way that the change that occurred in *Miller* could retroactively be applied to these petitioners. That would deny them due process of law." As for ex post facto considerations, this case cannot be distinguished from *Bouie* v. *City of Columbia,* 378 U.S. 347 (1964).

Mr. Justice Rehnquist: "Well, Mr. Solicitor General, as I understand the state of the law on this particular question, when it came here from the Sixth Circuit, the government had this case and another court of appeals decision with it, several other courts of appeals decisions against it. Don't you think the Solicitor General has some responsibility under the adversary system, when there is a plausible argument to make in support of affirming a judgment that has gone in favor of the government, to make that argument, rather than simply adopt what he thinks is the law?"

Bork answered yes. "And we have considered this case, this principle for at least three years now. And if I thought there were a plausible case to be made for applying *Miller* standards to pre-*Miller* conduct, I would certainly make that argument."

Mr. Justice Rehnquist: "What you're saying then . . . is that two courts of appeals, presumably consisting of judges appointed by the President and confirmed by the Senate, have reached a totally implausible result."

"That, in effect, is correct."

"Well, how is this Court supposed to function in that kind of situation? We are supposedly the beneficiaries of an adversary process. And I am sure we would look with great skepticism if Mr. Smith came here in the position that you are in now, and said that he represented his clients, and that he realized that he had a couple of courts of appeals cases going for him, but he just couldn't in good conscience say that their convictions should be reversed."

"Well," Bork replied, "I think the answer can only be that the government feels that it has an obligation not only to the adversary process but also to the law and justice. In a case where it thinks an injustice has been done, and that there is no intellectually defensible way of supporting conviction, I think the government must say so."

Bork agreed with Mr. Justice Rehnquist that this is ultimately the responsibility of the Court. Aren't we best served by an adversary presentation in making that determination? Mr. Justice Rehnquist continued.

Bork replied, "I trust that we also have an obligation to the Court to tell it when we think an adversary case can't be made." Confessions of error have been made in the past, and the Court has sometimes rejected them. We do not intend to impinge on the Court's ultimate authority—and we are sure we won't.

Mr. Justice Stevens asked whether the policy of confessing error was old or new.

Bork answered: "It has gone on since the memory of man runneth not to the contrary."

"My stand," he continued, "is that if the government has a respectable position, I will defend it regardless of my personal view in the matter. My personal views in this case are that I would dearly love to defend this conviction, but I don't think I can."

Mr. Justice Stevens observed that defense attorneys sometimes feel in good conscience they have no appealable points, and therefore in effect, so acknowledge to the Court.

Bork agreed, and said that the government's obligation to the Court is no different from private counsel's in this regard.

But Mr. Justice White asked whether Bork ever heard of private counsel making a confession like this on a point about which the circuits are split.

"I have not heard of it."

"And I doubt if you will either."

Mr. Justice Blackmun: "I trust, Mr. Solicitor General, that you are aware of the reaction of federal courts of appeals judges when the U.S. Attorney has prosecuted a case, and it is then affirmed, only to have the rug pulled out from under them up here."

"I'm aware of the reaction of the courts," Bork replied. "I'm also aware of the reaction from U.S. Attorneys. I have been made aware of that. Nevertheless, it seems to me that I have an obligation to do this. And, as unpleasant as it may be for me and for the Court and for the U.S. Attorney, I do it. Three years ago, I decided that this was the rule of law, and communicated that fact. Unfortunately, that decision was not communicated to the U.S. Attorneys."

Mr. Justice Rehnquist: "Do you think it might have been a good idea had we appointed counsel to argue in your stead?"

"It might have been. We confessed error in the brief, so that I think it comes as no surprise at all that we take this position here this morning."

Bork also agreed with Smith that the Sixth Circuit should have looked at these materials. He saw this as a statutory, rather than a constitutional matter, however. A viewing would not be necessary in all cases, but in this case there was almost no descriptive matter for the court to use. For effective appellate review, the court was required to view the films. The Supreme Court normally need not.

Community Standards

Bork then turned "with considerable relief" to the one issue on which he disagreed with the defendants. The defendants' argument on the definition of community does not support their conclusion, he asserted. The jurors here did not live throughout the Cincinnati area, and they came from a pool with a widespread geographic base throughout the Eastern District of Kentucky. *Hamling* makes clear that the community in a federal prosecution is ordinarily the federal district. Prosecution would become impossible, Bork argued, if every case involved a search for the single most relevant community.

But Mr. Justice Stewart thought such a search would not be a wild goose chase in this case. Anyone who lives in Newport lives in the Cincinnati community, he pointed out.

The point of the community standard, Bork replied, is to give the juror an extrinsic standard to which he can refer. The reference to the standard of the Eastern District of Kentucky served that purpose here.

Mr. Justice Stevens asked whether the purpose is to draw on the juror's normal frame of reference, or instead to look at the economic market in which the film is shown.

It is to refer the juror to something outside his own sensibilities, Bork replied. Second, the purpose is to refer him to something with which he is familiar.

But many would say Eastern Kentucky is not a community, Mr. Justice Stewart said, whereas the Cincinnati area is. The Eastern District of Kentucky is a geographic accident.

California may also be termed such an accident, Bork replied, but the application of statewide standards there has been upheld by this Court.

MARKS v. UNITED STATES

Supreme Court of the United States, 1977
430 U.S. 188, 97 S. Ct. 990, 51 L. Ed. 2d 260

The facts are stated in the opinion.

Mr. Justice POWELL delivered the opinion of the Court.

This case presents the question, not fully answered in Hamling v. United States, 418 U.S. 87 (1974), whether the standards announced in Miller v. California, 413 U.S. 15 (1973), are to be applied retroactively to the potential detriment of a defendant in a criminal case. We granted certiorari, 424 U.S. 942 (1976), to resolve a conflict in the circuits.

I

Petitioners were charged with several counts of transporting obscene materials in interstate commerce, in violation of 18 U.S.C. § 371. The conduct that gave rise to the charges covered a period through February 27, 1973. Trial did not begin until the following October. In the interim, on June 21, 1973, this Court decided Miller v. California. . . . Miller announced new standards for "isolat[ing] 'hard core' pornography from expression protected by the First Amendment." 413 U.S., at 29³. . . .

Petitioners argued in the District Court that they were entitled to jury instructions not under Miller, but under the more favorable formulation of Memoirs v. Massachusetts, 383 U.S. 413 (1966) (plurality opinion).⁴ Memoirs, in their view, authoritatively stated the law in effect prior to Miller, by which petitioners charted their course of conduct. They focused in particular on the third part of the Memoirs test. Under it, expressive material is constitutionally protected unless it is "utterly without redeeming social value." 383 U.S., at 418. Under Miller the comparable test is "whether the work, taken as a whole, lacks serious literary, artistic, political, or scientific value." 413 U.S., at 24. Miller, petitioners argue, casts a significantly wider net than Memoirs. To apply Miller retroactively, and thereby punish conduct innocent under Memoirs, violates the Due Process Clause of the Fifth Amendment—much as retroactive application of a new statute to penalize conduct innocent when performed would violate the Constitution's ban on ex post facto laws, Art. I, § 9, cl. 3; id., § 10,

---

³Miller held: "The basic guidelines for the trier of fact must be: (a) whether 'the average person, applying contemporary community standards' would find that the work, taken as a whole, appeals to the prurient interest . . . ; (b) whether the work depicts or describes, in a patently offensive way, sexual conduct specifically defined by the applicable state law; and (c) whether the work, taken as a whole, lacks serious literary, artistic, political, or scientific value." 413 U.S., at 24.

Under part (b) of the test, it is adequate if the statute, as written or as judicially construed, specifically defines the sexual conduct, depiction of which is forbidden. The Court in Miller offered examples of what a State might constitutionally choose to regulate:

"(a) Patently offensive representations or descriptions of ultimate sexual acts, normal or perverted, actual or simulated.

"(b) Patently offensive representations or descriptions of masturbation, excretory functions, and lewd exhibition of the genitals." 413 U.S., at 25.

⁴The plurality in Memoirs held that "three elements must coalesce" if material is to be found obscene and therefore outside the protection of the First Amendment: "It must be established that (a) the dominant theme of the material taken as a whole appeals to a prurient interest in sex; (b) the material is patently offensive because it affronts contemporary community standards relating to the description or representation of sexual matters; and (c) the material is utterly without redeeming social value." 383 U.S., at 418.

cl. 1. The District Court overruled these objections and instructed the jury under the Miller standards. Petitioners were convicted, and a divided Court of Appeals for the Sixth Circuit affirmed. 520 F.2d 913 (1975). We now reverse.

The Ex Post Facto Clause is a limitation upon the powers of the legislature, see Calder v. Bull, 3 Dall. 385 (1798), and does not of its own force apply to the Judicial Branch of government. Frank v. Mangum, 237 U.S. 309, 344 (1915). But the principle on which the clause is based—the notion that persons have a right to fair warning of that conduct which will give rise to criminal penalties—is fundamental to our concept of constitutional liberty. As such, that right is protected against judicial action by the Due Process Clause of the Fifth Amendment. In Bouie v. City of Columbia, 378 U.S. 347 (1964), a case involving the cognate provision of the Fourteenth Amendment, the Court reversed trespass convictions, finding that they rested on an unexpected construction of the state trespass statute by the state Supreme Court:

"[A]n unforeseeable judicial enlargement of a criminal statute, applied retroactively, operates precisely like an ex post facto law such as Art. I, § 10, of the Constitution forbids.... If a state legislature is barred by the Ex Post Facto Clause from passing such a law, it must follow that a State Supreme Court is barred by the Due Process Clause from achieving precisely the same result by judicial construction." Id., at 353–354.

Similarly, in Rabe v. Washington, 405 U.S. 313 (1972), we reversed a conviction under a state obscenity law because it rested on an unforeseeable judicial construction of the statute. We stressed that reversal was mandated because affected citizens lacked fair notice that the statute would be thus applied.

Relying on Bouie, petitioners assert that Miller and its companion cases unforeseeably expanded the reach of the federal obscenity statutes beyond what was punishable under Memoirs. The Court of Appeals rejected this argument. It noted—correctly—that the Memoirs standards never commanded the assent of more than three Justices at any one time, and it apparently concluded from this fact that Memoirs never became the law. By this line of reasoning, one must judge whether Miller expanded criminal liability by looking not to Memoirs, but to Roth v. United States, 354 U.S. 476 (1957), the last comparable plenary decision of this Court prior to Miller in which a majority united in a single opinion announcing the rationale behind the Court's holding. Although certain language in Roth formed the basis for the plurality's formulation in Memoirs, Roth's test for distinguishing obscenity from protected speech was a fairly simple one to articulate: "whether to the average person, applying contemporary community standards, the dominant theme of the material taken as a whole appeals to the prurient interest." Id., at 489. If indeed Roth, not Memoirs, stated the applicable law prior to Miller, there would be much to commend the apparent view of the Court of Appeals that Miller did not significantly change the law.

But we think the basic premise for this line of reasoning is faulty. When a fragmented Court decides a case and no single rationale explaining the result enjoys the assent of five Justices, "the holding of the Court may be viewed as that position taken by those Members who concurred in the judgments on the narrowest grounds...." Gregg v. Georgia, [428 U.S. 153] 169 n. 15 (1976) (opinion of STEWART, POWELL, and STEVENS, JJ.). Three Justices joined in the controlling opinion in Memoirs. Two others, Mr. Justice Black and Mr. Justice Douglas, concurred on broader grounds in reversing the judgement below. 383 U.S., at 421, 424. They reiterated their well-known position that the First Amendment provides an absolute shield against governmental action aimed at suppressing obscenity. Mr. Justice STEWART also concurred in the judgment, based on his view that only "hard core pornography" may be suppressed. Id., at 421. See Ginzburg v. United States, 383 U.S. 463, 499 (1966) (STEWART, J., dissenting). The view of the Memoirs plurality therefore constituted the holding of the Court and provided the government standards. Indeed, every Court of Appeals that considered the question between Memoirs and Miller so read our decisions. Materials were deemed to be constitutionally protected unless the prosecution carried the burden of proving that they were "utterly without redeeming social value," and otherwise satisfied the stringent Memoirs requirements.

Memoirs therefore was the law. Miller did not simply clarify Roth; it marked a significant departure from Memoirs. And there can be little doubt that the third test announced in Miller—whether the work "lacks serious literary, artistic, political, or scientific value"—expanded criminal liability. The Court in Miller expressly observed that the "utterly without redeeming social value" test places on the prosecutor "a burden virtually impossible to discharge under our criminal standards of proof." 413 U.S., at 22. Clearly it was thought that some conduct which would have gone unpunished under Memoirs would result in conviction under Miller.

This case is not strictly analogous to Bouie. The statutory language there was "narrow and precise," . . . and that fact was important to our holding that the expansive construction adopted by the State Supreme Court deprived the accused of fair warning. In contrast, the statute involved here always has used sweeping language to describe that which is forbidden. But precisely because the statute is sweeping, its reach necessarily has been confined within the constitutional limits announced by this Court. Memoirs severely restricted its application. Miller also restricts its application beyond what the language might indicate, but Miller undeniably relaxes the Memoirs restrictions. The effect is the same as the new construction in Bouie. Petitioners, engaged in the business of marketing dicey films, had no fair warning that their products might be subjected to the new standards.

We have taken special care to insist on fair warning when a statute regulates expression and implicates First Amendment values. . . . We therefore hold, in accordance with Bouie, that the Due Process Clause precludes the application to petitioner of the standards announced in Miller v. California, to the extent that those standards may impose criminal liability for conduct not punishable under Memoirs. Specifically, since the petitioners were indicted for conduct occurring prior to our decision in Miller, they are entitled to jury instructions requiring the jury to acquit unless it finds that the materials involved are 'utterly without redeeming social value." At the same time we reaffirm our holding in Hamling v. United States, 418 U.S., at 102, that "any constitutional principle enunciated in Miller which would serve to benefit petitioners must be applied in their case."

Accordingly, the case is remanded for further proceedings consistent with this opinion.

Mr. Justice BRENNAN, with whom Mr. Justice STEWART and Mr. Justice MARSHALL join, concurring in part and dissenting in part.

I join the opinion of the Court insofar as it holds that the retroactive application of the definition of obscenity announced in Miller v. California, 413 U.S. 15 (1973), to the potential detriment of a criminal defendant, violates the Due Process Clause of the Fifth Amendment. See Bouie v. City of Columbia, 378 U.S. 347 (1964).

I cannot join, however, in the judgment remanding the case for a new trial. Petitioners were convicted of transporting obscene materials in interstate commerce in violation of 18 U.S.C. § 1465. I adhere to the view that this statute is "clearly overbroad and unconstitutional on its face." See, e.g., Cangiano v. United States, 418 U.S. 934, 935 (1974) (BRENNAN, J., dissenting), quoting United States v. Orito, 413 U.S. 139, 148 (1973) (BRENNAN, J., dissenting). I therefore would simply reverse.

Mr. Justice STEVENS, concurring in part and dissenting in part.

There are three reasons which, in combination, persuade me that this criminal prosecution is constitutionally impermissible.

First, as the Court's opinion recognizes, this "statute regulates expression and implicates First Amendment values."

However distasteful these materials are to some of us, they are nevertheless a form of communication and entertainment acceptable to a substantial segment of society; otherwise, they would have no value in the marketplace. Second, the statute is predicated on the somewhat illogical premise that a person may be prosecuted criminally for providing another with material he has a constitutional right to possess. See Stanley v. Georgia, 394 U.S. 557 (1969). Third, the present constitutional standards, both substantive and procedural, which apply to these prosecutions are so intolerably vague that evenhanded enforcement of the law is a virtual impossibility. Indeed, my brief experience on the Court has persuaded me that grossly disparate treatment of similar offenders is a characteristic of the criminal enforcement of obscenity law. Accordingly, while I join the Court's opinion, I am unable to join its judgment.

The "Human Cannonball" Case

ZACCHINI v. SCRIPPS-HOWARD BROADCASTING CO.

Supreme Court of the United States, 1977
433 U.S. 562, 97 S. Ct. 2849, 53 L. Ed. 2d 965

Hugo Zacchini, an entertainer, performs a "human cannonball" act in which he is shot out of a cannon into a net 200 feet away. The entire performance lasts 15 seconds. On August 31, 1972, he performed at the fair grounds in Burton, Ohio; members of the public were not charged a separate admission fee to observe his act. A freelance reporter for the Scripps-Howard Broadcasting Company, the respondent and operator of a television broadcasting station, videotaped the entire act, despite Zacchini's request that he not film the performance. The film clip was shown on the 11 o'clock news program that night, together with favorable commentary. Petitioner brought a damage action in an Ohio state court against respondent, alleging an "unlawful appropriation" of his "professional property." The trial court granted respondent a summary judgment, but the Ohio Court of Appeals reversed on the ground that the complaint stated a cause of action. The Ohio Supreme Court, while recognizing that petitioner had a cause of action under Ohio law on his "right to the publicity value of his performance," nevertheless, relying on *Time, Inc. v. Hill*, **385 U.S. 374 (1967), rendered judgment for respondent on the ground that it is constitutionally privileged to include in its newscasts matters of public interest that would otherwise be protected by the right of publicity, absent an intent to injure or to appropriate for some nonprivileged purpose. The United States Supreme Court granted certiorari.**

Mr. Justice WHITE delivered the opinion of the Court.

* * *

... [I]f ... respondent had merely reported that petitioner was performing at the fair and described or commented on his act, with or without showing his picture on television, we would have a very different case. But petitioner is not contending that his appearance at the fair and his performance could not be reported by the press as newsworthy items. His complaint is that respondent filmed his entire act and displayed that film on television for the public to see and enjoy. This, he claimed, was an appropriation of his professional property. The Ohio Supreme Court agreed that petitioner had "a right of publicity" that gave him "personal control over the commercial display and exploitation of his personality and the exercise of his talents." This right of "exclusive control over the publicity given to his performance" was said to be such a "valuable part of the benefit which may be attained by his talents and efforts" that it was entitled to legal protection. It was also observed, or at least expressly assumed, that petitioner had not abandoned his rights by performing under the circumstances present at the Geauga County Fair Grounds.

The Ohio Supreme Court nevertheless held that the challenged invasion was privileged, saying that the press "must be accorded broad latitude in its choice of how much it presents of each story or incident, and of the emphasis to be given to such presentation. No fixed standard which would bar the press from reporting or depicting either an entire occurrence or an entire discrete part of a public performance can be formulated which would not unduly restrict the 'breathing room' in reporting which freedom of the press requires." 47 Ohio St., at 235, 351 N.E.2d at 461. Under this view, respondent was thus constitutionally free to film and display petitioner's entire act.

The Ohio Supreme Court relied heavily on Time, Inc. v. Hill, supra, but that case does not mandate a media privilege to televise a performer's entire act without his consent. Involved in Time, Inc. v. Hill was a claim under the New York "Right of Privacy" statute that Life Magazine, in the course of reviewing a new play, had connected the play with a long-past incident involving petitioner and his family and had falsely described their experience and conduct at that time. The complaint sought damages for humiliation and suffering flowing from these nondefamatory falsehoods that allegedly invaded Hill's privacy. The Court held, however, that the opening of a new play linked to an actual incident was a matter of public interest and that Hill could not recover without showing that the Life report was knowingly false or was published with reckless disregard for the truth—the same rigorous standard that had been applied in New York Times v. Sullivan [376 U.S. 374 (1964)].

* * *

Nor does it appear that our later cases, such as Rosenbloom v. Metromedia, Inc., 403 U.S. 29 (1971); Gertz v. Robert Welch, Inc., 418 U.S. 323 (1974); and Time, Inc. v. Firestone, 424 U.S. 448 (1976), require or furnish substantial support for the Ohio court's privilege ruling. These cases, like New York Times, emphasize the protection extended to the press by the First Amendment in defamation cases, particularly when suit is brought by a public official or a public figure. None of them involve an alleged appropriation by the press of a right of publicity existing under state law.

Moreover, Time, Inc. v. Hill, New York Times, Metromedia, Gertz, and Firestone all involved the reporting of events; in none of them was there an attempt to broadcast or publish an entire act for which the performer ordinarily gets paid. It is evident, and there is no claim here to the contrary, that petitioner's state-law right of publicity would not serve to prevent respondent from reporting the newsworthy facts about petitioner's act. Wherever the line in particular situations is to be drawn between media reports that are protected and those that are not, we are quite sure that the First and Fourteenth Amendments do not immunize the media when they broadcast a performer's entire act without his consent. The Constitution no more prevents a State from requiring respondent to compensate petitioner for broadcasting his act on television than it would privilege respondent to film and broadcast a copyrighted dramatic work without liability to the copyright owner. Copyrights Act. Pub. L. No. 94-553, 90 Stat. 2541 (1976); cf. Kalem Co. v. Harper Bros., 222 U.S. 55 (1911); Manners v. Morosco, 252 U.S. 317 (1920), or to film and broadcast a prize fight, Ettore v. Philco Television Broadcasting Corp., 229 F.2d 481 (CA3), cert. denied, 351 U.S. 926 (1956); or a baseball game, Pittsburgh Athletic Co. v. KQV Broadcasting Co., 24 F. Supp. 490 (W.D. Pa. 1938), where the promoters or the participants had other plans for publicizing the event. There are ample reasons for reaching this conclusion.

The broadcast of a film of petitioner's entire act poses a substantial threat to the economic value of that performance. As the Ohio court recognized, this act is the product of petitioner's own talents and energy, the end result of much time, effort and expense. Much of its economic value lies in the "right of exclusive control over the publicity given to his performance"; if the public can see the act for free on television, they will be less willing to pay to see it at the fair. The effect of a public broadcast of the performance is similar to preventing petitioner from charging an admission fee. "The rationale for [protecting the right of publicity] is the straightforward one of preventing unjust enrichment by the theft of good will. No social purpose is served by having the defendant get for free some aspect of the plaintiff that would have market value and for which he would normally pay." Kalven, Privacy in Tort Law—Were Warren and Brandeis Wrong?, 31 Law and Contemporary Problems 326, 331 (1966). Moreover, the broadcast of petitioner's entire performance, unlike the unauthorized use of another's name for purposes of trade or the incidental use of a name or picture by the press, goes to the heart of petitioner's ability to earn a living as an entertainer. Thus in this case, Ohio has recognized what may be the strongest case for a "right of publicity"—involving not the appropriation of an entertainer's reputation to enhance the attractiveness of a commercial product, but the appropriation of the very activity by which the entertainer acquired his reputation in the first place.

Of course, Ohio's decision to protect petitioner's right of publicity here rests on more than a desire to compensate the performer for the time and effort invested in his act; the protection provides an economic incentive for him to make the investment required to produce a performance of interest to the public. This same consideration underlies the patent and copyright laws long enforced by this Court....

The Constitution does not prevent Ohio from making a similar choice here in deciding to protect the entertainer's incentive in order to encourage the production of this type of work. Cf. Goldstein v. California, 412 U.S. 546 (1973); Kewanee Oil Co. v. Bicron Corp., 416 U.S. 470 (1974).

There is no doubt that entertainment, as well as news, enjoys First Amendment protection. It is also true that entertainment itself can be important news. Time, Inc. v. Hill, supra. But it is important to note that neither the public nor respondent will be deprived of the benefit of petitioner's performance as long as his commercial stake in his act is appropriately recognized. Petitioner does not seek to enjoin the broadcast of his performance; he simply wants to be paid for it. Nor do we think that a state-law damages remedy against respondent would represent a species of liability without fault contrary to the letter or spirit of Gertz, supra. Respondent knew exactly that petitioner objected to televising his act, but nevertheless displayed the entire film.

We conclude that although the State of Ohio may as a matter of its own law privilege the press in the circumstances of this case, the First and Fourteenth Amendments do not require it to do so.

Reversed.

Mr. Justice POWELL, with whom Mr. Justice BRENNAN and Mr. Justice MARSHALL join, dissenting.

Disclaiming any attempt to do more than decide the narrow case before us, the Court reverses the decision of the Supreme Court of Ohio based on repeated incantation of a single formula: "a performer's entire act." The holding today is summed up in one sentence:

"Wherever the line in particular situations is to be drawn between media reports that are protected and those that are not, we are quite sure that the First and Fourteenth Amendments do not immunize the media when they broadcast a performer's entire act without his consent." Ante, at ——.

I doubt that this formula provides a standard clear enough even for resolution of this case. In any event, I am not persuaded that the Court's opinion is appropriately sensitive to the First Amendment values at stake, and I therefore dissent.

Although the Court would draw no distinction,... I do not view respondent's action as comparable to unauthorized commercial broadcasts of sporting events, theatrical performances, and the like where the broadcaster keeps the profits. There is no suggestion here that respondent made any such use of the film. Instead, it simply reported on what petitioner concedes to be a newsworthy event, in a way hardly surprising for a television station—by means of film coverage. The report was part of an ordinary daily news program, consuming a total of 15 seconds. It is a routine example of the press fulfilling the informing function so vital to our system.

The Court's holding that the station's ordinary news report may give rise to substantial liability has disturbing implications, for the decision could lead to a degree of media self-censorship. Cf. Smith v. California, 361 U.S. 147, 150–154 (1959). Hereafter, whenever a television news editor is unsure whether certain film footage received from a camera crew might be held to portray an "entire act," he may decline coverage—even of clearly newsworthy events—or confine the broadcast to watered-down verbal reporting, perhaps with an occasional still picture. The public is then the loser. This is hardly the kind of news reportage that the First Amendment is meant to foster. See generally Miami Herald Publishing Co. v. Tornillo, 418 U.S. 241, 257–258 (1974); Time, Inc. v. Hill, 385 U.S. 374, 389 (1967); New York

Times Co. v. Sullivan, 376 U.S. 254, 270-272, 279 (1964).

In my view the First Amendment commands a different analytical starting point from the one selected by the Court. Rather than begin with a quantitative analysis of the performer's behavior—is this or is this not his entire act?—we should direct initial attention to the actions of the news media: what use did the station make of the film footage? When a film is used, as here, for a routine portion of a regular news program, I would hold that the First Amendment protects the station from a "right of publicity" or "appropriation" suit, absent a strong showing by the plaintiff that the news broadcast was a subterfuge or cover for private or commercial exploitation.

I emphasize that this is a "reappropriation" suit rather than one of the other varieties of "right of privacy" tort suits identified by Dean Prosser in his classic article, Prosser, Privacy, 48 Calif. L. Rev. 383 (1960). In those other causes of action the competing interests are considerably different. The plaintiff generally seeks to avoid any sort of public exposure, and the existence of constitutional privilege is therefore less likely to turn on whether the publication occurred in a news broadcast or in some other fashion. In a suit like the one before us, however, the plaintiff does not complain about the fact of exposure to the public, but rather about its timing or manner. He welcomes some publicity, but seeks to retain control over means and manner as a way to maximize for himself the monetary benefits that flow from such publication. But having made the matter public—having chosen, in essence, to make it newsworthy—he cannot, consistently with the First Amendment, complain of routine news reportage. Cf. Gertz v. Robert Welch, Inc., 418 U.S. 323, 339-348, 351-352 (1974) (clarifying the different liability standards appropriate in defamation suits, depending on whether or not the plaintiff is a public figure).

Since the film clip here was undeniably treated as news and since there is no claim that the use was subterfuge, respondent's actions were constitutionally privileged. I would affirm.

Mr. Justice STEVENS, dissenting.

The Ohio Supreme Court held that respondent's telecast of the "human cannonball" was a privileged invasion of petitioner's common law "right of publicity" because respondent's actual intent was neither (a) to appropriate the benefit of the publicity for a private use, nor (b) to injure petitioner.

As I read the state court's explanation of the limits on the concept of privilege, they define the substantive reach of a common law tort rather than anything I recognize as a limit on a federal constitutional right. The decision was unquestionably influenced by the Ohio court's proper sensitivity to First Amendment principles, and to this Court's cases construing the First Amendment; indeed, I must confess that the opinion can be read as resting entirely on federal constitutional grounds. Nevertheless, the basis of the state court's action is sufficiently doubtful that I would remand the case to that court for clarification of its holding before deciding the federal constitutional issue.

15.03 FREEDOM OF SPEECH

The License Plate Case

ORAL ARGUMENTS BEFORE THE U.S. SUPREME COURT*

Wooley v. Maynard, No. 75-1453; argued 11/29/76

In a lively argument the Court was asked recently to decide whether a New Hampshire statute that prohibits motorists from obscuring the "figures or letters" on any license plate is unconstitutional as applied to a pair of Jehovah's Witnesses who, for religious reasons, taped over the state motto, "Live Free or Die," which appears on all noncommercial plates.

A three-judge district court, ruling on the

---

*From 20 Crim. L. Rptr. 4101-4103 (1976). Reprinted by permission of the Bureau of National Affairs, Inc.

couple's 42 U.S.C. § 1983 Civil Rights Act suit, enjoined state officials from arresting them and held that their conduct in obscuring the motto constituted symbolic speech protected by the First Amendment. 406 F. Supp. 1381. The court also rejected the state officials' claim that *Younger* v. *Harris*, 401 U.S. 37 (1971), prevented it from hearing this § 1983 suit.

The Maynards contend that the message conveyed by the New Hampshire motto runs counter to their religious beliefs. They do not think that death is a reality for a follower of Christ. Nor do they believe a Christian should give his earthly life for the state, even if the alternative is living in bondage.

Robert V. Johnson, II, Assistant Attorney General of New Hampshire, began his argument by detailing the history of the motto. General John Stark, New Hampshire's most prominent Revolutionary War hero, apparently coined the motto in a letter to Vermont comrades assembled for the thirty-second reunion of the 1777 Battle of Bennington. At the conclusion of his letter General Stark proposed a toast for the reunion: "Live free or die: Death is not the worst of evils." In 1969, the New Hampshire legislature directed that the state motto appear on all noncommercial vehicle license plates, replacing the words "Scenic New Hampshire."

Mr. Justice Rehnquist: "If you had kept it just 'Scenic New Hampshire,' you would have avoided this litigation."

Requiring display of the state motto on noncommercial vehicles furthers legitimate state interests, Johnson argued. It fosters an appreciation of New Hampshire's long history, traditions, pride, identity and individualism as well as promotes tourism. Like most other states, Johnson pointed out, New Hampshire has also adopted a state seal, tree and flower.

The Chief Justice: "Is your case dependent on this having been declared the state motto by the legislature?"

The legislature has concluded that the motto is of importance to New Hampshire. Not only is the motto symbolic, it also serves other useful functions.

Mr. Justice Stevens: "Do you challenge the district court's finding that the appellees' motive (in obscuring the motto) was based on a fundamental interest?"

Sincerity

The state questions the appellees' sincerity in challenging this statute on religious grounds, he explained. "Mr. Maynard has been 'disfellowed' by the Jehovah's Witnesses."

Mr. Justice Marshall: "As to his sincerity, he went to jail, didn't he?"

"Yes, sir, that's correct." But counsel declined to concede that the respondents' beliefs were motivated by sincere religious convictions. Their conduct was more whimsical and eccentric than sincere, Johnson added.

The Chief Justice: "Do you rest on the fact that his departure from the faith undermines his sincerity?"

His sincerity, of course, does not resolve all the issues here, but it carries some weight, counsel answered.

The Chief Justice: "Could New Hampshire require its citizens to carry signs supporting the U.N.?"

"No, sir." That hypothetical is more "poignant" than the state's motto which is essentially a neutral statement furthering legitimate interests of New Hampshire.

The Chief Justice: "Couldn't the state just as well offer them an option if they didn't want the motto on their license plates?"

That would wreak havoc, counsel contended.

Mr. Justice Stewart: "Where are the state's plates made? In a prison?"

"Yes, sir."

Mr. Justice Stewart thought that ironic in light of the fact that these plaintiffs could have gone to prison and then been required to make the very license plates to which they object.

The presence of the state motto on license plates is not a "burning issue" in New Hampshire. "Most people accept it," counsel noted.

The Chief Justice: "What difference does it make that a particular person finds the motto objectionable?"

Little difference, if the state has adequate justifications. While counsel could envision some instances in which particular persons might have legitimate objections to a motto, he did not think this case poses such a situation. He suggested that the Court weigh the asserted interests of the state against those of the Maynards.

Mr. Justice Stevens: "Suppose Utah adopted the motto: 'The Mormon State'—would that be permissible?"

"I think it would be a closer issue." The words "Live Free or Die" do not have the same significance as such a motto would have, Johnson said. "Live Free or Die" is facially neutral.

Alternatives

Nothing in this statute prevents the Maynards from verbalizing their objections to the state motto. The issue posed here is similar to those in the draft card destruction cases, such as *U.S. v. O'Brien,* 391 U.S. 367 (1968), where the Court concluded that a government regulation barring destruction of draft cards rested on sufficient justifications. Similarly, the New Hampshire statute here furthers a legitimate governmental interest and does not attempt to suppress free speech.

Turning to the *Younger* issue, Johnson asserted that the district court should have refrained from exercising jurisdiction.

Maynard's failure to appeal his three state convictions for obscuring the motto bars his raising the First Amendment claims in the district court. His claims could well have been resolved by the New Hampshire courts, Johnson concluded.

No Pending Litigation

Richard S. Kohn, of Washington, D.C., told the Court that *Younger* v. *Harris* generally bars federal intervention in pending state criminal cases. At the time the respondents filed this § 1983 suit no state proceeding was pending. The *Younger* doctrine does not bar a federal civil rights action for declaratory and injunctive relief against threatened prosecutions merely because the federal plaintiff took no appeal from prior state court convictions, he maintained.

Mr. Justice White: "Your assertion is that this suit is wholly prospective?"

"Yes, sir." The plaintiffs asked for a prospective injunction. They are not attacking Mr. Maynard's state court convictions; the relief that they seek is purely prospective.

Mr. Justice Stewart: "Why was this a case or controversy?"

Mr. Maynard had already been prosecuted for obscuring the state motto. Without injunctive or declaratory relief, it was almost certain that he would suffer irreparable harm through another prosecution.

Mr. Justice Stewart: "Did you allege that in your complaint?"

"Yes, sir."

In response to a question from Mr. Justice Powell, counsel explained that Mr. Maynard did not seek expungement of his state convictions in the federal court. "Our case looked only to the future."

Counsel acknowledged that Mr. Maynard could have appealed his state court convictions and raised the federal constitutional issues there. But, Maynard, who represented himself, was not aware of all the legal options then available to him.

Mr. Justice Marshall: "But the point is that when he needed a lawyer he got one. He had remedies available in the state courts, but rather than use those, he went to the federal courts?"

But nothing suggests that he deliberately bypassed the state courts, counsel explained.

Moreover, New Hampshire's two-tier system did not afford Mr. Maynard the "opportunity to raise and have timely decided by a competent state tribunal the federal issues presented." The Maynards desperately needed temporary injunctive relief so that they could operate their cars while their claims were being litigated. But the state appellate courts offered no procedure for this.

Mr. Justice Stevens: "I am a little puzzled about the res judicata point (in your brief). You are not attacking these state judgments?"

"Right, your honor." The state suggests that res judicata and collateral estoppel doctrines barred the district court from adjudicating Mr. Maynard's claim because he failed to utilize the state appellate procedures.

These doctrines are simply not applicable here. Even if they were, Kohn argued, the state has waived them by failing to raise them as affirmative defenses in the district court.

As to the permanent injunction that the Maynards received, it suffers from none of the infirmities of the injunction condemned in *Rizzo* v. *Goode,* 423 U.S. 362 (1976).

Even if Mr. Maynard's failure to appeal his state court convictions barred him from instituting this suit, the claims that Mrs. Maynard, who shares her husband's religious beliefs, asserts remain open for resolution, Kohn contended.

Advertising Beliefs

Mr. Justice Rehnquist: "What if Nevada's license tags said 'Gambling Paradise'?"

Counsel thought this would present a serious First Amendment problem.

Mr. Justice Marshall: "You don't argue that the license plate belongs to the state?"

"That's correct."

Mr. Justice Stevens: "Do you think that an atheist could cover up the words 'In God We Trust?'"

Counsel thought not.

Mr. Justice Brennan drew laughter when he referred to his native New Jersey's motto, "The Garden State."

The motto requirement has created lively and sometimes heated discussion in New Hampshire, Kohn argued. "People are well aware of the controversy around the motto," which, he said, has raged for years.

Moreover, there have been other successful prosecutions under the statute.

The motto furthers no real state interest, and little evidence exists for the proposition that it promotes tourism. Moreover, the state concedes that a workable registration system can exist without the motto requirement. Nor is this case analogous to *O'Brien*, which involved the war power. The interests that the state has advanced "come nowhere near the war power" in importance.

On rebuttal, Johnson stressed that New Hampshire was before the Court "seriously" and reiterated the state's justifications for displaying the motto on license plates.

WOOLEY v. MAYNARD

Supreme Court of the United States, 1977
430 U.S. 705, 97 S. Ct. 1428, 51 L. Ed. 2d 752

New Hampshire statutes make it a misdemeanor to obscure the motto "Live Free or Die" found on all noncommercial motor vehicle license plates. The appellees, George and Maxine Maynard, who are Jehovah's Witnesses, viewed the motto as repugnant to their moral, religious, and political beliefs and covered up the motto on the license plates of their family automobiles. Mr. Maynard was subsequently convicted in state court on three separate charges of violating the misdemeanor statute. He refused to pay the fines imposed and was sentenced to serve 15 days in jail. The Maynards brought a 42 U.S.C. § 1983 action in federal district court seeking injunctive and declaratory relief against enforcement of the New Hampshire statutes. A three-judge court enjoined the state from enforcing the statutes and from arresting and prosecuting the appellees in the future for covering the motto on their license plates. The United States Supreme Court noted probable jurisdiction.

Mr. Chief Justice BURGER delivered the opinion of the Court.

The issue on appeal is whether the State of New Hampshire may constitutionally enforce criminal sanctions against persons who cover the motto "Live Free or Die" on passenger vehicle license plates because that motto is repugnant to their moral and religious beliefs.

* * *

The District Court held that by covering up the state motto "Live Free or Die" on his automobile license plate, Mr. Maynard was engaging in symbolic speech and that

"New Hampshire's interest in the enforcement of its defacement statute is not sufficient to justify the restriction on [appellees'] constitutionally protected expression." 406 F. Supp., at 1389. We find it unnecessary to pass on the "symbolic speech" issue, since we find more appropriate First Amendment grounds to affirm the judgment of the District Court. We turn instead to what in our view is the essence of appellees' objection to the requirement that they display the motto "Live Free or Die" on their automobile license plates. This is succinctly summarized in the statement made by Mr. Maynard in his affidavit filed with the District Court:

"I refuse to be coerced by the State into advertising a slogan which I find morally, ethically, religiously and politically abhorrent." App., at 5.

We are thus faced with the question of whether the State may constitutionally require an individual to participate in the dissemination of an ideological message by displaying it on his private property in a manner and for the express purpose that it be observed and read by the public. We hold that the State may not do so.

A

We begin with the proposition that the right of freedom of thought protected by the First Amendment against state action includes both the right to speak freely and the right to refrain from speaking at all. See West Virginia State Board of Education v. Barnette, 319 U.S. 624, 633–634, 645 (1943). A system which secures the right to proselytize religious, political, and ideological causes must also guarantee the concomitant right to decline to foster such concepts. The right to speak and the right to refrain from speaking are complementary components of the broader concept of "individual freedom of mind." Id., at 637. This is illustrated by the recent case of Miami Herald Publishing Co. v. Tornillo, 418 U.S. 241 (1974), where we held unconstitutional a Florida statute placing an affirmative duty upon newspapers to publish the replies of political candidates whom they had criticized. We concluded that such a requirement deprived a newspaper of the fundamental right to decide what to print or omit....

The Court in Barnette, supra, was faced with a state statute which required public school students to participate in daily public ceremonies by honoring the flag both with words and traditional salute gestures. In overruling its prior decision in Minersville School District v. Gobitis, 310 U.S. 586 (1940), the Court held that "a ceremony so touching matters of opinion and political attitude may [not] be imposed upon the individual by official authority under powers committed to any political organization under our Constitution." 319 U.S., at 636. Compelling the affirmative act of a flag salute involved a more serious infringement upon personal liberties than the passive act of carrying the state motto on a license plate, but the difference is essentially one of degree. Here, as in Barnette, we are faced with a state measure which forces an individual, as part of his daily life—indeed constantly while his automobile is in public view—to be an instrument for fostering public adherence to an ideological point of view he finds unacceptable. In doing so, the State "invades the sphere of intellect and spirit which it is the purpose of the First Amendment to our Constitution to reserve from all official control." Id., at 342.

New Hampshire's statute in effect requires that appellees use their private property as a "mobile billboard" for the State's ideological message—or suffer a penalty, as Maynard already has. As a condition to driving an automobile—a virtual necessity for most Americans—the Maynards must display "Live Free or Die" to hundreds of people each day. The fact that most individuals agree with the thrust of New Hampshire's motto is not the test; most Americans also find the flag salute acceptable. The First Amendment protects the right of individuals to hold a point of view different from the majority and to refuse to foster, in any way New Hampshire commands, an idea they find morally objectionable.

B

Identifying the Maynards' interests as implicating First Amendment protections does not end our inquiry however. We must also determine whether the State's countervailing interest is sufficiently compelling to justify requiring appellees to display the state motto on their license plates.... The two interests advanced by the state are that display of the motto (1) facilitates the identification of passenger vehicles, and (2) promotes appreciation of history, individualism and state pride.

The State first points out that only passenger vehicles, not commercial, trailer, or other vehicles, are required to display the state motto. Thus, the argument proceeds, officers of the law are more easily able to determine whether passenger vehicles are carrying the proper plates. However the record here reveals that New Hampshire passenger license plates normally consist of a specific configuration of letters and numbers, which makes them readily distinguishable from other types of plates, even without reference to the state motto. Even were we to credit the State's reasons and "even though the governmental purpose be legitimate and substantial, that purpose cannot be pursued by means that broadly stifle fundamental personal liberties when the end can be more narrowly achieved. The breadth of legislative abridgment must be viewed in the light of less drastic means for achieving the same basic purpose." Shelton v. Tucker, 364 U.S. 479, 488 (1960) (footnote omitted).

The State's second claimed interest is not ideologically neutral. The state is seeking to communicate to others an official view as to proper "appreciation of history, state pride, [and] individualism." Of course, the State may legitimately pursue such interests in any number of ways. However, where the State's interest is to disseminate an ideology, no matter how acceptable to some, such interest cannot outweigh an individual's First Amendment right to avoid becoming the courier for such message.

We conclude that the State of New Hampshire may not require appellees to display the state motto upon their vehicle license plates, and accordingly, we affirm the judgment of the District Court.

Affirmed

[Mr. Justice WHITE, with whom Mr. Justice BLACKMUN and Mr. Justice REHNQUIST joined, wrote an opinion dissenting in part.]

Mr. Justice REHNQUIST, with whom Mr. Justice BLACKMUN joins, dissenting.

The Court holds that a State is barred by the Federal Constitution from displaying the state motto on a state license plate. The path that the Court travels to reach this result demonstrates the difficulty in supporting it. The Court holds that the required display of the motto is an unconstitutional "required affirmation of belief."...

I not only agree with the Court's implicit recognition that there is no protected "symbolic speech" in this case, but I think that that conclusion goes far to undermine the Court's ultimate holding that there is an element of protected expression here. The State has not forced appellees to "say" anything; and it has not forced them to communicate ideas with nonverbal actions reasonably likened to "speech," such as wearing a lapel button promoting a political candidate or waving a flag as a symbolic gesture. The State has simply required that *all* noncommercial automobiles bear license tags with the state motto, "Live Free or Die." Appellees have not been forced to affirm or reject that motto; they are simply required by the State, under its police power, to carry a state auto license tag for identification and registration purposes.

* * *

... [T]here is nothing in state law which precludes appellees from displaying their disagreement with the state motto as long as the methods used do not obscure the license plates. Thus appellees could place on their bumper a conspicuous bumper sticker explaining in no uncertain terms that they do not profess the motto "Live Free or Die" and that they violently disagree with the connotations of that motto. Since any implication that they affirm the motto can be so easily displaced, I cannot agree that the state statutory system for motor vehicle identification and tourist promotion may be invalidated under the fiction that appellees are unconstitutionally forced to affirm, or profess belief in, the state motto.

The logic of the Court's opinion leads to startling, and I believe totally unacceptable, results. For example, the mottos "In God We Trust" and "E Pluribus Unum" appear on the coin and currency of the United

States. I cannot imagine that the statutes, see 18 U.S.C. §§ 331 and 333, proscribing defacement of U.S. currency impinge upon the First Amendment rights of an atheist. The fact that an atheist carries and uses U.S. currency does not, in any meaningful sense, convey any affirmation of belief on his part in the motto "In God We Trust." Similarly, there is no affirmation of belief involved with the display of state license tags upon the private automobiles involved here.

I would reverse the judgment of the District Court.

15.06 OTHER DECISIONS OF INTEREST: THE FIRST AMENDMENT IN ITS CRIMINAL CONTEXT— 1976–1977 TERM OF COURT

Obscenity and Pornography

In *Splawn* v. *California,* 431 U.S. 595 (1977), the Supreme Court granted certiorari to decide whether the instructions given to the jury during petitioner's 1971 trial for the sale of two reels of obscene film violated the First Amendment. The trial judge instructed the jury that in determining whether erotic materials had any "social importance" under the then-applicable obscenity test it could "consider the circumstances of sale and distribution, and particularly whether such circumstances indicate that the matter was being commercially exploited by the defendants for the sale of its prurient appeal." The petitioner contended that such an instruction permitted the jury to consider motives of commercial exploitation on the part of other persons in the chain of distribution. In addition, the petitioner contended that the instructions violated both the constitutional prohibition against ex post facto laws and the rule announced in *Bouie* v. *Columbia,* 378 U.S. 347 (1964), that a criminal statute must give "fair warning" of what conduct is prohibited.

The United States Supreme Court affirmed. Writing for a 5–4 majority, Mr. Justice Rehnquist held:

1. The instructions violated no First Amendment rights of the petitioner. The Supreme Court had upheld a similar instruction in *Hamling* v. *United States,* 418 U.S. 87 (1974).

2. Both *Hamling,* supra, and *Ginzburg* v. *United States,* 383 U.S. 463 (1966), make clear that evidence of pandering is relevant to the determination of obscenity; and the Supreme Court has less power to question jury instructions in state cases than in federal prosecutions.

3. The Ex Post Facto Clause and "fair warning" requirement were not violated by the fact that California had changed its procedural law, which included the pandering instruction, between the time of the alleged offense and petitioner's trial. The new law neither created a new offense nor changed the elements set forth in the statute under which the petitioner was convicted.

Mr. Justice Stevens, joined by Justices Brennan, Stewart and Marshall, dissented, stating that petitioner's statements about his films were neither false, misleading, nor offensive; that such speech was protected by the First Amendment; and that the films could not lose their protected status by being truthfully described.

In *Smith* v. *United States,* 431 U.S. 678 (1977), the Supreme Court granted certiorari to review the relationship between state legislation regulating the distribution of obscene material and the determination of contemporary community standards in a federal prosecution.

Petitioner was indicted in the Southern District of Iowa for mailing obscene materials in violation of 18 U.S.C. § 1461. The mailings took place entirely within the state. During the trial, petitioner unsuccessfully moved for a directed verdict of acquittal on the ground that the Iowa obscenity statute in effect at the time of petitioner's conduct, which proscribed only the dissemination of obscene materials to minors, set forth the applicable community standard and that petitioner had not violated that standard. Petitioner was convicted and the court of appeals affirmed.

Writing for a 5–4 majority of the Court, Mr. Justice Blackmun held:

1. State law cannot define the contemporary community standards that under *Miller* v. *California,* 413 U.S. 15 (1973), are applied in determining whether or not materi-

als are obscene. In federal prosecutions, the issue of obscenity is a question of fact for the jury to be judged in light of its understanding of contemporary standards.

2. State legislatures retain significant power to set substantive limitations in criminal obscenity cases, but they cannot declare what community standards shall be in a federal prosecution.

3. It is immaterial that the mailings were solely intrastate, because § 1461 was enacted under Congress' constitutional postal power, not its commerce power.

4. Although a state statute, which is not conclusive on the issue of contemporary community standards, does not nullify state law, a state cannot compel the federal government to allow the mails to be used to send obscene materials into that state.

Mr. Justice Brennan, joined by Justices Stewart and Marshall, dissented and stated that 18 U.S.C. § 1461, under which the petitioner was convicted, is "clearly overboard and unconstitutional on its face." Mr. Justice Stevens wrote a dissenting opinion stating that "criminal prosecutions are an unacceptable method of abating a public nuisance which is entitled to at least a modicum of First Amendment protection." Criticizing the community standards theory, Justice Stevens stated that "the guilt or innocence of a criminal defendant in an obscenity trial is determined primarily by individual jurors' subjective reactions to the materials in question rather than by the predictable application of rules of law."

In *Ward* v. *Illinois,* 413 U.S. 767 (1977), the Supreme Court noted probable jurisdiction on appeal to review the constitutionality of the Illinois obscenity statute. Petitioner was convicted in a state court for selling two sadomasochistic publications deemed obscene under Illinois law prior to the United States Supreme Court's decision in *Miller* v. *California,* 413 U.S. 15 (1973). Petitioner's conviction was affirmed after *Miller,* by the Illinois Supreme Court, which rejected petitioner's claim that the Illinois obscenity statute was unconstitutionally vague and failed to explicitly state that sadomasochistic materials come within the purview of the statute.

In a 5-4 decision, the United States Supreme Court affirmed. In an opinion by Mr. Justice White, a majority of the Court stated:

1. The Illinois obscenity statute is not unconstitutionally vague, as Illinois cases have long made it clear that sadomasochistic materials come within the sweep of the statute.

2. Sadomasochistic materials may be proscribed by state law even though they were not expressly included within the examples set forth in *Miller* of patently offensive depictions of specifically defined sexual conduct.

3. The materials were properly found by the Illinois courts to be obscene under the *Miller* standards even though the statute retains the stricter "redeeming social value" test held not required under *Miller.*

Justice Stevens, joined by Justices Brennan, Stewart, and Marshall, dissented, stating that by abandoning the specificity requirement of *Miller,* the petitioner was denied the notice to which he was constitutionally entitled. Justices Brennan and Stewart also stated that the Illinois obscenity statute is "clearly overbroad and unconstitutional on its face."

APPENDIX A

A REPORT CARD ON SUPREME COURT*

The direction in which the U.S. Supreme Court has moved under Chief Justice Warren E. Burger wins overwhelming approval among the nation's judges and leading lawyers.

That is the finding of a comprehensive nationwide survey by *U.S. News & World Report.*

The survey drew 508 replies from: 211 judges of the U.S. district courts and courts of appeal, 110 justices of State supreme courts and 187 lawyers who rank high in their profession. The major results:

• More than 3 out of 4 of those jurists and lawyers—78.1 percent—prefer the Burger Court to the Court that was headed by the late Chief Justice Earl Warren.

• Nearly 99 per cent described the Burger Court as more conservative than the Warren Court—with 78.4 per cent approving of the conservative philosophy.

• The Burger Court is viewed—approvingly—as less likely than the Warren Court to step into fields of public policy to make decisions that should be left to the legislative or executive branches of government.

• The quality of opinions written by the Burger Court is rated slightly higher than that of Warren Court opinions. But most of those polled think that even the opinions of the present Court are often too long, too often unclear.

• Justice Lewis F. Powell, Jr., gets the highest rating among individual Court members for the quality of his opinions, with Justice Thurgood Marshall rated lowest.

• On almost every controversial issue, the majority of those polled approved of "recent decisions or directions the Supreme Court has taken." The sole exception was on obscenity and pornography, where 51.4 percent disapproved. The vote was close on mandatory busing for school integration, with only 51.1 percent approving of the way the High Court has handled that issue.

• About three fourths of the lawyers and judges think that the federal courts are carrying too heavy a load of cases, and favor the addition of more judges—at higher pay. But 55.2 per cent oppose the creation of a new National Court of Appeals to lighten the Supreme Court's load, an idea that has been widely discussed in recent months.

• Although many criticized the selection of federal judges as often "too political," 69.6 percent approved, in general, the present system of choosing those judges.

All this is set out in detail in the tables on following pages. The reasoning of the respondents is explained in the written comments that accompany those tables. Most of those comments are quoted anonymously, because the questionnaires were designed so that the persons replying could not be identified unless they voluntarily signed their names. Thirty-three signed their names.

Nearly all of the jurists and lawyers answered every question in the long questionnaire. In the tables showing the votes on various questions, the percentages given are based on the number who answered that particular question, disregarding those who did not.

Against Court "Making Law"

"The present Court seems to be moving toward greater restraint, avoiding the posture of a superlegislature. This is to be encouraged."

This statement by Jeffrey B. Smith, a Baltimore lawyer, expressed a view widely held among the lawyers and judges responding to the *U.S. News & World Report* survey.

From a federal judge came this: "I'm not sure of the Court's philosophy, but I think the trend of the present Court is to interpret the law, rather than enter the legislative field of 'making the law.'"

Comparing the Burger Court with the Warren Court, a State supreme court justice said:

"The philosophy of the present Court more accurately reflects the philosophy of the American people."

*Reprinted from U.S. News & World Report, March 7, 1977, pp. 59–67.

That today's Court reflects the philosophy of most lawyers and judges was shown by the survey's statistical results, as set out in the table below. There was 78.4 percent approval of the Burger Court's more conservative philosophy and 78.1 percent preferred it to the Warren Court's more liberal philosophy. Of the three groups polled, lawyers were slightly less approving of the philosophy of the Burger Court than were the federal judges or State supreme court justices.

The Warren Court was criticized frequently for its judicial "activism."

One State justice said: "The Warren Court was a dark era in American jurisprudence—poor decisions in fields they should never have entered. The present Court is like a light at the end of the tunnel."

From others came such comments as these:

- "The Warren Court had a tendency to be a legislative, political Court—which ignores the separation of powers."
- "The Warren Court construed the Constitution to mean what it chose to have it mean."
- "While I approve of many things the

Among Judges and Lawyers
MORE THAN 3 OUT OF 4 PREFER BURGER COURT TO WARREN COURT

Question: In comparison with the Supreme Court headed by the former Chief Justice, Earl Warren, would you describe the present Court, headed by Chief Justice Warren E. Burger, as more liberal or more conservative?

More conservative	98.8%
More liberal	1.2%

Question: In general, do you approve or disapprove of the philosophy of the present Court?

Approve	78.4%
Disapprove	21.6%

Question: In terms of their judicial philosophies, which do you prefer—the Burger Court or the Warren Court?

Burger Court	78.1%
Warren Court	21.9%

Question: Do you feel that the present U.S. Supreme Court has a tendency to take jurisdiction of questions involving public policy that might better be left to the legislative or executive branch of Government?

Yes	40.7%
No	59.3%

Question: Do you feel that the Burger Court is more likely or less likely than the Warren Court to have such a tendency?

More likely	2.4%
Less likely	84.2%
About the same	10.4%

Note: 3% don't think that the Warren Court had such a tendency.

Reprinted from *U.S. News & World Report*, March 7, 1977. Copyright 1977 U.S. News & World Report, Inc.

Warren Court did, it went too far in several areas and entered several areas best left to others.

Some of the judges and lawyers defended the Warren Court's "activism" as necessary for its times.

"Both the Warren Court and the present Court were responding to the needs in existence at the time they sat," said one lawyer. "The Warren Court was more activist because at the time the legislative branch of Government was too inactive. The recent increase in the activism of the legislature is reflected in the greater restraint of the present Court."

Another lawyer put it this way: "It was necessary for the Warren Court to move us off center in the 1950s and 1960s—to take legislative types of action in view of the failure of the executive and legislature to reform. Perhaps it is wise to let the pendulum swing back now, even though much remains to be done. In this sense, perhaps one can approve of both Courts—each for its time."

A majority of those surveyed, however, agreed with the general idea expressed by one State justice who said: "The Warren Court was moving a bit too far—too fast. Some retrenchment was necessary."

Chesterfield Smith, of Lakeland, Fla., a former president of the American Bar Association, said: "Courts are ill-equipped to solve all of society's ills. They should resolve disputes rather than supplant legislatures in problem solving."

A federal judge expressed this view: "The Warren Court decided to face issues regarding segregation, rights of defendants, etc., that had been avoided for years. It played a vital and necessary role then. There is a need now for some balance and a greater weighing of society's interests and its needs at this time."

Some expressed concern that the Burger Court might be going too far in reversing the trend of the Warren Court.

"A period of consolidation after the motion of the Warren Court is probably essential," said one lawyer. "But there seems to be a danger that the present Court will retreat, rather than consolidate and refine, particularly in the area of civil rights." A State supreme court justice said: "The Warren Court did well in the field of personal liberties and constitutional rights. I agree with the momentary restraint of the present Court, but would not like to see them take any backward steps in this field."

A federal judge complained that "the present Court tends to be regressive." And from a lawyer came this criticism: "The Court's philosophy seems to look backward to the source of their appointments—a phony 'law and order' and 'strict construction' description manufactured by [former President Richard] Nixon and [former Attorney General John] Mitchell for political ends."

Two federal judges described the present Supreme Court as "still too activist." A lawyer said, "The Court still creates constitutional questions when none exists." A State justice complained "there is still too great a hangover from the Warren Court." And a lawyer charged there is still "too much 'judicial legislating.'"

One lawyer saw this difference between the two Courts: "The Warren Court had a tendency to exalt individual rights over the society's rights—that is, over the rights of other individuals. The Burger Court is balancing the individual's rights without seriously compromising them."

From another lawyer came this observation: "Although the Burger Court is in our opinion less active than former Courts, its philosophy is more in tune with what I feel is the present state of the national mood: restraint and a wait-and-see attitude."

Closing Courthouse Doors?

Controversy has developed in recent months over charges that the Burger Court is unduly restricting access to federal courts and making it harder for citizens to sue in defense of their constitutional rights. Chief Justice Burger has publicly denied such charges.

On this issue, 48.4 percent of the judges and lawyers polled by *U.S. News & World Report* agreed that "recent Supreme Court decisions have made it more difficult for citizens to use federal courts for redress of grievances." But 55.1 percent of all those responding said that they approved of such a policy. Lawyers were the only group to disapprove—by a majority of 51.7 percent—while State justices were the strongest in favor—by 63.7 percent—and federal judges approved by a vote of 56.8 percent.

"Essentially," wrote a State justice, "the Burger Court has simply recognized a more

CITIZENS' USE OF THE COURT

Question: Do you think recent Supreme Court decisions have made it more difficult for citizens to use federal courts to obtain redress of grievances?

Yes	48.4%
No	51.6%

Question: Do you approve or disapprove of making it more difficult for citizens to use federal courts?

Approve	55.1%
Disapprove	44.9%

Reprinted from *U.S. News & World Report,* March 7, 1977. Copyright 1977 U.S. News & World Report, Inc.

---

traditional and proper relationship between the State and federal courts and made the State courts the final arbiters of grievances, as I believe in most cases they should be."

Congress was blamed by some for forcing the High Court to weed out more appeals. U.S. District Judge Morell E. Sharp of Seattle wrote:

"Much has been written recently about the tendency of the United States Supreme Court to limit federal court jurisdiction, thereby decreasing citizens' access to the courts. It seems to me this criticism misses the point.

"Congress, without providing additional manpower, continues to increase the Court's jurisdiction by leaps and bounds. As a consequence, most of the federal courts are so bogged down with matters that could better be handled by the legislative process, by executive departments and agencies and by the State courts that citizens with legitimate federal claims cannot be heard.

"The Supreme Court is reacting to this problem by insisting that jurisdictional and 'standing' requirements be met by would-be litigants, and by limiting access to claimants seeking broad social reform through the courts rather than Congress."

In the view of one lawyer: "The present Court's philosophy in making it more difficult to use the Court is the only way the judicial system can survive." Said another: "The Court is overloaded, and therefore must turn down cases or spend too little time on them." And from a third lawyer: "The fact that the Court exercised judicial restraint by avoiding infringing upon the legislative domain does not mean that it shrinks in any way in deciding those issues which constitutionally are within its jurisdiction."

Some, however, were sharply critical of the Burger Court for turning away suits. A federal judge said: "The majority of this Court is engaged in shutting the federal courthouse doors, abdicating its responsibility to enforce the Constitution, generally favoring the wealthy, well-educated and well-entrenched."

Said a lawyer: "I am disturbed by the present Court's preoccupation with case load and questions of administrative efficiency. Where the Court has been required to balance the interests of litigants seeking to vindicate constitutional and other federally protected rights against the legitimate concern over increasing case loads in the federal courts, the Court has regularly favored the latter interest by denying litigants access to the federal forum."

From other lawyers came these criticisms:

• "The present Court does not appear to be concerned with the individual or the little guy. Given the opportunity, the Court supports big business or the Government."

• The Burger Court's philosophy "appears to be one of preferring State sovereignty or prerogatives over individuals' federal constitutional rights."

A State justice said: "I personally think the present Court, primarily influenced by President Nixon's appointees, has cut back measurably on Bill of Rights claims by individuals."

Another State justice said: "I am very

much opposed to the decisions of the present Court, the substantive effect of which is to restrict or deny access to the federal courts. Example: their rulings on class suits."

Tougher on Criminals

Virtually all of the judges and lawyers polled agreed that the Burger Court is tougher on criminals than the Warren Court was, and 73.6 percent approved of that policy.

"The further the present Court departs from the Warren Court, the more I approve," wrote lawyer Jeffrey B. Smith of Baltimore.

"The Warren Court was obsessed with the rights of people accused of crime," said the chief justice of a State supreme court. "Some of their decisions corrected some abuses, but the over-all impact of the Warren Court was to make it virtually impossible to end litigation in criminal cases. The Burger Court has made some notable success in reversing the trend started by the Warren Court."

Here are some other comments:
- "The Warren Court went too far. The rights of the victim and the police are overlooked."
- "Victims also have rights."
- "Society should have more protection."
- "Procedural acquittal of the legally guilty makes mockery of the law."
- "Warren Court responsible for crime waves. Present Court O.K."

Some judges and lawyers disapprove of the present Court because they think that it has not gone far enough to reverse the trend of the Warren Court's decisions.

Others fear that the Burger Court is going too far in backing away from Warren Court precedents. "I think that the pendulum had swung too far," said a federal judge. "Now I hope it doesn't go the other way."

Lawyers, as a group, were less approving of the present Court's trend on criminal cases than were the federal judges or State justices.

Some accused the Burger Court of not giving enough protection to the rights of accused criminals.

On the whole, however, there was wide agreement with the recent trend. "The Court is becoming more pragmatic in its approach by considering all facts and circumstances surrounding criminal cases, rather than relying solely upon highly legal technicalities—all without interfering with defendants' rights," said a federal judge.

"The pendulum swung too far left under the Warren Court—for example, rulings favoring criminals or the accused unreasonably," said a State supreme court justice. "The noncriminal public is lucky the pendulum is coming back and the Court is considering the rights of others as well as the rights of the accused."

"The Court is trying again to balance the rights of criminals and the rights of society," said Hector Reichard, Jr., of Aguadilla, Puerto Rico, a lawyer who is a member of the ABA board of governors.

On Death Penalty: Confusion

Although the Supreme Court's recent rulings on the death penalty won a narrow vote of approval—57.5 percent—many judges and lawyers complain that the net effect of those rulings is confusing. "All the Court did was create chaos," wrote one federal judge. "The decisions in this area have muddied the waters to such an extent that the States can't tell what is permitted and what is prohibited," said a State justice.

"I really don't know what the Court will approve," commented John L. Carey, a South Bend lawyer who is president of the Indiana State Bar Association.

"Court's opinions are contradictory and confusing," complained another lawyer.

Such complaints came from those who oppose capital punishment as well as from those who approve it.

Of those who clearly indicated their attitudes, about 2 out of 3 favored the death penalty, at least in some cases.

"The death penalty is a deterrent to crime, and for some crimes no other penalty is adequate—especially when a life sentence does not mean life and the defendant has a long history of other heinous crimes," observed a federal judge.

Among those opposing the death penalty, several disagreed with the Court's finding that it is not cruel or unusual punishment if it is properly applied.

Some judges and lawyers disapproved of the Court's death penalty rulings on the ground that this is a matter that should be left to the States.

ON MOST ISSUES: A MAJORITY APPROVES THE TREND OF HIGH-COURT RULINGS

Question: For each of the subjects listed below, will you please indicate whether you approve or disapprove of recent decisions or directions the Supreme Court has taken on that subject?

	Approve	Disapprove
Abortion	65.3%	34.7%
Mandatory busing for school integration	51.1%	48.9%
Death penalty	57.5%	42.5%
Rights of defendants in criminal cases	73.6%	26.4%
Racial discrimination	80.4%	19.6%
Sexual discrimination	71.9%	28.1%
Obscenity and pornography	48.6%	51.4%
Labor unions	73.0%	27.0%
States' rights and federalism	68.7%	31.3%
Antitrust laws and suits	72.6%	27.4%
Free speech	75.8%	24.2%
Freedom of press	70.8%	29.2%
Protection of environment	72.4%	27.6%

Reprinted from *U.S. News & World Report,* March 7, 1977. Copyright 1977 U.S. News & World Report, Inc.

Question: What Is Obscene?

The only issue on which the Supreme Court fails to win a vote of approval is that of obscenity and pornography.

The *U.S. News & World Report* survey shows that 51.4 percent of the judges and lawyers polled do not like the way the Court has handled that subject. Only State justices approved, and they were outvoted by the lawyers and federal judges.

But the survey answers do not clearly show why the critics disapprove. Some say that the Court is "too permissive," "too lenient," permits too much "filth" and "smut." Others charge that the Court is practicing unconstitutional censorship when it attempts to apply any curbs. And many complain that the Court's various rulings are too confusing to provide workable guidelines.

"This is an area in which the Supreme Court has failed to give clear and decisive leadership," said Judge Gerald W. Heaney of Duluth, Minn., a member of the U.S. Court of Appeals for the Eighth Circuit.

"The Court's holdings are impossible to understand or apply," in the view of another federal judge.

Lawyer Carey of South Bend expressed the dilemma that many legal experts face in passing judgment on Court rulings that have permitted some types of alleged pornography: "As a lawyer, I approve; as a father, no!" he said.

"A close question, but I favor more protection of society over individual excesses," wrote another lawyer.

"If I don't like smut, I don't have to buy a ticket," was the comment of Nevada supreme court justice David Zenoff.

Some who thought that the "Warren Court went too far" in permitting pornography described the present Court as moving in the right direction. Said a federal judge: "Although as a legislator I would be inclined to let consenting adults read and see what they want, I doubt that the Founding Fathers thought that the First Amendment barred the regulation of what we now know as hard-core pornography. I think a sensible balance has now been achieved."

Disagreeing, a lawyer complained that the Court still "leans too far to protect freedom at [the] expense of ordinary citizens." And a federal judge described the Court as "still too broad-minded."

Expressing the view of those who oppose any censorship, U.S. District Judge Don J. Young of Toledo, Ohio, said: "I take the position that the First Amendment [guaranteeing freedom of speech and the press] is absolute. The courts should have nothing to do with these sumptuary matters, nor should the legislatures."

A Close Vote on Busing

It is by a bare majority—51.1 percent—that judges and lawyers approve of the present Supreme Court's stand on mandatory busing for school integration.

Here again, the reasons for approval—or disapproval—are mixed, and often unclear. Some approvingly perceive the Burger Court as "backing away" from busing. Others think, as one State justice put it, "this Court hasn't gone far enough in getting federal courts out of the school business."

Most of those who attached written comments to their votes on the Court's busing decisions made it clear that they oppose "mandatory" busing—especially if it is designed to create fixed racial quotas in each school of a district.

"Mandatory busing of children is wrong, and busing for racial balance is even more so," said a State justice.

"Mandatory busing only for racial quotas is hampering education and driving the whites from the cities to the suburbs and definitely injuring the public schools," said a federal judge.

From another federal judge: "Since the Court has ordered less busing, I agree with the decisions recently entered. School busing should never be a tool to do anything other than improve the quality of education and never as an instrument to force integration of the races."

Some who approved of busing made such comments as "Justified in some but not all circumstances, as the Court recognizes," or, "Enforce antidiscrimination law but with busing as a very last resort."

A few insisted that there is "no other way to remove the curse of segregation," or that busing "is the only way to dismantle segregation in some cases."

One lawyer charged that recent Court curbs on busing "are capitulations to mob rule."

Sharp Dispute Over Abortion

Abortion is another subject that stirs sharp controversy among lawyers and judges—just as it does among the general public.

Although 65.3 percent of those answering the *U.S. News & World Report* poll approve of the Supreme Court's rules that permit abortion early in pregnancy, many either oppose any court regulation or think that all abortions should be prohibited. And still others say it is a question that should be settled by legislation, not by a court.

"What the Court is doing here involves judicial legislation instead of constitutional interpretation," said one State justice. "It practices medicine, not law," said a federal judge.

Many appeared to agree in general with a State justice who described the Court's decision as "a practical accommodation of conflicting views on a highly complex and emotional subject," or a federal judge who said, "A reasonable balance has been achieved between individual freedom of choice and the right to life within an acceptable legal framework."

On Discrimination: Wide Approval

Discrimination suits have provided some of the major controversies of recent years. Yet, even in this area, the Supreme Court wins a resounding vote of approval.

Of judges and lawyers surveyed, 80.4 percent approved of the present Court's decisions on racial discrimination, and 71.9 percent liked its trend on sexual discrimination.

"The more recent decisions bring earlier decisions within more rational bounds in both the racial and sexual discrimination areas," in the view of one lawyer.

In racial cases, said a federal judge, "the Court continues the Warren philosophy of striking down discrimination in public situations, and I favor this course." On equality for women, the Court's position was frequently described as "reasonable," or "balanced," or "legally sound," and moving "toward equality." But some thought the Court has moved too far, and others thought not far enough. Examples: One federal judge said that the Court "ignores common sense and the fact that there is a difference between men and women." Another judge accused the Court of "effectively retarding the move toward equality."

In the racial field, the most frequent criticisms were about decisions approving "quotas" or "reverse discrimination." A federal judge complained that "some decisions border on approval of quotas." Another judge said "racial discrimination should be eradicated, but this does not mean allocation on a quota basis, regardless of qualifications." From yet another judge: "Affirmative-action programs are often unconstitutional in discriminating in favor of minorities."

Clearer, Shorter Opinions

Although the great majority of judges and lawyers gave the Supreme Court's written opinions "high" or "average" ratings for quality, most agreed that the opinions are "often too long" and "too often unclear."

"Too verbose, too complex" was the terse way one federal judge described the Court's writing.

It is not uncommon for opposing sides to rely upon the same Supreme Court opinion to support their position," said another federal judge. "It is therefore obvious that the opinions are confusing and 'fuzzy.'"

"Shorter, clearer, more concise opinions would frequently eliminate need for further litigation to obtain elucidation or clarification," said Joseph E. Spruill, Jr., a Tappahannock lawyer who is president of the Virginia State Bar Association.

There were many complaints about the number of separate "concurring" decisions written by Court members.

"The insistence of the individual judges in having their say in most cases creates unnecessary uncertainty," said one State justice. From another State justice: "The real problem lies in the various concurring opinions in order to arrive at a decision. It becomes difficult to arrive at what the consensus of the Court is on a given issue."

There were also frequent complaints about the number of dissenting opinions written by Court Justices. Said one federal judge: "There are too many dissenting opinions which are meaningless, as the majority opinion is the controlling law."

As the table shows, 84.4 percent of those replying to the survey believe that most Supreme Court opinions could be shorter

RATING THE QUALITY OF COURT OPINIONS

Question: In general, how would you rate the legal quality of opinions written by the present Supreme Court?

High	33.7%
Average	59.7%
Low	6.6%

Question: In comparison with opinions written by the Warren Court, how would you rate the opinions of the present Court?

Better	33.6%
About the same	51.9%
Worse	14.5%

Reprinted from *U.S. News & World Report,* March 7, 1977. Copyright 1977 U.S. News & World Report, Inc.

ARE COURT OPINIONS TOO LONG AND UNCLEAR?

Question: Below is a list of statements which have sometimes been made about the Supreme Court's opinions. Do you agree or disagree?

Statement: Opinions are often too long.

Agree	75.2%
Disagree	24.8%

Statement: Opinions are too often unclear.

Agree	65.3%
Disagree	34.7%

Statement: Lack of clarity in Court opinions often creates serious problems of confusion and misinterpretation.

Agree	69.9%
Disagree	30.1%

Statement: Most opinions could be shorter and clearer without risking the creation of other faults.

Agree	84.4%
Disagree	15.6%

Reprinted from *U.S. News & World Report,* March 7, 1977. Copyright 1977 U.S. News & World Report, Inc.

and clearer without risking the creation of other faults.

Many of the judges and lawyers who answered other questions were reluctant to rate the individual Justices as to the quality of their written opinions. Almost 1 in 5 refused to do so. And those who did rate the Justices generally refrained from commenting on the reasons for their ratings.

However, as the table shows, Justice Powell got the most "excellent" ratings, followed in order by Justices William H. Rehnquist, Byron R. White and Potter Stewart. Chief Justice Burger ranked fifth, followed by Justices John Paul Stevens, William J. Brennan, Harry A. Blackmun and Thurgood Marshall.

The Justice with the most "poor" ratings was Marshall—with Powell getting the fewest.

How to Improve Justice?

In spite of the high ratings given to the Supreme Court, many judges and lawyers are deeply concerned about the federal court system as a whole.

"I strongly believe that action must be taken now to save the federal judicial system from collapse," said a U.S. judge. "The action requires restructuring the jurisdiction of the federal courts, carefully developing new machinery for final disposition of many administrative-agency cases and prisoner cases without permitting appeal to the federal courts as a matter of right."

A major concern among the legal experts surveyed by *U.S. News & World Report* was the growing number of cases that have clogged the calendars of the U.S. district courts, the circuit courts of appeal—and the Supreme Court as well.

As the box on this page shows, about 3 out of 4 agree that federal judges are being asked to carry too heavy a workload, and that more district and appellate judges are needed.

But many see the need for changes going far beyond the mere addition of more judges. Some complain that Congress keeps passing laws that create more work for the courts.

"Year by year, Congress is constantly increasing the load of U.S. courts by statutes involving indigents, civil rights, habeas corpus, freedom of information, truth in lending, etc.," said a federal judge.

"Congress *must* remove many of the

HOW INDIVIDUAL JUSTICES ARE RATED

Question: In general, how would you rate the quality of opinions written by each of the present Justices on the Supreme Court?

Justice Lewis F. Powell, Jr.

Excellent	60.3%
Average	36.6%
Poor	3.1%

Justice William H. Rehnquist

Excellent	43.9%
Average	43.2%
Poor	12.9%

Justice Byron R. White

Excellent	37.3%
Average	57.2%
Poor	5.5%

Justice Potter Stewart

Excellent	35.0%
Average	60.6%
Poor	4.4%

Chief Justice Warren E. Burger

Excellent	29.4%
Average	59.1%
Poor	11.5%

Justice John Paul Stevens

Excellent	29.2%
Average	65.0%
Poor	5.8%

Justice William J. Brennan, Jr.

Excellent	29.1%
Average	53.5%
Poor	17.4%

Justice Harry A. Blackmun

Excellent	24.3%
Average	68.1%
Poor	7.6%

Justice Thurgood Marshall

Excellent	11.2%
Average	56.5%
Poor	32.3%

Reprinted from *U.S. News & World Report,* March 7, 1977. Copyright 1977 U.S. News & World Report, Inc.

WIDE AGREEMENT THAT LOAD ON JUDGES IS TOO HEAVY

Question: Do you think that the work load carried by the Supreme Court is too heavy, too light, or about right?

Too heavy	71.4%
Too light	1.0%
About right	27.6%

Question: Do you think that the work load carried by federal district and appellate courts is too heavy, too light, or about right?

Too heavy	76.8%
Too light	0.4%
About right	22.8%

Reprinted from *U.S. News & World Report,* March 7, 1977. Copyright 1977 U.S. News & World Report, Inc.

---

trivial matters which it has increasingly imposed upon the federal court system," wrote Don M. Jackson, a Kansas City, Mo., lawyer who is a member of the ABA house of delegates. "These are making the federal courts in many respects no more than a justice-of-the-peace court."

"More judges will not solve these problems," Jackson asserted. "The basic laws must be reviewed and some administrative finality must be enforced."

Long, drawn-out proceedings in criminal cases were cited frequently as a cause of trouble.

"Frankly, it is my view that the failure to promptly dispose of criminal cases by the courts, both State and Federal, forms the weakest link in the judicial system and has been a contribution to the crime wave sweeping the country," wrote B. K. Roberts of Tallahassee, a former chief justice of the Florida Supreme Court.

"Stop the interminable litigation in criminal matters," said a State supreme court justice. "Have a little more good common 'horse-sense.'"

Improved methods of court management were suggested by several. One federal judge called for "adoption of modern management techniques, including computerized management of case load and computerized research." He charged that "too many judges are back in the days of quill pens."

A lawyer urged: "A thorough review should be made to streamline procedures, particularly in criminal cases, to speed up the trial process and to eliminate the requirement that witnesses make multiple appearances in court. New technology, such as videotape, should be used more extensively." Another lawyer suggested that efficiency could be improved "by providing in each district and in each circuit a strong, well-trained administrator with authority to install improved methods of administration...."

Of the judges and lawyers responding to the survey, 55.2 percent opposed the creation of a new National Court of Appeals to help the Supreme Court by screening appeals and deciding some cases.

One federal judge called such a court "unnecessary" and predicted "it will result in additional delay and expense without corresponding benefit."

Several who supported the idea of a new National Court of Appeals warned that its sole job should be to decide cases referred to it by the Supreme Court and that it should not be empowered to screen appeals and decide which cases the High Court should handle.

"Control of its docket should be retained by the Supreme Court, and review by it should continue to be available," said James D. Fellers of Oklahoma City, a former president of the ABA. "No one is proposing a court to screen cases for the Supreme

NEEDED: MORE JUDGES, BUT NO NATIONAL COURT OF APPEALS

Question: Should a National Court of Appeals be created to screen appeals to the Supreme Court and to decide some cases?

Yes	44.8%
No	55.2%

Question: Should the Supreme Court's jurisdiction be narrowed?

Yes	36.5%
No	63.5%

Question: Do we need more federal judges at the district court level?

Yes	84.0%
No	16.0%

Question: Do we need more federal judges at the appeals court level?

Yes	74.1%
No	25.9%

Question: Should salaries of federal judges be increased?*

Yes	89.0%
No	11.0%

Question: Do you approve of the present system of choosing federal judges?

Yes	69.6%
No	30.4%

* Note: This survey was made before the pay of federal judges was increased on February 20.

Reprinted from *U.S. News & World Report*, March 7, 1977. Copyright 1977 U.S. News & World Report, Inc.

Court," said another lawyer. "The viable proposal is one to help the [Supreme] Court decide cases and to enlarge the unity of national law."

Former Chief Justice Roberts of the Florida Supreme Court suggested a different solution: Enlarge the Supreme Court from nine to 15 Justices, with two divisions—one to handle civil cases, the other to handle criminal appeals.

The survey, taken before the recent pay raise given U.S. judges, showed wide support of such an increase.

Ways to Get Better Judges

Better judges would improve the administration of justice, in the opinion of many legal experts.

But how to get better judges? On that question, there was a wide diversity of opinion.

One idea, frequently suggested, was put this way by a Blytheville, Ark., lawyer, Oscar Fendler: "Selection of judges on merit basis rather than political."

Said another lawyer: "A merit system should be devised to eliminate political patronage." A third lawyer suggested: "A nonpartisan commission should nominate a panel from which the President appoints lawyers."

Only a few favored election of judges. Another few favored limited terms, instead of lifetime appointments to the bench. After a judge has served a limited term, it was suggested, that judge's record could be reviewed for possible reappointment or reconfirmation by the Senate.

"Because of life tenure and arrogance of uncontrolled power, some judges lose perspective," wrote J. Allan Crockett of the Utah Supreme Court. "There should be some method of periodic review of the performances of judges."

Another State supreme court justice, Stokes V. Robertson, Jr., of Mississippi, said this: "Power seems to go rather quickly to the head of the average district judge. He thinks there's no wrong that he can't personally remedy. I think judges should be answerable to the people every eight years."

"Have a six-year recall," proposed one lawyer. "Get rid of those who decide they are 'anointed' instead of appointed."

A frequent suggestion was that there should be some way to remove an unfit judge besides the only present method—impeachment—which one lawyer described as "impossible" in most cases. Another idea was to get judges off the bench at an earlier age by forcing their retirement.

Many legal experts insisted, however, that the constitutionally prescribed method of appointing judges for life is the only way to insure the independence of the judiciary.

"The method of selection of judges is totally immaterial," said U.S. District Judge Young of Toledo, "for it must always, and properly, be a political matter. What is important is tenure of judges. If the tenure is short or insecure, the best qualified will not accept judgeships. And impartiality of those who become judges will be impaired."

"What would elected judges have done when confronted with desegregation problems?" asked another judge.

In spite of all the criticisms, 69.6 per cent of those who answered the *U.S. News & World Report* questionnaire approved of the present system of choosing federal judges.

"Actually, from a practical point of view, it is about as good a system as can be evolved," said Caleb R. Layton, III, a U.S. District judge in Wilmington, Del.

There also was general approval of the way federal courts dispense justice. "I think the federal courts do a very good job on the whole," said Fred R. Winans, a justice of the South Dakota Supreme Court. "Of the three branches of Government, it does its allotted job best."

"Basically," in the opinion of William H. Copeland, a Clayton, Mo., attorney, "our judicial system is unequaled in the present history and unexceeded in world history."

From John C. Pickett of Cheyenne, Wyo., a senior judge of the U.S. Court of Appeals for the Tenth Circuit, came this: "As an assistant U.S. attorney and a U.S. circuit judge for over 40 years, my observation is that, with few exceptions, the work of the federal judiciary has been excellent."

Copyright 1977 U.S. News & World Report, Inc.